HOW
DO
YOU
FEEL?

John Wood

is a free-lance journalist and a staff member and group leader at the Center for Studies of the Person, La Jolla, California. He also directs the Center's Project on More Human Journalism.

John Wood

HOW
DO
YOU
FEEL?
A Guide

to

Your Emotions

A SPECTRUM BOOK

PRENTICE-HALL, INC., *Englewood Cliffs, New Jersey*

Library of Congress Cataloging in Publication Data

MAIN ENTRY UNDER TITLE:

How do you feel? A guide to your emotions.

(A Spectrum Book)
Contains a collection of recorded interviews and conversation.
1. Emotions. I. Wood, John II. Title.
BF561.H68   152.4   73-22179
ISBN 0-13-396630-5
ISBN 0-13-396622-4 (pbk.)

Cover Photograph by Ted Lau

© 1974 BY PRENTICE-HALL, INC.
ENGLEWOOD CLIFFS, NEW JERSEY

A SPECTRUM BOOK

10

Printed in the United States of America

PRENTICE-HALL INTERNATIONAL, INC (LONDON)
PRENTICE-HALL OF AUSTRALIA, PTY. LTD. (SYDNEY)
PRENTICE-HALL OF CANADA, LTD. (TORONTO)
PRENTICE-HALL OF INDIA PRIVATE LIMITED (NEW DELHI)
PRENTICE-HALL OF JAPAN, INC. (TOKYO)

CONTENTS

This Book

is about me and some people I know and I am presumptuous enough to believe it is about you. This is a collection of reflections, reactions, wonderings and learnings about human feelings. The people in this book have shared themselves with me, and you, in a way that I have not seen in print before. Today I feel very good that they trusted me enough to do that. It's a hard thing sometimes to be so personal, so open; it is equally hard to put those personal feelings into words.

To those who make up this book: Thank you, deeply.
To you: Welcome. I hope you in-joy your journey.

John Wood

*I should not talk so much about myself
if there were anybody else whom I knew as well.*

Henry David Thoreau

HOW
DO
YOU
FEEL?

INTRODUCTION

I think this is an important introduction. I've read many introductions that don't add one whit to the book they introduce; they are an occasion to thank lots of people or for someone other than the author to say what it is he thinks the author is saying.

I hope this will help you enjoy the book. It is an explanation of the process of putting this book together, what I think the book is, what I think the book is not, what my hopes are for it and some ways you might use it.

This is an unusual book. Sometimes it seems so simple to me; it is merely people sharing their own feelings. But, as some of you surely know, "merely" sharing feelings is not an easy thing to do. Just being aware of what we're feeling, after years of covering up many of our emotions, is hard enough. Discovering an accurate, effective way to put those feelings into words is equally difficult; we have not developed a very good vocabulary for talking to each other about our feelings. Finally, finding the right time, place, people, *and* the courage to share those tender parts of ourselves makes the whole process complex and very hard for most of us to do with any regularity and satisfaction.

On top of all that, this is a society that does not honor feelings; ideas are fine, rational thinking is rewarded, but the expression of our feelings is systematically denied.

The feelings expressed here are responses to my requests either to talk or write about one's own feelings in 31 categories. You may find some of your "favorite" feelings missing; I hope not. I don't believe I chose the feelings in a very scientific way, which is appropriate. These 31 are honed down from various lists of emotions, feelings, moods, and states I found myself in, observed in others or picked up from one medium or another.

Each feeling receives pretty much the same attention, though I consider some more important, more prevalent than others. I didn't want to arbitrarily decide which feelings to emphasize though; what's important to me may not be to you. So much for the sections.

I believe the people in the book have something in common. They are all aware of their feelings, at least some of the time; they know, to varying degrees, the value of expressing themselves about their feelings and they are explorers of a sort, in search of new parts of themselves.

I came into contact with most of the people at or through the Center for Studies of the Person. CSP is a loose-knit amalgamation of people who are interested in human growth and the enrichment of individuals' lives in our society. In one way or another they express this in their work. Some are psychologists, sociologists, and counselors—loosely categorized in the "helping professions." Some are artists, teachers, or writers, and some are without any kind of professional title. But the point is not so much what they do, but who they are.

To me, a good number of them are very good friends and I count myself fortunate to be able to say that. One of the things we try to do at CSP, perhaps the most important thing to many of us, is build a personal community of sorts, an extended family, so there is a place we can come and let it all hang out with friends and colleagues. At the same time, often in the same meeting, we can share our feelings about a recent "upper" or "downer" in our lives, then move on to a business agenda similar to other corporations with large professional staffs.

This sense of what the Center is is important to the book because, in a way, I have taken advantage of who we are and the way we live our lives to get this book done. I have horned in, with a notepad and tape recorder, and taken word pictures of people's feelings. The expressions in this book are similar to the way we talk to each other at CSP most of the time, but not in specific categories and not under such systematic questioning.

In most cases, the statements were taped. Getting people to sit down and write fairly lengthy statements about their feelings proved to be a bit like persuading strangers to give me $10 out of their pocket. So I went into my friends' homes and offices with my tape recorder and we talked about being afraid, sad, joyful, attracted, and scores of other things human beings can be. A few of the statements were written, without much questioning; they are the shorter ones.

The process of putting this book together has been a very satisfying and expanding one for me; I recommend it. In the early part of the going, I was working on one emotion a week. After several months, I stepped up to two emotions a week and finished the interviewing and transcribing in six months.

I would wake up on a Monday morning and say, "Okay, this is my week for competition." I would begin to notice myself in competitive situations: Who do I feel most competitive with? Why? How does it make me act? What are the consequences of being very competitive?

Writing about that feeling would put me into it for a while. If I was scheduled to be aware of my sadness for a while and write something meaningful about it, I became sad. There was no way out of it. For people close to me, it was an unusually emotional, moody, and scattered six months.

The influence on the people I interviewed was weaker, but much the same. I found myself talking people into certain moods, helping them feel anxious, for instance, so they could talk to me about it. It got so some people refused to submit to interviews when I was doing certain sections; others would eye my approach warily, until they learned what emotion was being run through the wringer that week.

However, the occasion of sitting down at the typewriter or over the tape recorder was a growing one for both me and the person interviewed. It was a time to look down inside ourselves, search out parts of ourselves and bring them out in some kind of organized way so that someone else could understand and learn from them. I have learned very much by doing it—about myself, my friends, and about people in general.

I had some standard questions I asked that it might help you to be aware of: How does it physically feel when you're afraid? What happens to your body? How do you act it out? How do you behave? What kinds of things typically make you afraid? Do you know why? What have you learned about your fear? How is that different than you were, say, five years ago? What do you wish for yourself the next time you're afraid?

These questions weren't in every interview; sometimes they didn't need to be asked. They served as rough guidelines for a conversation. You'll see that my questions are edited out of the interviews. In most cases, they did not add to what was being said, but established, a direction which is evident in the statement itself.

I took very few liberties with what people said in these statements. Sometimes the way we talk is not as organized as we would like it to be, but I thought it was important to preserve the flavor of the way a person was talking about himself or herself. Confusion is left in, of course; we don't have it all together. Contradictory statements are left in; we contradict ourselves all the time. Often you can see a person's realizations about himself or herself in that particular emotion as the interview progresses.

These are words. That is important to remember. When I chose a book to communicate with you, there are certain things I had to give up, important things . . . movement, facial expressions, tone of voice, gestures, posture, vibrations. Those things are very important in interpersonal communications and, while you'll see many references made to them, you'll miss experiencing them. Sorry.

There are several ways you can use this book. Let me suggest a few. There's a certain amount of value in just identifying with some of the things that are said, a kind of "Wow, you-mean-someone-else-feels-that-way-too?" feeling. Sometimes that's enough to give you some courage.

I hope you learn something about yourself too; that is, you see new possibilities, new ways to grow. Only you will know what those ways are.

You can imagine yourself feeling the same way as the person talking. You can imagine being on the receiving end of the same statement. And you can jot down your reactions to that . . . how you are different, how you are the same.

Though our feelings are individual and distinct, there is commonality, which is a nice thing to keep finding out. So you can learn something about other people, people in your family or at your office, who have these emotions operating in them.

Some words of caution. These feelings represent parts of multi-dimensional people. They are parts that bubble to the surface sometimes; later, a contradictory part may surface. We change.

I am not an expert. The people in this book are not experts, at least not about you. I think it would be a mistake to take our feelings, our reflections, and our actions and make them yours. We don't know what is best for you. You might treat this book as a mine, full of iron ore, gold, silver, zinc, some granite to pick through and even some fool's gold. Take from it what you will.

Remember, you are the only expert on yourself. Ultimately you are the only one responsible for yourself. Some people know more about themselves than others, but there is *always* something to be learned, always a way to grow.

We are incomplete. And that's good.

The Decline and Fall of Our Feelings

The whole image of a man in America today is: You can't feel.
I say, goddammit, let me feel.

A Vietnam veteran

All of us, men and women, get the message: "Don't cry; things will be all right!" "Don't get mad; it won't do any good." "Be happy. There's no use walking around sad." "Hey, control yourself; lets not lose our heads."

Our heads we are not losing. On the contrary, the head is worshipped in America. Rationality rules. Clear, logical thinking is rewarded. Feeling and expressing feelings is mostly for children—when it's appropriate. Women have certain feelings reserved for them, but others are not acceptable. Men are "allowed" even fewer feelings.

In the first few years of our lives we experience and express a wide range of feelings. We get angry, sad, confused, stubborn, needy, joyous, jealous, and anything else we damn please. It doesn't matter much that our parents or others around us aren't ready for that feeling and it upsets the pattern of their living. As babies, when we got mad, people knew it, and quick.

But Archie Bunker's message to his wife, "Edith, stifle yourself!", starts coming in loud and clear, in different ways, as we get a bit older. "Don't cry, you'll upset your mother." "Will you shut up! Everyone is looking at us."

Parents, teachers, aunts, uncles and in-laws start to have their effect.

They tell us it's appropriate to have certain feelings at certain times, otherwise, don't rock the boat.

As we get older, the media, schools and other institutions start to influence us. From an early age until we reach the time when we have the guts and wherewithal to break out of the mold, many of our feelings are systematically denied or stuffed back down our throats. All that stuffing and stifling makes it awfully uncomfortable down there.

The schools get to us early on. Here is a short poem by a fourth grader in the San Diego City schools, published in an annual creative poetry book. It seems typical of the influence he's under already.

Babies howl
Children whine
Bears growl
Owls moan
Losers weep
But big boys
Don't cry!

This "big boy" is all of nine years old. He has already learned, as well as he has learned any of his more formal lessons, that if his sadness or emotional pain results in tears, his peers and some adults will think less of him. More important perhaps, he begins to think less of himself for yielding to what are in fact healthy expressions of emotion.

While schools cannot be totally blamed for repressing our emotions, it is certainly true that they do not allow enough time or encouragement for healthy emotional expression by individual human beings. They too often, in fact, reinforce the unhealthy attitudes found in the media, the military, business, and other institutions.

This neglect of so much of our very human-ness prompted the Carnegie Commission to report: "Public schools are quite literally destructive of human beings."

The situation hasn't gone totally unrecognized. In a recent National Education Association paper, Arthur Combs, professor of education at University of Florida, wrote:

"What makes people human are matters of feeling, belief, values, attitudes, understandings. Without these things a man is nothing. These are the qualities which make people human. They are also the qualities which, in our zeal to be objective, we have carefully eliminated from much of what goes on in our public schools. The problem of dehumanization is no accident. We brought it on ourselves. We have created a Frankenstein's monster which has broken loose to run amok among us. We have become the victims of our preoccupations with the wrong problems. But we got into this fix because of our intelligence and it is our intelligence which can get us out again if we truly believe that humanization is important. We can find ways to humanize our schools. As a matter of fact, we had better do so. Anything less means that we have failed everyone, ourselves, our students, and society itself."

Edgar Dale, the Ohio State University educator, also addressed the problem in his monthly newsletter:

"We have become more concerned about the minds of our students than we have about their hearts, more concerned with their intellect than we have with their emotions. We examine intellectual growth more than we examine growth in values. We have emphasized what students *know* but underemphasized a concern for what they deeply *care* about, their attitude toward life, their zest for living."

The schools *could* take more of a part in our emotional development —for the better, that is. It is time that administrators, teachers, school boards, and PTA's recognized that learning about interpersonal communication, self-actualization, emotional expression and the psychological development of ourselves is more important, even to elementary school students, than the geography of Kenya, how wheat is turned into bread or that seven times seven is 49.

Learning is much easier when any individual has a sense of his or her self-worth, has learned some things about how they communicate, how to take risks, grow, and go after what they want. That person has a zest about reaching out and exploring things, extending, sharing. It is, at the same time, sad, maddening, and frustrating that in my own children, I see this discouraged instead.

Though the schools have a frightening influence on our emotional development, other institutions make their mark as well. The news media, through which we learn about other human beings in our global and local communities, does little to encourage personal expression and more human contact among us.

Newsrooms in newspapers, news magazines, and television stations are serious, emotionless places. There is no room for feelings in the "news." That would be too "personal," too "subjective." Our daily diet of information about our neighbors and institutions, in the eyes of the news editors, has to be "objective."

"A reporter learns early to separate himself from the story," NBC newsman John Chancellor, said in a recent interview. "As a young reporter, I was told time and time again, 'Keep yourself out of a story; who the hell cares about you?' "

To anyone who knows news editors, that's not an atypical remark, and if that's the message reporters and editors keep getting, how can we expect them to do a better job at transferring information that brings us closer together as human beings? The point is not so much that a reporter is taught to keep his own biases and prejudices out of his stories—any communicator should be aware of those and state them. But, as a person, he learns over and over again that professional rewards come from detachment, aloofness and a preoccupation with hard facts. As a person and a professional, then, he becomes less and less sensitive to people's feelings and less apt to communicate about them.

Our news media rely on facts, events, eruptions, and changes for its daily bread, but in personal behavior as well as group behavior, those events are often merely symptoms of underlying attitudes and feelings. Those attitudes and feelings are saved for occasional editorials or "think pieces" in most of the media that supply us our news. "Human interest" stories are sometimes used, but they are supplemental to "hard news."

The resistance by many newsmen to "personal journalism" is only one indication of how the expression of emotions, opinions or anything "subjective" is regarded by the media. Blacks, students, poor people, "hippies" and, more recently, women, have discovered that the strongly defended "objectivity" of our media is but one more subjectivity and that it is, for the most part, white, middle-aged, middle-class, male, and affluent.

The next time you read a newspaper or watch television news take a good look at the information we as a society are passing on to each other. How does it improve your life? How does it affect your human-ness? What does it cause you to think and feel about the people who live in your community? The Frankenstein monster Arthur Combs saw in the classroom is loose in the newsroom too.

While the media and the schools affect nearly all of our lives, only some of us are touched directly by the military, but to those who have served or are members of the armed services, the impact of the military and military training on their emotional lives is deep and permanent.

I shudder when I think about the millions of young men who have gone through military training in this country, the men and women who are spending their working lives in military installations and the number of children growing up in a house run like a platoon.

In my conversations, discussion groups and encounter groups with military personnel or veterans, there is almost unanimous agreement that the military way of life not only puts one in situations that discourage feeling and expressing emotions, but that feelings are systematically and purposely denied.

In a New York City "rap group" for returning Vietnam veterans, one vet said:

"After all that physical and verbal abuse (in training) you're humiliated until you're emotionally at the lowest level that you can possibly be—until you feel like hiding in a hole in the ground. So the next time, you want to do everything correctly, just to please your master, just to avoid that abuse. In bayonet practice, I went at those dummies like crazy—though I'm not even a hostile person. Then they put a machine gun in my hands."

From the same article about Vietnam vets in *The Progressive,* Nora Sayre talks more about the military and feelings:

"Above all, the military told them that men must not have emotions of any sort; also, 'Don't be afraid, you're a man.' This is called the 'John Wayne image.' One said: 'The whole image of a man in America today is: You can't feel. I say, goddammit, let me feel.' "

Hundreds of thousands of veterans have returned to a complex, rapidly changing civilian life in the past few years with training and experiences that tell them their feelings should be stuffed down and held in their stomachs. It is a massive understatement to say that this is unhealthy, not only for the individual lives of the men and women, but for us as a society.

Military training and military experience by nature require a certain amount of dehumanization in an age where we desperately need all the humanization we can get.

Men suffer this experience the most. Our mold is made for us. Our image of the ideal man is cast and stressed over and over every day, and in order to be accepted, we fit into it. Crying is out. Tenderness is out. Sadness is out. Uncertainty is out. We must be cool, strong, in control, know what we're doing and know what is right for others around us who don't know.

American women, for the most part, don't go through military training. Yet they go through "training" of a different sort. Parents, teachers, the media, et al., tell them what they can feel and can't. Anger is out. Aggressiveness is definitely out. Superiority is out. Open expression of attraction to the opposite sex is out. Tenderness and crying is *in* (somebody in the family has to have it, I guess) but strength, control, and assertiveness are the domains of the man.

In the remarkable book, *Our Bodies, Our Selves,* by the Boston Women's Health Book Collective, the women who put the book together felt it was important to talk about their emotional health and they said some things we can all learn from:

"We realized that as women we had been raised to be nice to everyone, to please everyone, and that we had not allowed ourselves to experience ambivalent feelings about ourselves and others. Facing this allowed us to be more honest with ourselves and others.

"As we were changing, we found we were frequently angry. This surprised us and embarrassed us. We had grown up feeling that we needed to love everyone and be loved by everyone. If we got angry at someone, or they at us, we felt in some sense that we were failures. We shared memories of our pasts. Nearly all of us had had a hard time expressing anger verbally or physically . . . We began to admit that we felt angry during our lives, but we had been using the anger against ourselves in hating ourselves. There are many ways we had learned to cover up our anger. It has built up for so long inside us that we were afraid we would explode if we let it out. We have come to realize that there are many aspects of our lives and our relationships that make us angry . . . The anger that is in us is a starting point for creative change and growth.

"Probably the most valuable learning for each of us was learning to feel good about speaking for ourselves and being ourselves."

Speaking for ourselves is a hard thing to do and it is made a lot harder by the roles we're asked to play by people close to us and society at large. Some of those roles, as we've seen, are downright blunt about discouraging any feelings at all. Some of the roles, particularly in the business worlds, ask us to be pleasant and professionally personal. Airline stewardesses, bank tellers, public relations people and restaurant personnel are trained to be pleasant at all costs. This costs them a part of themselves.

What is the toll we pay for thinking we have to behave in certain patterns all our lives and repeatedly denying our own emotions?

We miss discovering. We miss the unexpected. We miss a richness in life. We miss touching other people, really touching them. We miss exploring the unknown, the undiscovered in ourselves. We miss being fully human.

The tragedy of our lives today will be not so much what we suffer, but what we miss, what we don't experience, and there is so much we are repeatedly cutting ourselves off from. Self-denial has become a way of life for us.

It is our feelings that we rely on to tell us what is important in our lives. According to Carl Jung, "Sensation establishes what is actually given, thinking enables us to recognize its meaning, feelings tell us its value." Our physical senses and our intellects can only tell us so much. The values in our lives, the impact, the passion are cut off when we repress our feelings.

I don't want to suggest that we surrender and be governed only by our emotions. I want to be able to bring all of myself into being . . . my intellect, my will or spiritual self and my feeling self. It is when I can take stock of and act on my whole self, that I am most joyous.

But we have gotten out of balance. We are out of touch with our selves and it follows that we are out of touch with each other. Our emotional self is sadly neglected, tagging along behind our heads, still, without our control or even acquaintance, it subtly but pervasively manipulates our lives and the lives of those around us.

When we deny that we are mad at someone or hurt by them, we are not only cutting ourselves off from our own feelings, we are putting distance between ourself and another human being. When we are unwilling to admit and report our own insecurity, we are increasing its hold on us.

We cannot pick and choose the emotions we can have. We cannot pull out only the good ones and share those so everyone will like us. We can't, that is, without paying the price of not being known—by ourselves or others—not being understood, not being loved.

Where all this self-denial gets us in the end is loneliness. We are the lonely people. Psychiatrists, psychologists, sociologists and journalists are spending a lot of time these days writing about our loneliness and how closed we have become. It seems it is one of the by-products of a rapidly changing technological age.

We all open and close. We all have suffered scars in our growing, wounds that are tender and not easy to expose. We all have suffered pain, are afraid of suffering pain, been close to someone who has. None of us wants to be lonely. Yet to admit that, to share that part of yourself with someone is hard.

I once wrote about my own opening and closing in this way:

Poem for everyman

> I will present you
> parts
> of
> my
> self
> slowly
> if you are patient and tender.
> I will open drawers
> that mostly stay closed
> and bring out places and people and things
> sounds and smells, loves and frustrations, hopes and sadnesses,
> bits and pieces of three decades of life
> that have been grabbed off
> in chunks
> and found lying in my hands.
> they have eaten
> their way into my memory,
> carved their way into
> my heart.
> altogether—you or i will never see them—
> they are me.
> if you regard them lightly,
> deny that they are important
> or worse, judge them
> i will quietly, slowly,
> begin to wrap them up,
> in small pieces of velvet,
> like worn silver and gold jewelry,
> tuck them away
> in a small wooden chest of drawers
>
> and close.

Awkward and afraid we set out to meet each other. Our first attempts are slow and hard. We make small offerings at first, a word, a smile, a feeling shared. If they're received with acceptance and warmth, we go a little further. So it is with all of us who want love. Some are encased in a harder, thicker shell than others, but a human is in there just the same.

I want to tell you who I am. I want to be understood and loved. But I'm afraid you won't like me. I'm afraid you will not accept my inconsistency, my sexual feelings, my failures, even my fears of you.

If I am that tender, that afraid, how do I begin to share myself with you? What kinds of things do I say? What will happen when I start sharing my feelings with you?

Insides Out

Often the shortest distance between two people is a straight line, a straight line like: "I need you." or "That really hurts me." or "I'm afraid to tell you what I'm feeling now because you may not like it."

For a lot of us, those kinds of straight lines are unusual. We talk to each other about the weather, yesterday's football game, how things went at work, the neighbors . . . things outside ourselves. It's not that those things are not important, but all too many of us go no deeper.

We know how to talk about things outside of our being, but we don't know how to talk about ourselves. Underneath our talk about other things, other people, other events, are feelings that are only ours. Behind our opinion of how the neighbor treats her children is our feeling about our own children. Behind our accusations of our wife may be our own frustration with how the day has gone. Underneath our aloofness, our distance, is a feeling that no one really loves us.

Why should we share those kinds of things with anybody? What is the profit in continually sharing yourself with others?

Let me answer for myself. I am not alone. In between the aloneness of my birth and my death, I may be by myself in space and time, but my existence here is with other people. I am a social animal and my time here is best spent encircling my relationships with others.

I don't mean to deny in one the need to be alone, to have a relationship with myself, in a sense. I do know, however, how much payoff comes in interaction with others.

There are very deep drives in me to communicate with others, to be understood, to be loved. I've learned how very much of my life—my hopes, my fears, my growth, my rewards—has to do with deepening personal relationships. I believe most of us are like this; underneath a lot of other urges—for money, power, property, security—are deep human needs to be *with* another person.

The best way I know to be with other people, to go as deep as I need to go and gather the riches in a relationship, is to be in an open process of communication of my feelings. I share my ideas, my opinions, the "facts" I know about, the rumors I've heard, the things I've read and seen, all of those too. But my real investment is in sharing my feelings. That's the part of me, and of most of us, that seems the most neglected.

We live in an age in which we've accumulated more technical knowledge than we know what to do with. We know more about each other than we ever have before, yet we remain alienated and lonely. For me, coming together is what this book is all about. Sharing your feelings is a way of coming together.

What happens when I share my feelings? One way I could tell you about the consequences of living a more feeling-full life, that is, sharing one's feeling in a more open, honest, non-manipulative way than most of us are used to, would be to tell you about some of the things that have happened to me and my friends. These have to do with my relationships with my colleagues at Center for Studies of the Person, my children, my close friends and loves.

These learnings have come out of the last four years of my life when I've been a teacher some of the time and a student some of the time. In either case, I've been learning.

Things have surely changed. I've changed and will continue to change. That is the first thing, the most obvious thing, I think of. I think I'm fortunate to be in relationships with people who are changing too. As we all change, and share that with each other, it changes the dynamics between us. It changes the way I see them, the way they see me and the way we react to each other.

I am often surprised. There are things about me I didn't know, things about my children, my friends I didn't know. The surprises I have had have both delighted me and scared me.

I have been afraid and have tried, as much as I can, to face my fears. Sometimes I have seen the fear of changing things paralyze people so that they tighten themselves down into a knot and, as near as they can come to controlling things, will not let people or situations around them change in the slightest. The new is scary as well as exciting.

I feel like I've gotten more involved with people, really involved . . . mixed up, confused, entangled in some real messes. Feelings are unpredictable, irrational, sticky things and sometimes I've felt like I've had my hands in a batch of salt-water taffy. It takes a great deal of time and energy to work those things out.

I've been confused a lot. Feelings are often confusing, especially when I hadn't been used to admitting them to myself and sharing them with others. Confusion led me to exasperation, frustration and hopelessness. I cry a lot more than I used to.

I've gotten deeper. I've reached down deeper into myself and gotten deeper into the lives of people around me. Now I have a real hunger for that and I don't think I could do without it. I can't be superficial anymore. This is sometimes scary too. When you've been paddling along on the surface for so long, merely looking at what's going on, it's hard to dive down and get involved in what's below.

"Facts" have lost their hard edge for me; things have become more vague. The meanings of the words "right" and "wrong" are hazy to me and I discover more and more that everyone has their own truth they are living by.

As I've shared my feelings with others, I've been responded to in the same way. I get what I give. People have shared more of themselves and I have gotten some unexpected pain and some unexpected pleasures.

One result of this reciprocal sharing is a mutual trust building between friends and colleagues. Our fear of each other and what we could do to hurt each other keeps going down the more we share. At the Center, we've gone deeper than I thought was possible for a group of that size that meets that infrequently.

The structures in my life and the lives of others have changed—marriages and divorces, jobs, religious affiliations, lifestyles. Things seem to go up in the air and come down again looking quite different. The structures that I leaned on, depended on, have lost their meaning. Marriages take more work, more time, as do more of your relationships. It became harder and harder for me to stay in a professional role I had been in for many years. I got so I couldn't settle for the same level of response and companionship I had been used to. I wanted more.

I feel much more free than I ever have, determining what is right and wrong for me and letting others take care of themselves, for the most part. That doesn't mean I have come to care less about others, on the contrary I have come to care more, but I am not responsible for them.

There are times in the last three or four years when I have felt personally more powerful than ever. I have watched the same thing happen to others. It's as if you get in touch with things you didn't know you had.

I think it's not just a product of age that I have gotten more mature. I speak out for my own needs more and do something about getting them met. I found out that I am the *only* one responsible for my accomplishments and my mistakes.

It's funny. I feel more free and independent but have discovered that I am more interdependent than ever. I need and use the friends I have around me.

I feel as if I've gotten away from most roles and titles and the expectations that go along with those roles. At the same time, I find myself a little lonely at times because my identity is not as sure as it used to be. Who I am is determined by me now, not by being "father," "husband," "editor," "instructor," or "member."

I've started touching people a lot more and found out how much fun that is and how much people respond to it. I've looked at the rest of society and felt how sad it is that we don't touch each other more.

I think all of these things have made me more joyous, more full. I don't mean to suggest that instant joy comes from sharing your feelings; it doesn't. But I do think that most of us have gotten out of touch with a lot that's rumbling around inside. When I started to be more aware of that, I saw how full of things I was, how endowed with life I was. Good things and bad bubbled up to the surface. I want all of those things to come up and out; they are me.

Those are some of the things that happened to me after I had some experiences and made some conscious decisions to share more of my feelings with the people I valued. I learned that sharing my truth with someone is a way of showing them how much I value them. It is a gift I can give them.

Often this way of sharing your feelings with others seem to have no rules at all, but there are some suggestions of productive and nonproductive ways of talking to yourself about other people. We're not born with a natural skill of communicating with each other, it's something we have to learn and keep working on.

I think the most important thing I've learned is not to deny something in myself. I don't want to lie to myself, battle myself, condemn myself . . . or lie to you. To deny something in me, to repress it, only increases its strength and tightens its hold on me. I want to admit it, at least to myself; I want to explore it, turn it around and look at it, go to it and let it run its full course. Then perhaps I may want to share it with you. When I do, I want to keep some of these things in mind.

When I try to talk about myself I want to realize that I am talking about something *inside me,* not you, not the guy over there, not something I read, but just my self. That means I don't try and tell you who you are, should be or what you should do. To open myself in this way, only me, by myself, takes courage.

I want to understand that my feelings are neither good or bad, they are just my feelings. Feeling a certain way does not make me a good person or a bad person, just me. The same goes for you.

I want to know and want you to know that what I'm telling you is only a part of me; it is not my whole self and it may not last. Part of me may be mad as hell at you while a larger part still loves you. But don't try and deny my anger because you only want the other part of me.

I want you to know that I can admit feelings to myself and express them to you, but that I don't have to act on them. I may be sexually aroused by a woman, feel that deeply, think about it, report it to you and realize that I'm not going to do anything about it. Your acceptance of that feeling in me helps me.

It is usually much better to talk about something while it's going on than to wait. I might lose something important while I'm waiting; I might tuck it down inside, along with some other "stale" emotions and they will explode, all smelly and mixed up, later. Someone may miss a part of me they want.

I want to report as fully as I can. I don't want to drop a bomb and run. I want to say as much as I can about the feeling I have, no matter how unimportant or silly it seems. Then I want to stay for a response.

A lot of this business of communicating feelings depends on the responses I get from others listening and that I give to others when I'm on the listening end. It's important to remember that the person talking and the person listening are mutually responsible for making things truly understood. We all need help.

It's always good for me to give the speaker my version of what he or she has said. This feedback seems more important when you're talking about feelings since there seem to be so many nuances to be misunderstood. It's up to the speaker then to correct what the listener didn't receive.

As a listener, I try and regard the person speaking in a nonjudgmental way. This means dropping my defenses, withholding my evaluation and forgetting my investment in what is being said. This is very difficult, but very important. It is the difference between hearing what someone really means and closing them up altogether.

When I feel like I've heard the person I search myself for my true, personal response to what has been said. This may sound like a contradiction to what I just said, but I can give a response to people without judging them. If it starts out "You are" instead of "I am" it's probably wrong. What I want to give them is a message about me.

I try to be aware of all the person who's talking to me. I listen not only to the words, but the tone of voice, body movements, eyes, anything else that is expressing something. I might find myself saying something like this: "Tony, your words say that you feel perfectly okay about seeing Marcia today, but you seem really nervous and unsettled. What is that about?"

I try and let the message get to me. I take the words and meaning in and be aware of how it makes me feel. This might lead to an empathetic kind of response. If I can put myself in the other person's shoes, it will probably turn out to be a learning for both of us, but I want to resist the temptation to give advice.

If I don't totally understand what was said, I say so. There may be things that have nothing to do with the subject at hand that have to be cleared up before I can communicate with someone else. But I don't want to go away not understanding. I don't want to walk away without being understood either. I want to see that my listener has understood what I wanted to say.

When I'm busy defending myself, no matter how subtly, it is impossible to keep efficient communication going. As the sender of the message, I get wrapped up in ways of dancing around the message without really revealing myself. I am afraid to say what is really going on inside. As a listener, I become occupied with what I'm going to say or do next to convince the speaker he or she doesn't feel that way and why it's good or bad.

Psychologist Jack Gibb has a marvelous story about defensive communication. A mother and her young son are in the house alone, in separate rooms, when a mild earth tremor shakes the building. The windows rattle, the hanging light in the kitchen sways. The mother cries out: "Bobby, where are you?" Bobby, playing quietly in his room, shouts back: "Mommy, I didn't do it."

Sometimes just questions make us close our gates and prepare our defenses.

There are climates you and I can set for others, and for ourselves, to help feelings come out. I think these "personal environments" are equally applicable to couples, friends, families, classrooms, clubs, and offices.

These are some situations or atmospheres that make it hard for me to say what I'm feeling: I'm feeling constantly judged or evaluated for what I say. The person I'm with feels superior to me (or inferior) and lets me know that. I am not really listened to. People don't care about what I say; they merely listen and don't react. Everyone seems certain about what they say, the decisions they make and the way they lead their lives; they are not confused. When I say something serious, even if it is veiled, I get laughed at. No matter what I say, people have me in a box and try and fit me into that box for their own purpose.

These are things that help me express myself: The people I'm with really want to hear what I'm saying, even when it may say something painful about them. They give their attention to my message, spoken and unspoken. They take time with me. They accept me for what I am and don't evaluate me or the feelings I have. They respond; they are genuine and spontaneous in conversations with me. People don't try and manipulate me. They don't think they're better or worse than I am, but can see our differences. They can understand my point of view and empathize with me. Most of the time they are not afraid of me and if they are they let me know.

These are not meant to be rules; we couldn't remember all of them when we're talking to each other anyway. These are guideposts, things I've learned (but have trouble always applying) about getting in touch with the people I care about. Stated this way, they seem pretty basic to me, but it's ignoring or not knowing these basics that get us into such messes with each other.

If you care, you can get a lot done.

Knowing all this, at least in my head, I still question sometimes whether or not it's worth it. Sharing myself with someone or lots of someones is hard work; make no mistake. It takes time and energy and caring.

Sometimes, when I get in a bad place, it seems very easy for me to retreat into myself. It seems so easy to draw in, pull in all my playthings, cover up my tender spots and stop trying.

Often I feel like an explorer, but instead of charting new waters, I am sailing through the darkness of the spaces inside of me. I'm trying out new ways of being. I'm looking for answers and knowing at the same time there are no answers I'll settle for. I'm walking over mountain tops, not knowing what I'll see on the other side. I feel like I'm going into my own unknown.

It's hard sometimes. It helps to read things like this, by e.e. cummings:

> to be nobody-but-yourself—
> in a world which is doing its best,
> night and day,
> to make you everybody else—
> means to fight the hardest battle
> which any human being can fight;
> and never stop fighting.*

My isolation, or wishes for it, doesn't last long. I need too much. I need you; I need myself. When I start to shut down and pull in, I am numbing the parts of me that are human, giving, loving, expansive, joyous. I want to know and use all parts of me.

The more I know myself and use different parts of myself, the fuller I become. The fuller I become, the more I have to say and do . . . the more creative I am. I have more to share with you. I gain more courage to live in a complex world that whirls around me. The more I have of myself, the easier it is to reach out to you.

Are you there?

How are you feeling?

* From *E. E. Cummings: A Miscellany,* ed. by George J. Firmage. Reprinted by permission of Harcourt Brace Jovanovich, Inc.

ACCEPTED

You say you want me to change. I will change easier when you accept me as I am.

John Wood

᠕᠕᠕

Terry Van Orshoven

How does it feel to be accepted? . . . good, warm, comfortable, relaxed. It feels secure, important; takes away demands and expectations. With acceptance I give myself the opportunity to be with someone without demands or with a great lessening of demands on me. When I don't feel accepted I will place demands on myself to be something other than I really am, or want to be.

I think about acceptance as a comfort zone; I am comfortable, yet I'm still accountable. Like in my work, management consulting, I'm meeting new groups of people and new individuals week after week. I feel the most potent in those cases when I accept myself and feel accepted for who I am. That happens when the expectations going in are either clear or low, when the demands on us all are reduced, when there are no "hidden agendas" and criteria for what is needed for success are not so strict. Then I am not floundering around sorting out criteria for so-called responsible behavior in our relationship; I'm not computerizing or fantasizing inputs and needs from others and sorting them out. I am focusing on what I want to do with them; I can be more aware of myself, more present, through acceptance. It just turns my creative thinking on.

When that's not present what I most often do is start talking to the expectations; it has become almost a ritual. I start talking about my expectations, why I'm there, what I intend to do, what I want to learn, what I want from them.

Somehow it seems the same when I think of more intimate, one-to-one relationships, such as marriage. When Marcia and I are more clearly running out our expectations on each other, it seems to raise the acceptance we have of ourselves and of each other and the environmental set we're working in. Like with the children, if she expects me to be "Daddy" or expects me to be disciplinarian or wrestler, it's really helpful for me to know what those expectations are and then I can accept them or reject them. And it seems that sometimes rejection is part of acceptance for me; that is when I am really accepted I can say "no" and have that accepted too. I can reject a demand or expectation of her and still be accepted.

After those expectations are out front, it seems that the issues and the priorities start getting talked about and it becomes a process of talking about needs and satisfactions and conflicts. This may sound like a very constructed, artificial thing, but I don't experience it that way. Acceptance is not a ritualistic pattern to be gone through.

There are certain kinds of people who make me feel more accepted . . . people who are congruent with their own personalities, people who are "together," that are doing most of what they need to do for themselves. I feel a lot of self acceptance when others feel a lot of self acceptance for themselves; it's very contagious in that way. ⤸

Howard Saunders

Acceptance means different things to me. I think about the difference between being accepted and being liked. Acceptance is bigger than liked; it takes in being liked *and* disliked. And it takes in more than being tolerated too; I don't like it so much when I feel I'm being tolerated. I'd much rather feel truly accepted.

I want to be accepted by everybody, but mostly I want to accept myself. If I'm accepting myself I feel good. If I'm not changing my behavior based on what other people want from me then it seems like I'm accepting myself. And when people accept me, whenever I'm doing my crazy number, then I know I'm cared about. I seem to operate in some crazy ways sometime that really put a demand on people to accept me. Sometimes I think I'm a really difficult person to feel accepting towards and the people that I like best are the people that can accept me and all those crazy places I can get into. If I'm not accepted at those times, I go crazier, I mean it gets worse.

Other people's acceptance affects me depending on how I feel about myself. If I feel great, really feeling good about myself—not just accepting myself, but feeling good about myself—than it almost doesn't matter about the acceptance of others. I'm just oblivious to it. Sometimes when I get into those really good places, really high and wide, I'm as difficult to be with as when I'm really hurting, sometimes even more difficult. Sometimes there's just not much for another person to say when I'm into feeling really bad, I share that too, but it's harder for other people to hook into a real high . . . unless they're feeling that way too. And if someone else is feeling that way too, you can get into some really neat places.

It's important for me to be accepted when I am in a bad place—and I think I'm good at accepting myself at those times—but it's hard for me when it involves others accepting my really negative trips. Like one day last week I went home wanting to feel welcome and warm, hoping someone would be there, and Patsy was holding the women's group there that night, which meant I had to go sit in my room by myself and not disturb what was going on. It made me feel horrible, homeless . . . really awful. I was really miserable. When we talked later she got mad at me for laying a trip on her about closing off the house. What I really wanted was to be accepted for feeling awful; I really needed that. And I got kind of hysterical about that; I kind of freaked out. I understand how she felt, but I couldn't slough off that horrible homeless feeling I had. I just really needed to be accepted. Those are the kinds of times, when I'm really bad like that and I can't get out of it and if it affects someone else, that's when I need most to be accepted instead of having it turned back on me.

Sometimes it seems like those situations for me are a microcosm of the whole rest of society; people are not willing to accept others' bad places, their negative numbers. I mean it's really hard to and I'm not so good at it myself at times. But knowing that about myself, how much I need that acceptance, how important it is, makes it easier for me to accept others in their bad places.

It seems like the good times take care of themselves and in the bad times I really need the acceptance of people around me that I care about; that's when it's most important.

Ralph Keyes

When I feel like I'm accepted, it feels like an emotional sauna. It feels good, warm; it makes me relax. I let down my guard and don't consider so much what I am saying and what affect it will have. The tension of how I'm going over with others seems to disappear.

I think of a couple of ways, situations in which I feel accepted . . . one is good, the second is better. The first is to be with people who feel like accepting people, saintly figures who accept me because they accept most everybody; that's a good feeling to be with people like that. But even better, for me, is to be with people I've known over a period of time (and who may or may not be saintly figures) that know me. They know me well enough to know what's right with me, but more important, they know what's wrong with me. I feel like they've seen enough of what's wrong with me, the worst that they're going to see and still consider me a friend, someone they like to be with and love, not for lacking faults, but despite my faults. That to me is acceptance, acceptance by someone who knows the worst I'll let them see and come back for more.

Sometimes after sharing an intense emotional experience with someone, and I've seen this happen in encounter groups, you will come to a point of real acceptance, of being in love with each other in a way. At that point, anything you say and do is okay. No one will judge you or condemn you; that's a very pure kind of acceptance, born out of a real sharing of intense good and bad things. But that can't last; it seems to die soon after the experience.

You meet the same people later and you are on guard again, as they are. That can show you what it's like, but it seems temporary.

More long range is the acceptance of a few friends who I have trusted enough to let them see a lot of different things in me, a lot of different sides of me, and I know they won't split; they'll hang in there with me. I can think of specific times when I feel like I've really blown it completely with someone, been scared to see them a day or two later and been pleasantly surprised they are still my friend. Not that they've liked what I did, or a way I was, but that they realize its part of being human, or even better that they see that I did what I did because I was hurting in some way.

When I'm not accepted I'm just not natural at all. It seems to make me behave in a lot of strange ways, some of which I'm not even aware of. I'm not what I think of as me; I'm playing out roles, acting so that I'll be accepted or so I can hold people off until I can get away. It means tensions, muscles tightening, stomach hurting to me; a tensing up to protect.

I think I have spent most of my life not feeling accepted, to the point where that's been like a natural state of things for me. I think I've spent much of my life behaving in very odd ways, most of the time not realizing it, because I felt unaccepted. It seems only recently that I'm taking chances, making true friends and feeling accepted.

The whole question of acceptance has become more and more important to me, perhaps more important than love or like, in a way. I can like or love a number of people in particular circumstances in different ways, but the acceptance and the accepting of a long period of time seems more important.

There's a real question in this whole acceptance thing . . . it seems we all want to be accepted, but do we want to accept? Sometimes I don't know.

Another one, that I wrestle with constantly, is when to accept someone and when to call someone, when to say, "That's who you are and that's okay" or when to say, "You're bullshitting me and you're fucking around and you're hurting me and I'm *not* going to accept that." It's really hard and I think I'll be wise when I can figure out which is which.

John Wood

The best way I can think of to describe how I feel when I'm accepted is to say that I flow. There is little or no hesitation, no censoring of things I'm going to say or do, I just flow out into the situation and into the people I'm with. Being with people that I feel accept me helps me be spontaneously me.

I have this on-going fantasy to do with acceptance; I have found myself into it several times in group situations. I imagine that all of us in the group are Indian chiefs in an important council. We are all very important people and whatever we say is listened to with attention by each of the other chiefs. I value all the other chiefs and their wisdom— in whatever way it is expressed—as they value me and mine. Each of us accepts the notion that whatever another says is true; we do not deny it, laugh at it, or defend an opposite point of view. We *accept* each other.

I wish more people had this feeling about the various times and ways they come together for meetings. That kind of acceptance seems to bring out my uniqueness, my creativity, my own best self to the issue or situation at hand.

When I am with a person who truly accepts me, I have the feeling he or she is pulling things out of me, almost like they were pulling in a fishing line, hand over hand. Words and images, hopes and fears just seem to keep coming out of me. I am not being judged, I am not being made fun of, I am not being argued with.

On the other hand, it seems that all too often I am fighting to present myself. I am choosing my words carefully, to make sure what I say is not going to be jumped on for poor word choice; I must say exactly what I mean. I look for openings in the conversation. I feel as if I have to be something to the other person or persons, as if I have to fit into a role that they need. It is during these latter occasions and immediately after them that I feel discouraged, bound up, and not known to the people I've been with.

By contrast, being with people who accept me makes me feel more powerful, more natural, and more in love. Writing this makes me realize how important that is.

When I think about that and look at myself, I realize how hard it is for me to feel completely accepted. Like I was home alone this morning with some really good music on and I was dancing in the living room, really letting go. But I'm self-conscious about my dancing and if someone would have walked in I would have stopped immediately, even, or maybe especially, someone I knew well. I think that they'll judge the way I dance. It hits me that I feel that way in a lot of other situations . . . If I do what I'm really feeling, people are going to judge me for it. They'll say, "He's crazy," or "He's selfish," or "He can't dance very well." That really restrains me and I wish it wouldn't. It also leads me to say, to my-self, "What the hell am I putting this on other people for?" If I accept myself, I'll dance the way I want to.

AFFECTIONATE

Affection is the broadest basis of good in life.
George Eliot

‿‿‿

Jack Bowen

Most often I feel affection physically; I want to reach out and hug. It's like a body surge toward someone. If I can't complete that, can't get in touch with the object of my affection, I'm left with a very incomplete feeling. It's like being angry and not being able to hit someone.

With Andy, my little boy, it's like all my stops are out when I'm feeling affection for him. I can feel just as excited and physical as I want to. And act on it. We have this little game we play, almost a ritual. I'll say to him: "Andy, I'll bet you don't know who loves you." And he'll smile and say: "Daddy loves me." Then he'll hug me. That really feels good to me.

With adults it's not quite so wide open. I feel more distance from adults. I sometimes feel uncomfortable about it because of what other people might think. Or I hold back because I might offend the other person. Sometimes it's hard for me to know what to do.

There are signs or cues that I see in people that I feel affectionate toward. One of these is touching. If I reach out and touch someone and they draw back or stiffen or seem cold to it, that can make me withdraw. I look for cues that they too feel affectionate, that they value me. I don't think I invest really warm feelings like that very often. I tend to be more standoffish and don't let myself get involved with people very easily. Part of that, I'm sure, is the fear of being rejected; the sexual aspects of that are scary too, of being sexually rejected. Very often my feelings of affection are sexual, but sometimes it's just a warm, cozy feeling inside and I don't need to do much about it. That is, sometimes I feel I need to be physical; other times I don't. For instance with Bob; I feel a lot of affection for Bob, but I don't very often want to be physically close to him. With you, I really like what I see . . . the way you move, the way you conduct yourself, the way you're living your life, things like that. When I feel affection for you it's almost always wanting to be physical with you.

Most of the time I'd prefer not to have to make that distinction, whether it's sexual or not. I'd like to just go ahead and let my feelings go. Perhaps they'll turn out to be sexual, perhaps not.

But that being physical with people is my best way of showing affection. Letting my body go with others and having them do the same leaves me feeling, clean, alive and refreshed. It's almost like a ritual that I need. A lot of the time I catch myself sitting very stiffly, looking very much my pious, competent self, when what I'd really much rather do is curl up in somebody's lap and just lie there. Nothing going on. It just feels good lying there, listening to their belly rumble.

Tony Rose

It may sound funny, but I feel like a very affectionate person. I find myself repeatedly getting these warm feelings, having a happy, teary-eyed smile and wanting to hug somebody, cuddle somebody or snuggle into somebody. If it's someone I know, I just let myself do that. If it's someone I don't know well, I feel it in my eyes . . . and kind of a gulp in my throat and a warm bubble in my stomach. That feeling really fills me and fills a lot of my life.

If I let that go and it kind of flows down through my body and starts to go into my genitals, then I know I'm into a different kind of affection. There's more energy there. There's still a softness, but there's a kind of drive to be sexual with that person, to enter. I only let that happen when I'm with women. I could let that happen with some men I guess, but I don't. I usually take someone in with my eyes and let them go down into my chest, but I cut it off in my belly; I don't let my feelings for anyone get beyond that now except for Sandy.

There's a definite change in the energy when it does get below and into my genitals; it's almost like my center of gravity changes. When my emotions are up in my head or throat or chest, I'm kind of leaning over to someone, enfolding them, kind of protecting them. When it goes down, when that energy flows down into my genitals, everything shifts and I want to thrust, to enter. It's almost a penetrating instead of an enfolding. Or they both can go on at once. I talk about that in physical terms because that's what happens with me, but I think those same kinds of feelings can go on when I'm sitting across the room from someone.

When I think about what draws me to people and makes me feel affectionate, I think about eyes. I attach a lot to eyes, warm, inviting eyes, to start. Then if a smile comes, I can melt. If the person moves closer to me, I melt even more. If they talk softly and move gently and we have a tender physical contact—a hand, a shoulder, a knee—those are definite signals that I'm with an affectionate person, that I can be affectionate.

I wish people could be more that way. I think I could be that way with just about anybody I've ever met. If we give ourselves a chance to relax, we will find that in each other.

But obviously things cut that off in us. The strongest thing I think about is roles . . . all the different roles we have that rule out affection as a way of relating. So many of the traditional roles we have leave very little room for affection. There's some room for it between a male supervisor and a female employee, for instance. But between a female supervisor and a male employee, it's taboo. Just ticking off in my head some of the roles that limit our affection . . . teacher-student, student-student, male-male, almost all the roles in the military services . . . you can think of others. When I'm in situations where that's operating, I like to try and break it down. I like people to know that I like them, that I care about them. It turns out that things do change when that kind of energy gets going.

When I'm feeling soft and affectionate and can't act that out for one reason or another, I start to feel alienated and I withdraw. I begin to feel rejected when I haven't even been rejected. I'll be feeling warm and wishing we were talking softly and cuddling up to each other and I'll hear a big intellectual trip going on that's so far removed from where I am, I feel like they're rejecting me and don't even know it.

Another side of it is, I have this pervasive feeling that my affection is a place of vulnerability, of almost weakness, for me; that when I'm soft and affectionate, I can be hurt easily. On the other hand, the impact of my affection on others is very strong. Sometimes it's a threat. If I come in gushing and loving when a group is in the midst of something else— they're in their head and I come in out of my heart—it just jerks them all around. It's something people want very much, that affection, but they don't want to be vulnerable in that way. They're not at all sure they want to be open to this flow of feelings. I think there's a real potency in softness in that way.

John Wood

I have a real sense of softness when I feel affectionate. I'm receptive somehow . . . gathering in, taking people in. I feel open and available to the person or people I'm with. There's something large about it too. "There's enough of me to have you in here. I am large, come be a part of me. Come into me." I seem to be saying.

Women, smaller people, children and soft men bring up these feelings in me. Maybe that has something to do with seeing them as needing affection and/or protection. I can enfold them and be something fatherly to them.

I have gotten to the point where most of the time I'll act on my affectionate feelings. It doesn't seem to matter much what observers will think of my being physical, *as long as* the person that's the object of that is in tune with me. When the person I'm feeling that way towards is ready to receive me, I could care less about others, but it's a damn lonely feeling to want to give that to someone and get a cold shoulder or a shield of some kind out front. I can be affectionate to someone who doesn't want to be affectionate in return, but I can't give it when they don't want it. The nicest thing, of course, is when it's working both ways, when we're both open and available to each other; that's really contagious.

Thinking about being that way with someone receiving, accepting, soft, helping, allowing them in, gathering them in—makes me think about the opposite way of being with someone. I think about something physically between people, a shell or shield. There's an uptightness, a pushing away, a denial. Those kinds of things seem the opposite of affectionate to me and, unfortunately, the way most of us relate to each other. It strikes me that because of social taboos and roles that we lock each other into and other things, that it is hard to be affectionate with each other. It's hard to be soft. It's hard to make my way through the world being open and vulnerable, which is part of being affectionate, when I learn over and over again to close and defend. It seems a paradox saying it this way, but it feels like I have to be strong to remain soft. But when the alternative is to be stiff and cold with people, it doesn't seem much of a choice to me.

Joann Justyn

When I feel affection I feel really warm and excited. It kind of bubbles up inside of me and pushes me forward. It feels very good and I don't like to have to keep it inside; I want to go with it. When it's really strong I can physically feel it, like champagne bubbles in my stomach, floating up to my chest, up to my face, making me smile and giggle. It's one of thet best sensations I have.

I think one of the things that makes me hold that back is a fear of being rejected. And when I can't express it, or am afraid to, it's a terrible feeling just to keep it locked up inside, to control it. Other things that might keep it inside are thinking I shouldn't feel that way about someone or places or situations that don't seem appropriate. When I hold it in, it kind of freezes me altogether; I don't know what to do and can't operate fully until I get rid of that locked-up feeling.

I was thinking about being affectionate at home, with my parents and my sister. We have never been very physically affectionate, ever, and the more I like that feeling and become more that way, I act that way when I visit. Like I'll be really glad to see my sister and reach out for her and she'll do a really funny thing with it; she'll pull back and give me a "what's wrong with you?" look. Sometimes that will shut me down and I'll pull back from her. But more and more lately I'm feeling comfortable being that way and letting my family handle themselves.

I believe I'm getting more and more affectionate. I think that has to do with liking myself better, feeling okay about me and saying that's a good way to be in the world. I know I won't be destroyed if I offer affection to someone and they back away from it. I feel stronger, better about me and more able to face that rejection, if it comes. And I've gotten a lot of strokes for being that way; that helps.

I feel particularly affectionate about someone if I like their body, the way they look and feel, but also the way they move through the world . . . kind of their whole physical aura. That will happen with someone I don't know at all . . . it's all non-verbal. Sometimes I will start out on that affectionate level with someone and come to know them in other ways. Other times I will begin to feel affection for someone after getting to know them in other ways. I don't know which of those things I trust more; both seem okay. They are just different with different people.

Being with people who are physically affectionate and express it helps me a lot. I think being in encounter groups helped me; that was my first experience with being affectionate with someone I didn't know all that well and I learned that it was a rewarding way to be. But when I'm not sure of myself or uncomfortable in a situation, it's hard for me to come out with my affection.

I'd like to be more comfortable with those feelings in different settings, in all situations. At home, for instance, where it's not the norm, or in places where other people aren't acting that way. For me, being affectionate is a primary way of relating to people. It's tied up with wanting to be closer to people. I want to be closer with people and that seems my way of doing that.

There's another part of it; it's like giving what you most need. It seems like I want to give affection out because I need it the most. I expect it in return. In a way, it has to do with my way of seeing the world and regarding people the way I regard myself. It is my reality to be affectionate, to give it and to need it, and I see other people as being the same as I am. But sometimes I forget that or I'm scared off.

There are days when I seem to have an affectionate feeling for the whole world. I walk down the street—in the sunshine, the wind in my hair, the birds are singing to me, I feel loving and open and it is during those moments that I believe I can fly.

AFRAID

ᔪ᷁ᔪ᷁ᔪ᷁

John Wood

What am I afraid of? I am afraid of not saying all I want to; of withdrawing. I am afraid, deeply, of not being able to give myself in love. And I am afraid of doing things that I care about but think will fail.

I think I protect myself pretty well, that I don't let myself get into many situations that I am afraid of. Maybe that's true. I know that I don't experience, or let myself feel, fear very often. But *I know* when I'm afraid.

The situation I'm thinking about is perhaps the worst kind of fear for me—someone discovering something about me that I'm certain they won't like; more—they will be repulsed.

I'm remembering the discovery my wife made once when I had an overnight stay with a girlfriend. As my wife began to realize what had happened, I caught myself looking quickly for a way out. None. The irretrievability of it hit me. I am in and can't get out—about to be exposed for what I really am. About to be accused. My breath rate stepped up and I was sure anyone could have seen my heart leaping around in my chest. Timidly, reluctantly, I started to talk about it. Wincingly, I said things I wished I was saying to an empty room. It was a stormy, painful talk and I knew the dregs would be around for months, or longer.

I remember how fear quickly leaped into my chest, how I folded my arms to hide it. Fear and hiding. Crouching away somewhere under a bush or ledge, afraid to be discovered. That's the kind of fear that means the most to me—that I'd like to be rid of the most. The fear seems to be that what I am won't be loved.

I think (hope) I handle that differently now. I try to act on all of my own best instincts, knowing that I am responsible for my own actions and knowing that I want to be able to be open about myself.

Then, I have come to know there are people who aren't going to accept me no matter what and I live with that. More important, there are people who will accept me as I am, including the parts I am afraid no one will like. But the first one who counts in that acceptance of me is me. If I can really live with myself and take the consequences of my own actions, what do I have to be afraid of?

ᔪ᷁

Chris Ross

The first flicker of fear comes into my mind . . . there is an instant alarm inside when I recognize something that could hurt me. It could be seeing my car start to slide across an icy road or realizing that my father dislikes what I just said. A dull sensation grows behind my eyes. I become aware that other parts of my body are already changing. It feels as if my blood is flaming or draining away and my limbs feel vibrant and unsteady. My heart quakes and my chest seems to sink. My fear sinks down and the stomach and abdomen become the focus of the storm as muscles turn against each other.

Then, it seems, one of two things can happen. If my eyes and ears declare that the signal from outside was a false alarm, the intensity decreases, leaving a somewhat meandering knot of tension. This may linger for some time and in this state I feel vulnerable to danger in the surroundings or from someone whom I feel may hurt me. I sometimes try and distract myself with cigarettes, drinks, or nervous munching.

But if eyes and ears confirm the dangers, the muscles in the center of my body gnash on, tighter and tighter. For protection I may fold my arms over my stomach or put my hands between my legs to allay the quaking that has started in my balls and rectum. Or else I just try and contract my body into as small a ball of fear as possible.

My attention has become riveted on the exact source of fear in the surroundings. My mind is running at an accelerated rate, working through a thousand alternatives. I may seize one. It doesn't work. I can't steer the car out of the skid! My God, my dad will see how weak I am and throw me to the ground! So I search out other actions.

When my fear is of another person, I may gain temporary respite by realizing: "I am afraid. I am still me. This is happening to me but in is only a part of me." If I am feeling strong I may own my fear and tell the other person. But my voice will be trembling, the sound strained as I try to control those shaky insides.

Once I get some kind of reaction, I feel better. It's not perfect but at least I have something to work on for a while. My self has been preserved; I am not lost. I can move on.

Charlene Mackowiak

I think that fear is the emotional catalyst that turns off and on many of my other feelings and actions. It's the biggest and the most; therefore it seems the most "unsolvable." Fear even keeps me from responding to fear.

I guess I see it as a series of steps, right down the road on the way to doing something that indicates change. Change. I guess that's what I fear.

I think this realization in myself has caused me to be impulsive—I *must* toss out the fear in order to *do* whatever that challenge is. It's like jumping into cold water; you're afraid to do it; but you're not going to let it get the best of you so you do it quickly and get it over with. Prolong it and the discomfort lasts longer. Then, being impulsive about pushing through those fears can create problems that perhaps wouldn't have been there had I proceeded in a more "rational" way. But when I don't respond to the fear quickly, I keep it and carry it around and become indecisive.

I guess my biggest fears are not being able to meet expectations of others, being alone, unknown, but mostly, not being able to love.   ↝

Bob Johnson

I get afraid when I do not know what is expected of me—what others expect of me. I feel afraid that they expect me to be a certain way, to be able to perform in a way they want. Mostly, I feel that their happiness at the time I'm with them depends on my acting a certain way. If I am paying attention and really care about the person I'm with, I will do the "right" thing and this will make them happy. If I "fail," they will be unhappy and angry with me.

So I have to check out what those expectations are. If they are things I can do, I am relieved. If they are things I want to do, I relax.   ↝

Paula Ripple

What is it that I am doing when I experience myself as closed off and out of touch, with myself and those around me? Something in me blacks out and locks in at the same time. It prevents me from changing at all or from being open. I am aware that my own insecurities are often responsible for this. Fear cripples me, as any paralysis might. It reduces me to immobility and I feel I can't grow, or reach out or just be. When I am afraid, my vision is altered. I am less capable of choosing well. When I am afraid of people, I sometimes retreat from them instead of going out to meet them. At other times fear is at the heart of an over-response to someone, which distorts the way I feel and the other person's response as well.

Of all my emotions, fear is the one which seems the most insidious and harmful. It will not let me walk with ease as my pilgrim feet want to do. It causes me not to risk the life-giving choices which make new life possible.   ↝

Chuck Lee

Of what am I afraid? I wish I knew more about that; perhaps then I could face it.

I often see myself running in all directions, away from those things I'm afraid of. Or is it to something I want and can't ask for? I don't like being there—in that scrambling around, fragmented state—and I seem to strike out at people whom I think put me there. I try to get even and use all my weapons to hurt them, even my most effective—withdrawal. And when I am alone, without anchor or support, without being able to touch or be touched, my biggest fear swells up inside—that I can't love. Because I don't. And that's the fear that means most everything to me now.

I stop when I say that because it is hard for me to face. It is easier to reach out in small ways and love a little and then say, "See, I do love," but underneath that kind of social reaching out is the spectre of, "Do I really love anyone? Will I ever love anyone?"

I have other fears: People seeing my stomach and thinking I'm fat.

People thinking, "Did he say that dumb thing?"

My inability to say those negative things I carry around some times.

My maneuvering to get to a point because I can't say it in a real way.

My needs—will they be met?

You . . . do you like me?

Maria Bowen

Usually the thing that scares me the most is the unknown. I am scared sometimes by things I know are going to happen, but the things I don't know about bring me the most anxiety and the most physical reactions.

For instance, when I started therapy, I was very scared about what I was going to change into, what I was going to become and whether or not I was going to like that. There was a lot of fear that I was going to find out some very ugly things about myself and would end up not liking myself. That's an unknown that scared me.

In my relationship with Jack, I sometimes worry about his growth. He goes after what he wants and he becomes different and I get afraid of what that will do to our relationship and to me. Those are unknowns that sometimes scare me, sometimes even paralyse me.

Every time I meet a large group, I'm scared. My voice is lower, I'm inhibited, and I don't feel sure of myself. Whenever I teach before a large class, I get a little scared. I *know* that's going to come out all right, never the less, I experience some fear every time I get before a group.

I used to put myself down for being afraid. Now it feels much better to admit to myself, and to the people I'm with, that I'm feeling that way. I think fear is all right as long as it doesn't stop me from doing what I want to do. When fear stops me, I don't like it.

For instance, when we took that small plane over the Grand Canyon I was *so* scared, but I knew that wasn't going to stop me. It's kind of uncomfortable but I'm able to live with it and do what I want to do. The fear that I don't like is the fear that prevents me from doing what I want.

There's a difference I think between fearing the unknown and having expectations or making predictions that I am afraid of. Fritz Peris used to talk about what he called "catastrophic expectations." When I expect terrible things to happen to me and I can be fairly specific about those, that's not really "the unknown," but something I am predicting for myself and that I have some knowledge of. When I experience a fear of *any* change, that might be called fearing the unknown.

Sometimes I will start out with a general fear and not know too much about it and I'll say "I'm afraid of what's going to happen." But when I talk about it and work down to what it is I'm really afraid of, it turns out to be a specific fear. I think that's the best way I have of dealing with fear, is to sit down and face it and talk about what it really is that I'm afraid of. When I start talking about specifics, I can see what's rational or irrational, what things I have control over and what things I don't. Then I can see what is stopping me.

If I do that, get down to specifics, it usually eases the fear and I am reassured. Even if it doesn't, I have defined it, it gives me perspective and I can prepare myself to deal with it in some way.

One of the things I'd like to be able to do is be quicker to realize what I'm feeling is fear. Obviously I can't deal with it until I know it. A lot of times it takes me a while to say to myself, "Hey, I'm scared." I might avoid doing something or tell myself I can't do it, all the while not admitting that I'm afraid to do it.

The way I want to deal with fear is to not avoid what I'm afraid of. I can't deal with it until I face it. That's the only way I can conquer it, to walk into it, whatever it is.

ANGRY

You don't learn to hold your own in the world by standing on guard, but by attacking and getting well hammered yourself.

George Bernard Shaw

ᔐᔐᔐ

Bob Lee

The first thing I think about in getting angry is excitement; my body is more excited than usual. I feel a real force, a powerful, strong kind of feeling coming up in me. It's a physical feeling of going forward.

I like anger; I value it, I respect it.

Historically, I was taught not to be angry. I can remember having temper tantrums as a child and was told that it was not okay for me to have those feelings, in a variety of ways. I remember one instance when, after one of my tantrums, my mother put me in the corner and made me stay there "until I could behave myself." I was terrified. She left the house and I was terrified she was going to leave me because of what I'd done.

Then it seemed like I went for 20 years of my life being a nice guy. Anger was a no-no. But an outlet I had for it, a way to discharge that angry energy was sports. Getting mad in sports was okay; I could really smash a volleyball or hit a tennis ball or tackle somebody with all the aggressiveness I wanted. All that was legitimized. It wasn't okay to be directly, spontaneously angry until recently in my life.

The fear of getting angry, the image that was in my head, was one of murder. A few times I would let go and it was a murderous rage. I remember a fight at Memorial Jr. High where I used to teach. Two girls were fighting and the kids had all gathered around them in the courtyard. I saw the fight and I knew both the girls and I just went into a rage. They were tearing each other apart and everyone, teachers and students, were just standing around watching. I just went through the crowd, knocking people right and left, and I grabbed those girls with such strength and with all the force of my rage and they just froze. Later, when just the three of us got off by ourselves, everything was okay. We all were calmed down and I got teary eyed. I had gotten in touch with that powerful, murderous rage. People around me were scared of it and I was really scared of it. It seemed like I was going into that circle to kill them both.

What that is, I think, is having absorbed so much anger as a child and young man. I just absorbed it like a sponge . . . my mother and dad

33

fought, my sister and my mother, my grandparents . . . I just soaked all that up without letting go of it. Then when fights came up, I was afraid to get in there because I was afraid I'd just go in there and kill people.

I see anger now as a result of being abused or misused. I can do that to myself, others can do it or my environment can abuse me. And it's like my organism responds spontaneously struggling against that abuse. The extreme of it is a life-death struggle.

I remember two years ago, in the encounter groups in the La Jolla Program, my whole theme was anger. Anytime there was any anger I let it come. Once it was really murderous. I was in a group where a woman asked all the men in the group to fight with her and they all refused. She came to me and she kind of knew and I kind of knew. "Yeh, we'll fight." And I knew there wasn't going to be any holding back. And in the next moment I attacked her and just drove her up against the wall; I was going to kill her. And I didn't kill her. That was the release. I found out that I wouldn't kill anyone and it started something for me, a real release to be angry.

My anger is just stored up inside of me. It accumulates, over years sometimes, and is just there waiting for someone to set it off, to tap into it. But I feel much better about that now; I feel like I've arrived. I want to express my anger and want to express it as strongly as it is and I know I can do that now. It's really in me; others don't make me angry in a literal sense, I let myself be angry.

What I want is to get it out, not hold it in, to fully be my anger in your presence and not put that on you, but get it out. And I'm more and more able to do that. I can do that when I trust; when I trust the people and the situation I'm in. I want the people I'm with to be able to handle my anger. Where I judge, often mistakenly, that people can't handle it or I'm going to be judged for it, I hold it in. The kind of situation I like is where I'm really able to be freely me, including my anger.

John Wood

When I get angry I feel very resolute, unyielding, forceful and strong. There is a sense of focusing on the issue or person that is making me mad and somehow of not letting go of that until it's resolved.

Sometimes those seem good ways to be, yet I don't seem to let myself get angry very often. My guess is that I'm afraid of it; afraid that I will let go of an awful lot of energy and anger that perhaps belongs somewhere else and physically hurt the person at whom it's directed. Or that my anger will be disproportionate to the issue and that will emotionally hurt and confuse the person I direct it to. I guess I don't want to be seen as an angry person. I generally don't like people who fly off the handle easily and always seem to have a ready supply of anger just below the surface.

I think I carry that too much to the other extreme though. I think of myself as too controlled as far as my anger goes and I wish I could let my anger come out more spontaneously, when the occasion demanded it.

There seem to be two ways, in general terms, for me to be angry. I can be angry at something specific . . . a person, an incident, a condition I see. Its at those specific times that I want to allow my anger to show and that's when I seem to get those strong, forceful feelings I mentioned. The issue seems clear and most times I can confront it.

Another way I recognize is when I seem to maintain a posture of being angry. I am mad at the world. I am short tempered. Others might call this a bad mood. I think this has something to do with reservoirs in me; I think about this for anger and sadness as well. There seems to be a deep well, or reservoir, of anger—or at least space for it—inside of me. If I deal with the things that make me mad as they come up instead of stuffing them down inside of me, my "angry reservoir" seems to stay clean, empty. That's a good feeling for me; it feels like I'm taking care of myself. But if I keep stuffing angry things down into that well, it soon is full to the point of overflowing at just about anything. And the amount of anger that flows out isn't always proportionate to what caused it. I want to be more the first way I mentioned and stay "clean." It's when I try and hold all that anger inside that it crowds out other feelings and emotionally constipates me.

It seems risky for me to get angry. Besides the fear of hurting someone, there's the fear that the person I'm angry with won't take it and will put distance between us. I'll get mad at you and you'll leave me; you don't care enough to hang in there and work it out.

That means to me that I want to trust the people I get mad at, especially if I have some investment in our relationship. I want to trust them to receive my anger and not walk away without resolving it. But I also have to trust myself and take the responsibility for my own anger.

So often it seems my anger is not really directed at the person I'm with, but is a part of me I've been collecting and carrying around for a while. When I'm that way, a way I don't like, it would help to have someone around who would let me be, help me be, my crazy, angry self and not take it as a personal attack on them.

David Mearns

Anger seems just beyond annoyance for me. A lot of things annoy me, but not many of them go beyond that to real anger. I don't think I let them.

Often things frustrate me and annoy me and I do something to head it off before it becomes anger. I deal somehow with the frustration or decide that it's not that important. That makes me think about anger as a way of saying that something is important to me and maybe I'm not ready to admit that too often.

Someone hurting me, someone trying to get the best of me, someone playing games with me, something frustrating me . . . all those make me angry.

When I get mad I feel a welling up inside of me; I seem to grow bigger and taller and stronger. I get a feeling of energy coming up and out, making me bigger and stronger.

It's been a long time since I've been really angry, a long time. About four years ago I got into a fight, actually two fights, with the same guy during a soccer game. He just kept tackling me—hard, poorly timed tackles—and he just seemed to keep egging me on. After a while of that I went for him and it was a totally consuming feeling. Nothing else mattered except beating him into the grass. He was bigger than me and I didn't really think I could beat him but that didn't matter. It's funny how strongly that feeling overcame me.

A lot of what makes me angry has to do with my inferiority, or my belief that I'm not as good as the next guy. And when it gets to the stage where I'm up against that admittance, I seem to have to fight, physically fight, to prove that it's wrong.

It seems to be a matter of cutting it off in early stages or my anger reaching such a point that I feel I have to fight about it. There doesn't seem to be much of a middle ground.

I like being angry. I can remember times when if I hadn't been angry, acted out my anger when I felt it, I would have felt really weak. Getting angry made me feel more myself, more potent.

And, oddly enough, what I want to do is control it more, not to let it out as it happens, although it makes sense to me to advise other people to let it out. But my reaction for myself is to control it. It's funny; I know I control it too much, but I am a bit afraid to let it all out. If I keep it in, I think I can let it out in other less harmful ways.

If it comes out, if I really let myself get angry, I'm afraid I'll lose. I'll lose the fight, I'll lose the angry argument and I'll have given it all my energy, all I've got and still lose. That's my fear. If I don't; if I hold back, that can be my excuse. I can say to myself, "well, I didn't give it all I had."

A lot of that has to do with coping with the differences getting angry would make in my relationships. Getting mad would risk the possibility of losing friends or family. Perhaps when I feel much better about taking that kind of risk, I'll be able to get angry more often. I'd like that.

Terry Van Orshoven

I have a friend who says, "It's better to be pissed off than pissed on." That's kind of the way I feel about anger; I think of it as a nourishment, a gift you can give someone.

So often I see people taking their anger and using it against themselves . . . holding it back, storing it in their bodies, rolling their guts around and around, getting more and more rigid, jaws clenching, faces getting red . . . all those things start happening when you keep energy like that stored up inside instead of letting it go.

I see anger as a kind of warmth. If I'm indifferent, it's from not caring. Anger at least means I care. It's a gift, a gift to myself to let go of a feeling I have and a gift of my true emotions to another person. At least those are my values.

In a way, anger can be as nourishing as affection or praise; I can be very manipulative and destructive with affection. For instance, I can be manipulative in loving someone by holding back my anger. I can hold back my anger but keep in the "hooks" I have going for me . . . warmth, praise, affection, all those "positive" things. I can set up a loyalty based on what a good guy I am being to you; how good I am to never give you that shitty thing called anger. Then you're indebted to me. But that's a phony setup. How much better it is for you to know me, to know my hurt and my anger and not have you set up, propped up, in a way, with just my positive warm emotions.

One of the ways I get angry is when I'm hurt. Another way is when I don't get something I want. Like when I'm feeling sexual and my partner is not and I don't get laid, I take the disappointment and the ego blast and turn it into anger. When I do that I can't really speak to it and own all of it because I know it's screwy to be putting that demand on someone else. But I still get angry; like the kid and the cookies. My head tells me that it's not legitimate or valid, but it's there.

Sometimes the anger is a labeling or a judgment about someone else . . . "those guys are all screwed up" or "she doesn't know what she's doing anyway." When I start judging someone like that I know it's a judgment of my own inability to pull off what I wanted to pull off according to my own standards.

I would really like it to be a world where people could beat up on each other, to pound, slug, punch, kick and fight—but nobody get hurt. I really think that would be healthy.

That goes back to the first thing I said. I think anger is a way of caring. Somewhere along the line I think anger has gotten screwed up . . . we think it's a no-no because we think we're harming other people. I think that's what our culture says. But I think we don't want people to know we're angry because it reveals our vulnerability; it shows that we care. That seems to be kind of an unconscious should-not, to care. If we can be hurt by someone then that's an admission of caring and if we care, we're vulnerable and if we're vulnerable we feel we're dependent and after all who wants to be dependent?

So I think it's bullshit when it's said that anger is a no-no because we're mutilating someone else. I like to let my anger out. It's good for me. And, ultimately, it's good for the person I get mad at too.

Bill McGaw

Anger is a peculiar, intriguing feeling for me because, in myself and in others, it seems to be a blanket for so many other feelings. It's a cover-up in a way, a kind of secondary feeling. The valuable thing for me to do is get below the anger to the primary feelings and express those. That's a very hard thing to do sometimes because the anger can be so intense it scares the other person off.

Supposing Audrey is mad at me. Knowing the kind of things we value, we both would feel it would be good for her to own her anger, to let it out. But, depending on the intensity of her expression, I may respond in a productive way or not. If it's very intense I may get very guarded.

For example, take a situation at a party. I go out into the kitchen with all the guys—where the booze and the ice and the mix are—and we're out there saucing it up and telling jokes. Audrey is stuck in the living room with all the women and the knitting talk—she hates that situation. So we leave the party and she lays it on me: "I'm really raging at you." Okay, she's letting me know what her feelings are, but I don't have, or take, much of a chance to respond. In that case, it seems like it's tough to respond to her anger because it's a secondary anger, covering up so many other things. What's going on with her in that case might be a feeling of desertion, not feeling valued, feeling unimportant, bored, resentful, lonely, taken for granted . . . all those may be going on. If she would say those things, it would be much easier for me to respond, but unless she were an expert at looking inside herself at a time like that, the only one she legitimately comes up with is anger. When that's the only one she expresses, we're not going to have a very productive conversation. We have to get beyond that.

That's what makes it so tough about anger—there are usually a dozen or so things colliding at once to produce the white knuckles, the clenched fist, the tight jaws and all the stuff that comes with anger.

In the "good times" that I am angry, I like to be able to express the anger but also express in some depth why I am feeling that way; I try to get to some of the primary feelings that brought up the anger.

That's when I'm at my best. I can go all the way to being a martyr or punishing the person I'm angry with or sarcastic; that's when I feel defensive and angry. And there's hardly any way to predict how I'm going to be. It's impossible.

One of the things that seems to tap into my anger most of all is being taken for granted, not being appreciated. I sometimes have very little tolerance for that. Or for being misunderstood. Interactions with rigid people really get to me too, people who make no attempt to understand what I'm talking about. I find myself getting beyond impatience very quickly. It has to do with being a non-person . . . not making any difference, relegated to just a number with that person. That gets to me quickly.

I wish I were more tolerant, more forgiving, more accepting of other people's imperfections, but when I get angry I can't think of all those things. I really hope I can not only express my anger, but can get to the feelings below that, to the depth and the range of my feelings. I want to be able to say things like: "I feel taken for granted," "I don't feel understood or listened to," "I don't feel cared for." I'd like to be able to do that more, but I think I'm better than I used to be at it. I used to just react, boom, and that would often come out in destructive ways.

I think you're giving people a gift when you can give them your anger and give them the range and the whys of it too, not just your rage.

ANXIOUS

The state of man: inconstancy, boredom, anxiety.

Pascal

〜〜〜

John Wood

I'm anxious today. I see myself flit from small task to small task, not pausing long enough to get settled at any one thing. The pleasant warmth of the day and the calm way others seem around me seems only to accentuate my nervousness. Occasionally, I catch myself with a wrinkled brow and tight eyes, my shoulders sneaking in toward my neck—how can I head that off?

I prepare curt, testy replies to imagined encounters with others in the house; there seems to be a quick, hard-shelled defense right at the surface. What is under that? What am I worried about defending? I have brought out—superficially—some "borderline" worries; money, a general aimlessness. But deeper than that I know I am worried about Betsy coming back. A separation of five months, a trip for her of more than a month and now two days together before she leaves again. I'm sweating. I don't know what to expect. I don't want to expect too much and pressure us both so we can't relax with each other. And trying to expect little or nothing seems to make me apathetic. The waiting! That's what screws me up.

I seem to be suspended in some kind of powerless limbo, waiting for her to make up her mind, waiting for her to do something to respond to. And I begin to think that if I can stop waiting, take some power of my own, take responsibility only for myself and *do* what it is I want to, I will be less anxious. That is, my anxiety has to do with fearing the unknown and, in this situation, subtly giving up most of the power over what happens to Betsy.

The unknown is still there. But I will surely feel better about it if I can go into this in touch with my own needs and feelings and not so worried about and dependent on her actions or what will go on between us.   〜

Doug Land

Sometimes it seems almost like a superstitious fear; there doesn't seem to be any real reason to be anxious, but it's like a nameless fear that occasionally creeps into me. But I don't know what it is I'm afraid of; there's nothing there. If I could see what it is I don't think I'd get anxious.

I do recognize anxiety—it's one of the few—through some definite physical manifestations. I can tell I'm anxious when I get a tightness, a bunching of muscles in the back of my lower neck; I seem susceptible to pulling a muscle there, it seems so tight.

One of the things that I get anxious about is a fear of failure; it's like something coming up that I have to do. I might get afraid of it because I'm not doing what I need to to get ready for it and I can see myself "failing" at it. But there's part of me that doesn't want to get ready for it, to prepare for the future. So there's a kind of fight inside of me going on. Then I seem to get irritable with other people. I get withdrawn and preoccupied, thinking about this upcoming event, and somebody intrudes, then I can get irritable about it.

In a way anxiety is a good thing; it's not always bad. In fact, I don't have many anxiety experiences, when I don't recognize it as a kind of creative energy. My organism is telling me that I ought to be focusing on something, giving more attention to something than I am. If I'm watching TV and I've got something else that I'm anxious about, it creeps up on me and it keeps making me think "I shouldn't be here" and of course at some point I've got to break, I've got to stop doing the distracting thing and focus.

When something like that looms ahead, the bad thing I do is try and get out of it. Like I can agree to do something six months from now and I feel great about it when I agree and it sounds like an exciting thing, but then as the time approaches and the anxiety starts coming, then I start wondering about whether I really want to do it and I find it hard to know. Then since I'm anxious about it, my first thoughts start to be escapist ones, "How do I get out of this?" But the escape thing seems to pass and the anxiety feelings seem to push me into somehow preparing, learning something about it, getting ready for what I will do.

I think that one thing I get anxious about in a relationship is a fear of some kind of catastrophe . . . something happening to the kids or Elsie when they're not here. I have to work to get those things out of my head. They don't seem to be profitable thoughts to me. I am powerless to do anything about those kinds of occurrences. Again, I think I'm anxious about a situation in which I couldn't cope, where I'm helpless, where I'm not the master of it. The only way I know of heading that off is by saying I'll deal with it when it comes, by telling myself that I'm anxious about something that doesn't exist right now.

Because anxiety for me is also a physical thing, it can be worked out physically. I could go play football, or handball or tennis and really work it out by making my body tired, loose. But generally I think the way I work through any negative feeling I have—fear, despair, anxiety—is to recognize that I can just do what I can do, that I am what I am and I can only do my best. Then anxiety seems to dissipate. ↰

Paula Ann Engelsman

I am first aware of anxiety sometimes when I try to read a book and my mind wanders, but I don't want my mind to wander, so I try to get involved in other tasks, but can't. My mind won't stay with it. My energy and vitality are being directed inward and I don't like it. The harder I try to direct my energy outward the more fragmented and frustrated I become. I seem to be unable to control what I want to do. I am frightened. This anxiety is to me a huge, undefined fear. I don't know what I am afraid of so I don't know how to face it. I have a tremendous feeling of holding in, but I don't know what it is I'm holding in.

I stop trying to direct my energy. I go inward. I experience a churning through the center of my body. I am not "centered." I am confused and divided. My body does not feel together. I have the sensation that a small earthquake is disrupting my gut. I feel a trembling in my fingers. My hands are cold and clammy. I notice that my breathing is shallow and my back muscles are tense. I am afraid that the quiet, internal shaking will tear me apart.

I force myself to relax—to breathe deeply. The shaking becomes more obvious. I stay with the shaking. I experience it and let it come out. My body begins to shake. Now I start to cry. My crying becomes noisy with grunts and groans. Somehow during this discharge I become aware of my fear.

I can't really *live* when I deny my own feelings; living to me means fully experiencing my feelings. And since, ultimately, I am the one who denies the feelings inside of me, I am creating my own anxiety. I am cutting myself off from me.

I think I would never be anxious if I could always be aware of my feelings, let them run their course and be honest in my expression of them. But I guess that would make me perfect. I want to work toward being more open and honest, but thinking I have to be totally that way all the time creates another kind of pressure in me.

I am getting much better at realizing my imperfections, not expecting too much of myself and admitting my weaknesses. This seems to be a good thing. It seems to be reducing that split of wanting to be a totally perfect human being but knowing I can't. In a funny way admitting my weakness makes me stronger. ↰

Elsie Land

When I find myself getting anxious my heart starts to beat a little faster and my fingertips get cold. I kind of tighten up all over, but not to any extreme.

I'm anxious when kids don't show up from school on time. Or Doug isn't home when he's supposed to be. My anxiety mostly is about the people I care about and my fears of some tragedy happening to them. I don't seem to have much anxiety for the future. Or about Doug and I getting along.

Sometimes when others' demands start to come in on me, I can get anxious. Some neighbor down the street has been complaining because he thinks we have a dirty sidewalk. That starts to bother me. My next door neighbor has been asking that we cut down one of our trees because it's starting to lean into her yard; I can't ignore her, so I begin to get anxious about that.

I like to please people and when I'm not pleasing someone yet can't see how what I'm doing is wrong, that's hard for me to reconcile and I worry about it.

Sometimes anticipation will get me anxious. Last month when Geoff had to perform a trumpet solo, Doug and I were very much on edge because we just knew that he wasn't that well prepared. The day of his solo I really got busy; I occupied myself so I wouldn't have to sit and stew in my juices. It just kept going through my mind, "I'll feel awfully bad, for him, if he really makes a dreadful mistake. I wish I weren't so involved in this." Yet I had too much invested. I wanted him to really shine. One thing that helped, we kidded each other, the three of us, all day long.

Another thing that makes me anxious—I like to come across as being successful at what I do. So if people are coming over for dinner, I want to be able to give them a good time. And I don't often give them credit for being able to create a good time. So I worry about how I'm going to look if everyone has a lousy time.

I think that anxiety doesn't bother me too much because I seem to be free of limitations and pressures put on me from the outside. I don't have a job I have to worry about. Doug doesn't put pressure on me about the house so I don't feel any kind of demand to perform. Any kind of pressure on me is my own and I can short circuit it when I want to; I can just back off on my own demands.

ATTRACTED

*There are other things besides beauty with which to capti-
vate the hearts of men. The Italians have a saying: "Fair
is not fair, but that which pleaseth."*

Ninon de Lenclos

∿∿∿

Earl Burrows

A woman comes to mind when I think about being attracted to someone. It was a gal in a workshop I did in South Dakota; when I saw her I felt very attracted to her quickly. I felt warm, curious when I looked at her; there was a softness inside.

Then as I experienced her, the feeling changed. It became a feeling of hardness, resistance, in terms of what I experienced with her. I got a lot of mixed messages from her and gradually she became a person I would avoid rather than be drawn to.

Generally it seems I will "go with" my feelings of being attracted to someone. If I start getting other, negative feelings, it depends on what my investment is as to whether I'll work that out with the person. Mostly that means just talking about how my feelings are changing; that helps give those warm, attractive feelings a chance to come back into me. That's something I have to choose; if I get into a hard place with someone I have to make the conscious choice to talk about that hard place or walk away from it.

When I'm feeling good, when I'm pro-active in a situation with someone I'm attracted to, I start from an open-ness, a feeling of "I'll show you some of me and give you a chance to do the same." I'm going to share. Then I find out if I'm going to get some of that back.

I think a lot of people have the focus on the other person. They tend to want to have the other person share first, then they'll open up with something. That's partly a lack of trusting, I think. I was much more that way before I felt real good about myself. That resistance to opening, in a lot of cases, is a function of how I feel about myself.

There are times when I'll feel attracted to someone and won't follow it up. Right now in my life I am afraid that following up would mean someone else would have expectations of me and I just don't want to get into that kind of relationship right now. That's a conflict in me. I know that I have a desire for a close, sharing relationship, but now seems not the time.

44

When someone is really accepting of me there's no denial of ways that I'm feeling and no heavy expectations laid on me, that's when I feel the most attracted and the most like following that up.

John Wood

Being attracted to someone is like they are a magnet and I am a piece of steel; I am just drawn to them; I lean toward them; I can feel that happening physically. I just get locked in on that magnet.

Most of the time I am fairly controlled in showing that. I seem to sit on my feelings of being attracted, waiting for the feeling to prove out or something. It's not like zapping right into someone, going right to them. I hold back. I guess that's the safe way. With someone brand new, I don't have any basis to go to them on so I wait awhile.

In the last six months or so I have been learning, in a number of ways and from different people, that what I want from another person is what I want from myself. And that some of the things I am attracted to in others are things I don't have myself and want in my life. Sometimes it seems like a real yearning I have and look for in others. For instance, I am attracted to women who are spontaneous, bubbly and just seem to have a life-energy about them. That is something that I want for myself but a lot of the time I feel subdued and holding back; I see myself as cooler than the type of woman I seem attracted to. Now that seems okay—people complimenting each other and all that—until I start to lean on my woman to be bubbly when I want it; saying to her, in effect, "You've got to put the bubbly into this relationship because I don't have it. And if you're not bubbly, I'm not going to love you as much." I think that holds with a lot of other qualities people bring to relationships and often it's tied up with male and female roles.

Sometimes I try to find out what it is I am attracted to in a person. I feel this magnetized kind of leaning toward them and I want to follow it, to explore it. Part of my leaning too seems to be to present myself to that person, wanting to put some of myself out there. It seems very hard for me to be strongly attracted to someone and stay completely out of their emotional sight, their presence. Perhaps that's being *attracted* and wanting to be *attractive*.

I know one quality in a person that I'm strongly attracted to, that's acceptance. Part of me is very susceptible to being judged by others and I don't like that. I really flourish and feel much more natural when a person is able to set an atmosphere of acceptance for me with them, when I don't have the feeling that I am being judged. I am attracted to people who nurture me in that way; it's like a plant turning toward the sun.

Bill Stillwell

Being attracted is exciting. It's an arousing feeling, one of being curious, interested, attentive all at the same time. It's joyous to be attracted.

But then I don't think I could take being attracted, aroused, on a more or less constant basis. It's like being titillated all the time. That excites my life, but I don't want to feel like I have to follow through on everything/everyone that is attractive to me. Sometimes I just take the attractiveness, superficial as it may be, for what it is and let it alone.

Other times I will want to "go with it" but with women other than Anne I seem to cut it off pretty quickly. Perhaps a part of that is fear, but a bigger part of it is a healthy respect for how I see and want our relationship.

On some levels, I am attracted by too much in the world and I set some limits on things I just won't go any further with. I've been that trip before or I don't need that right now or whatever. I just choose to not make myself available to that which I'm attracted to.

It seems like about half of the people I'm attracted to are not that attractive to other people around me. I don't know much about that, but I have noticed it in me.

The things I pick up on first are the moves a person has, their walk or hand and facial movements. I like joyous people, people who seem happy about what they're doing.

One of the things about my feelings for Anne is that she is attractive to me in ways that other people are attractive to me; she has certain qualities that I in general admire. But when she is not those things sometimes I have a hard time being attracted to her, of a moment. For instance, one of the things I like about her is that she's really a happy person. Sometimes when she's not happy, I catch myself trying to joke with her and cheer her up so she'll be that happy, attractive person to me.

That attractiveness, though it changes and goes up and down with time, really seems to tap into something basic in me, qualities that I am strongly drawn to. When that person I'm attracted to changes, as they must, I know I have that strong feeling to bring back or bring out that quality that I need from them.

Bringing out that quality in Anne might be harmful sometimes though. It's one thing to develop a sharing with each other, a partnership and another to lock each other in ways of being. It's an adaptive system for a while but eventually it can trap both people.

Anne Stillwell

There's something very fast for me about being attracted; I like things like that.

It seems like I can be attracted to people quickly without knowing much about them. There must be a few key things that tell me "Hey, this might be one of my people." I'm not sure that I even know what these things are—movement, dress—I'm not sure.

I remember when I saw Muriel for the first time. I was pretty lonely at the time; I didn't have any friends here. I took one look at her and said to myself, "Wow. She looks like a friend. She looks like one of mine."

It was something about simplicity. She was dressed really simply amongst all these people who were into a California-ethnic-dressing-up trips. She put out a quietness that I was attracted to. It made me want to go over and make friends with her right then and there. I went over and we got into a conversation about dance. Muriel is really interested in dance and I was in a silly little Tuesday morning dance class that I didn't like at all. I was disappointed that the first thing I was going to talk about with this person who might be a friend was something I didn't like and that she seemed to like. I was afraid we might miss each other; it seemed to be a bad beginning. But it turns out we had time to get together and explore other things.

There is something else attractive to me . . . a person's sense of humor. I like people who laugh at what I think is funny, who say things I think are funny—someone on the same funny line as I am.

Generally I don't do too much with my feelings of being attracted, particularly when they are toward men outside my marriage. I seem to sit on them, hold them inside. I wish I had a better way of dealing with them. And though the feeling of being attracted to someone seems to come up fast in me, it dies much slower; it seems to last a while. But it can slip away without me noticing it.

BORED

. . . sitting.
spinning useless images that find no form,
building castles that mistily die as they are born,
touching no one nor anything.
useless probabilities in a world
of timeless spacelessness . . .

Bill Stewart

꒔꒔꒔

Bob Kavanaugh

Ever since I was a little boy and learned I had to eat everything on my plate—everything mother chose, even spinach—I have found it hard to make choices, to know what I really wanted to eat, to do, to dedicate my time to. Now that choices are possible everywhere, I find myself incapacitated in their presence. Herein lies so much of my boredom—so much I would like to like to do but none of the choices seem to satisfy my fear that something better is possible around the corner.

Boredom begins as a mental apathy and I react with physical edginess and fantasy. I am rarely bored by others—it is a condition in myself, an abiding feeling of blah-ness creeps over all of me. Emptiness. Futility. And the people I call bores are those who cannot or will not shake me out of my stupor and into touch with them.

As boredom settles I feel anger at myself, self-pity, a wonderment about what's going on in me and depression often comes from my self-deprecation.

I used to always run to things or people to alleviate my boredom, but more often now I am willing to be bored. All ultimate resolutions seem to be found in letting interest and purpose come back by themselves—without force or ceaseless running.

I must confess too, that underlying all of my "interesting" and "absorbing" tasks, I feel a layer of almost constant boredom—wishing that my life had more purpose, better meaning. This existential boredom can be overlooked for a while but it is always there, always promising or at least seeking new excitement, new rewards, something richer than what I now know. This boredom is part of me—it will never go away—and though I resent its continuing quest for more, I also appreciate it as the basis for all my hope and idealism.

꒔

Mary Bardone

Bored, I feel listless and empty, as if I have nothing to offer anyone or anything. I project that others also find me boring and so I avoid being around people. The only felt desire is to be shockingly stimulated—to have the senses and the mind reactivated—to have something outside come in to occupy my being. I fantasize traveling to exotic places, being constantly hit with new stimuli. Then I think that the change must come from within, that it is too simple to place blame on friends and activities that are not momentarily exciting me. I am the one not exciting me, not exciting others, not animating my activities. How then can I change these feelings about my present self?

I think of outside activities to get involved in, but that seems shallow; it seems like I'd be doing that just to alleviate boredom and not for the activity itself. Or sometimes that commitment or effort involved in getting into something new feels too great.

Sometimes the activities I could be interested in seem such solitary ones—piano, reading, yoga—and I become afraid that even though they might alleviate boredom, they will accentuate my aloneness.

I think of doing something physically exciting that will make me feel alive and vital and it usually does until my head tells me that I am only trying to divert attention; underneath that exhilarating physical feeling of expended energy is boredom only temporarily suspended. And none of these changes my feelings about myself and my environment.

Often I come out of a bored state with nothing in my external life changed. But I feel things differently. I have no cue to relate the change to, except that it was just "karmically" the time to feel differently. Sometimes it is an external factor that changes the way I feel about myself and my environment, but it is usually something that just happens and not something I have conjured up.

I am never too sure how it is I get in and out of boredom. I know when I'm there and I try and trust the process of changing emotions, yet I'm always amazed when it really happens.

Anne Stillwell

Boredom for me is a dissatisfaction. I am bored especially when I have had expectations of being excited, interested, stimulated, concerned, inspired and these expectations are not fulfilled. Something boring gives me no return at all for what I invest in it.

I have two kinds of boredom, with different implications for me. External boredom is being uninterested in some immediate, specific condition that I expected to find interesting or otherwise worthwhile to me—a political speech, for example, that I expected to be informative or stimulating but that ends up saying nothing. Because I tie this feeling to an external, immediate cause, I don't stay bored in this way for long and I think of it as a minor thing.

Internal boredom is a much bigger matter, more lasting and more involving to me. It is a generalized boredom, about the way my life looks at the moment. I make an interpretation about my whole life out of the disappointment of some expectation. I think I become bored in this way when I expect to gain something I want generally from life—feeling productive, creative, intellectually high, for example. From this kind of experience I think of other felt lacks in my life and come out with a generalized dissatisfaction. Then I usually blame the routines in my life for my boredom, even if the real specific cause is not at all routine. When I am bored with my way of living, I am bored with myself. This I can feel as small and temporary, when I'm just not excited by any of my usual activities for a while, but it usually feels absolutely momentous. I feel in need of a whole new structure for my life, dissatisfied with the whole thing. Then I get annoyed with everyone around me who expects me to follow my regular patterns; I become grouchy, withdrawn, and demanding of some kind of excitement.

Boredom, then, is very often self-directed. I see it as something most importantly internal to me and external events cause it only through my acceptance and reaction to them. I don't have good ways to deal with boredom. On the large scale, I usually do some activity which makes me feel some motion (a false change) or requires my attention. Occasionally, I really make changes in routine. But what I'm really after is adventure.

Marcia Jaffe

I'm bored. Standing still. Out of touch with any feelings. It is dissatisfaction without energy to want something new. Boredom usually precedes frustration in me. I look around me and everything seems old and void of meaning. Time seems to slow down. I have lost my sense of excitement and challenge. Things that once meant something valuable to me have ceased to raise the excitement I once felt. When I am bored I feel empty words floating through me. I feel detached and dead.

My body feels heavy. I tend to eat more, which makes me fat and slower. I am sleepy. My senses are dulled. I feel unaware of my surroundings. Colors and sounds seem muted. I feel like the world is spinning on its axis around me and I am looking upon it detached of feeling and meaning. I find myself staring into space, thinking and feeling nothing.

If I am around people who are not close to me, my boredom may come out as hostility. Around close friends I usually find a way to break the spell. I can release some of the boredom by voiding my state of being and having friends suggest something to do. I find boredom frightening as I become more aware of myself in this state. I try to do something physical to move from this inner deadness. If I get my body moving around and let go of my mind, I can feel energy start to flow again. My body begins to function, cleaning out some of the nonsense in my head and new energies seem to arise to further my desire for something new. I then often become frustrated for I am in need of something new to challenge me and have not yet found this outlet.

Boredom is the beginning of transition, the dying of old meanings to give room for the new challenges of my growth.

John Wood

Boredom is a very bad feeling for me to have. I have thought about it on two levels. The one is a rather superficial boredom with what others are doing in a situation—a meeting for instance. I recognize it first when I hear myself saying, silently, "Hey, you people are not doing what I expected/want you to do." I have gotten to the point where I can voice that and—most times—say what I expect from a situation. What that means to me most often is that I am not doing or saying what I expect from a situation. I am not doing or saying what I want to do. In other words, I am boring myself, or, at least, staying in a situation I don't want to be in.

The deeper level is definitely a boredom with myself over a long, drawn-out time and has to do with what I'm doing with my life, my creativity, my motivation. At these times I feel MEDIOCRE. I once told a close girlfriend in the 11th grade that I was going to be "cursed by mediocrity" and it is in these long spans of boredom that I do indeed feel cursed. It is a death-like feeling for me, a numb-ness. It frightens me to think I might stay that way. It begins to pervade my whole life—my job, wife, friends, children—I feel out of love with all of them and start to sink further into total apathy. I *have* to get out—I'm being sucked down—is the feeling. After a while I start casting about for things to pull me out of it, to excite me. A change of some sort is usually in order; the bigger the boredom the bigger the change. But it is easy for me to make mistakes here. When this mediocrity, this boredom so pervades my life, what is the element that needs changing? The house I live in? The city? My job? My profession? My friends? My wife? Myself?

This feeling is sometimes threatening to those close to me, who begin to think that they are in some way responsible for my boredom. This is hard to work through and paradoxically, in the midst of being out of love with everyone, it is when I need them the most. With their understanding and acceptance I can begin to make small changes—to listen to myself—to test out some new behaviors and see where they lead me.

COMMUNITY

Neighbors forced to exist together will end up as enemies unless they act and live animated by a hope one day to become friends.

Dag Hammarskjold

᭶᭶᭶

John Wood

There seem to be a lot of different feelings that go into my "feeling" of community and it makes it hard to say "I feel like I have community." Security, trust, not being lonely, mattering . . . all these seem to go into my sense of community. One of the first things I think about as a "requirement" for community is a gathering of people in which I can be completely myself and not have to be any certain professional way or be careful about how I am.

Community seems to be a basic need we all share and I have wondered a lot lately about whether or not any group of people can come together and achieve community. I think about people who move into and through different groups—the PTA, the bowling league, things like that. I don't think they are finding the community they want in those groups. Part of it seems to be because they're moving from group to group to group. In the past they might have been with one group . . . The Family or The Job, but now there are so many groups that aren't a real part of their lives that it becomes a fragmenting thing. I don't have the time or energy—or take it—to put my investment into any one of these groups, into that particular area of my life. That diversification, that fragmentation doesn't help to get me to the feeling of community I say I want so much.

Sometimes a problem I have is wanting community with everybody, with the total group I'm involved with. I get frustrated when that doesn't happen. Somehow I want everybody to love me; maybe I ought to just seek what I want from individuals that I want something specific from and with.

It seems as if our way of life discourages community, or makes us seek a different kind. If I am able to be here with you physically then I'm going to find community with you fairly quickly. If I'm able to leave, encouraged to leave, my building, my city, my state and it's easy for me to do that, and I'm able to leave you spiritually—by watching TV, reading, paying attention to all the stimuli coming in—all that keeps a distance between us. I see community feelings as a coming together of many parts and the way I and much of our society is living today is spreading us out, exploding us, in a way. That makes it harder and harder for me to achieve community.

When I think about how to achieve it, I seem to get simplistic. Just being more open, sharing more, more air time with each other. Can it be that simple? I know that some of the ways I am take me away from people rather than closer to them. But I need to be known. You may like me when I'm a good guy, but when I show you my bad parts . . . and they hurt and you have the tendency to split, that doesn't make it. I want to be able to show you all those ugly parts of me and know I'm not going to be rejected.

Tony Rose

I think about asking for what I want and getting it, when I think of community. If I want to share myself, usually I can get someone to listen or share with me or play with me or work with me.

For me it has a lot to do with being physical—not sexual necessarily —but being close, physically close, sending energy from one to another. That feeling has a lot to do with making up community . . . a whole psychological sensing . . . we are in common with each other.

I think there is something in us, something that we have evolved from ancient stone age families and bands of men . . . something deep within our genetic makeup that wants to propel us backwards into some kind of extended family. I sure do think that in our society today we have built structures and things that keep us from connecting. For instance, in our media we talk about how to sell more toothpaste or whatever, instead of ways we can be together.

There's something else that strains our community—there's something about reaching out of the community, for forbidden fruit, you might say, that changes the community. To me, in a sense, the fruit is the fruit of outside experience. I start traveling, working outside my community, my family and start tasting forbidden fruit. Suddenly my family changes, my perception of it changes, and I return home and I grieve. But I think that process is a natural one.

I don't feel I have to have everyone in a given community responding to me in a certain way. I think if I can look around, see the people I'm with, I can go about meeting my needs with certain individuals. I don't have to be with one person, nor do I have to be with everybody together to be satisfied. To feel that kind of community, where I can express my needs and have them met, that's like an extended family to me.

Earl Burrows

Community is a place where I can be what I am at the time. Sometimes that is more guarded, because of what goes on in my life. That's part of myself at that moment. I think to be accepted as me on days when I feel like is important. I don't want a thing over me that is the community's imposed norm, that says I must be a way that the people in the community are. The Center (Center for Studies of the Person) is the place that I feel more community than anywhere else. I get a community feeling a lot of times when I do workshops or weekend groups; that feeling rises that becomes a community for me. That's neat but it's a transient kind of thing.

Moving toward that community is a matter of sharing experience, whether it's just the verbal sharing or actually going through something together. There's a lot of different things that can go on that make me start to care for others, but I think that sharing, in varying degrees, is the way it starts.

My ideas about community also have a lot to do with where I am with the individuals around me. It's not a stagnant thing. I guess the reason CSP represents community for me is because it's a place where there are more people that I have had really deep experiences with. I don't have to have the same level of experience and feeling for everyone, as long as my needs are being satisfied, as long as there are a number of people I can do things with, people I can go to and get my strokes. I think that overall feelings of community comes out of my having ways of getting what I want.

One of the really good things about having community for me is to go to the Center and hear Tony talk and Terry talk and realize that I'm not the only one who has some screwed up things going on in my life. Other people let me know they've got some screwed up things going on too.

Staying with is important to me. That's maybe what the essence of community is. 'Course, I think that's what love is, a willingness to stay in the relationship. I feel like I may do things or say things that people really may not like, but they'll stay with me; they are not people that when that part of me comes out, they'll get up and split. Maybe that's more of what community is to me—people who I know will stay with me.

David Meador

I can talk about community as one way to experience feelings. When I think about community, I think about not being lonely. When I experience community, I feel a sense of belonging, or that I matter.

I don't want to play around with semantics, but it seems that community is another one of those words like guilt that we superimpose over a bunch of feelings. When certain emotions coincide in a certain way, then that combination, that bouquet, we describe as community. In that bouquet for me are acceptance, feeling I matter, having influence, feeling that I am able to respond to that group and it responds to me, that I can be open. And I need to be known.

There seems to be different levels of community for me . . . there's my country, my generation, people I work with, my family, my friends . . . and each of them mean different things to me at different times. It seems to me that it's a need everyone has, more or less; I need it more during stress situations.

It seems that commitment is a given in a community feeling for me. But I think about short term communities, conferences, groups, etc. Like an encounter group is a bunch of people contracting to have community for a weekend.

Another aspect of community that I think about is the "We-they" effect. The people I am okay with versus the others, the ones I don't feel okay with. When I am depressed, I feel very alone and although I remember that I have friends and community, I cannot use them or let them be with me in a nurturing way. A stranger I meet on the beach will probably feel most appropriate to open up to. As I move away from my feelings of helplessness, I am once again able to respond more totally to my community. As my strength and sense of well being grows, and the self-imposed alienation subsides, my community base expands. Some moments I stop being frightened. Taking a walk to, say, Peru, seems very pleasant. The world seems safe and the world is my community.

COMPETITIVE

Nothing is ever done beautifully which is done in rivalship.

John Ruskin

The way of the sage is to act but not to compete.

Lao Tzu

◡◡◡

Ralph Keyes

I am continually struck by how much competition, particularly among men, pervades our society. I'm reminded of reading recently about a group marriage in Berkeley breaking up; one of the main reasons cited was that the male partners in the marriage couldn't work through the competitive feelings they had.

From my experience with male consciousness raising groups, it seems to be a case of males competing to see who can admit to being the most chauvinistic. And in encounter groups, I have experienced a great deal of unspoken, un-dealt-with competition among the men to see who can be the most sensitive.

In each of the cases, there is a great set of ego games going on among the men. And though we can talk to those games, we don't take much action to overcome them. We go on playing them.

In general I lament that. I mostly see competition as a bad thing, if you want to attach a good or bad to it. First, I don't feel good when I'm competitive, whether or not I win or lose. That's especially true when it's in a setting that isn't overtly competitive, where there are subtle games going on. Secondly, being competitive keeps me cut off from people, especially from other men. It's very, very hard—impossible—to be open with someone you feel competitive with.

On the other hand, in a very clearly defined competitive situation, like our Saturday afternoon basketball games, I can really enjoy competition. I don't mind losing that much and I enjoy winning. For me that's one of the worst things about growing up. You lose these socially acceptable occasions to compete and the competitive situations you do find yourself in—work, for example—are deadly serious. They can get very bloody and they are so damn subtle and under the covers.

I think I am most competitive when I am least sure of myself in a situation. I really feel that in sports, for example. I don't feel like a very good athlete and so when I play I am aware of competing intensely because I don't feel that good about my ability. Somehow I have to make up for that; I have to show that I'm better. In general, I feel like I have to compete, to strive for a power position when I am just slightly underneath someone, just a little worse than they are. For instance, in a group setting, I'm terrible with a clear, well-functioning leader because I lay for him. I'll wait and get him in a very subtle way sometimes. In that way, I think I'm a good competitor because I've learned not to be real overt.

I think of it like wrestling. One guy will seem to be on top and have things pretty well in hand and, all of a sudden—bang—the other guy will have him flipped and straddled. I think of myself that way, just coasting along, fiddling around, letting someone else be on top—as long as I'm sure I can flip him—until, bang, I'll get him. In my experience, the least successful competitors are the most overt.

To feel that edge of competition, to lay in wait, makes me very tense; I have to be on my guard all the time, always watching and waiting for that right opportunity, afraid that I might miss it.

For me this feeling has a lot to do with my size. I learned very early that I wasn't going to compete head to head with most of the guys around me. That would be suicide. And since I still wanted to compete and win among men, dealing with my own physical inadequacies meant learning to be that much more subtle, patient and cunning.

But I don't like it; it does awful things for me. What I try and do now is remove myself from those deadly kind of competitive situations. I still feel like I want to win, to be the best at what I do, but now it doesn't feel like a win-lose thing. I can win and other people can win.

There's another part of that though. Remember when you were a kid and how the guy you had the worst fights with would often end up being your closest friend? There's something about that kind of contact, that kind of energy that I like. And sometimes I miss the camaraderie and compassion that goes along with that kind of competition.

Gaye Williams

I feel differently about competition with woman than I do with men. I don't feel like I've ever been competitive with women. I can only remember being jealous once. Mostly I feel very comfortable with myself as a woman, so that's never been an issue for me.

But with men I think I am competitive, in an intellectual way. And I was raised to be that way. My father comes from a long line of lawyers and we used to sit around the dinner table and a topic would be announced and we would all argue about it. If I didn't know what I was talking about, I was wiped out, by my father or the rest of the family and it was my job to go find out about that subject. He wasn't one to let us win because we were kids either, or women. Like he always won unless we *really* won.

I think that's still operating for me. I never felt like I had to be a dumb blonde because that's the way you're supposed to be with men. We were brought up to compete, and win. That seems bad and good. I know now that it's hard for me to respect someone who isn't as capable intellectually as I am. I really respect a man that can win; that can hold his own in areas I don't know about.

I think I am much less likely to compete with men who I feel are fairly knowledgeable. I want less to compete in that case then when I sense a guy who is on my level or one who doesn't know what he's talking about. Then I'm more likely to compete.

I've noticed lately in tennis—we were also raised to be very competitive in sports—that I'm not nearly as competitive as I used to be. It certainly seems different and I don't know if I can generalize that to other areas of my life or not. I think what changed it is my becoming comfortable in other ways with myself; then I didn't have to battle to be so good in that one area. Like a certain amount of my identity was tied up in being a good tennis player so I had to strive to keep that up. And it's hard to know now how much of my identity is tied up in being bright with men. It's certainly very important to me.

When I feel competition coming up in me I get very aggressive. And again I flash on my family. We would strike our fist on the table or throw water to make a point. I become much more demonstrative and active when I feel a challenge. When I charge out to meet that challenge I somehow feel more competent; that intellectual challenge is ground I feel familiar on and I'm ready to do battle.

I seem to like competition, in that way; sometimes it brings out good things in me. I don't like it when it becomes an angry thing and people start putting each other down. I think there can be competition, in discussions for instance, and people can go away without angry feelings.

I know one thing; I respond to a challenge. I feel charged up, a little wicked, and looking for the fun involved. Sometimes I think I need that contact, that interaction; maybe it's like the battle before loving.

The funny part is, I think I want to lose. ⤸

Tony Rose

I don't feel competitive very often. Maybe it's just a "should" with me because I know my family taught me that I should not compete. In a way competing is saying "you gotta win." I was never encouraged to try and win; I was encouraged to do my best and live up to my potential but not to beat someone else. In a sense I was competitive in that though; I lost respect for those who I saw competing. I would say to myself, "They're wrong and I'm right."

But the atmosphere I was brought up in, set up largely by my mother, was "Get along, children, let's not have violence. No fighting." We could disagree, but the pressure was to avoid coming to blows. Cooperation was valued; competition was not.

Most competition still is not comfortable for me. I don't like it. In certain sports I like it; it seems like it's acceptable when everyone can play and winning is not the only goal. If we can play well and enjoy each other, that's ok. I like playing with people who want our team to win, but it's ok to lose too. I like playing with people who enjoy losing a good game.

When I do start to feel competitive I seem to tighten up in my neck and shoulders. My jaw gets tight, I squint my eyes and I feel a kind of viciousness coming up within me. Then I start to feel physically aggressive, like wrestling or throwing somebody. I feel like a leopard, tightening for a spring on someone.

Competition makes me very intense and focused on a person or a goal; everything else seems to be blotted out. It carries a package of being goal-oriented, aggressive, strong, and violent when it's carried through. I like that and I don't like it. There's a feeling of energy inherent in it which seems good. It can unify. I can feel it from my toes all the way to my head. At the same time it's scary; I wonder if I'm in possession of myself, my competition, or is my competition in possession of me. So far I believe I can handle it, but I worry about hurting someone else, physically or emotionally. When I sense that kind of ruthlessness coming up in me, I recognize ways that I head it off. I try, for one thing, to try and tune in to the other person . . . his softness, his vulnerability, and see where I could be hurting him. Then that rears in me the ugly specter that I am really going to hurt someone and lose a friend, or a potential friend. I put that above winning. I put fear in the way, I put my other values in the way and it serves to head off the viciousness of the completion.

It seems there are people who say, and I find myself wanting to say sometimes, "Competition can be constructive and creative." But inside I feel like that's bullshit. I think that competition essentially is destructive. At best, it kind of comes out even; an individual may lose and one may win but there is no gain for man in that. Only in cooperative situations is there gain for humanity, for life. One of the most important things for me in my life is to help people cooperate and stop competing. It is one of my strongest beliefs, a strong experience of life for me. It seems even more tragic to see intense competition when I know what beautiful things can happen in a cooperative situation, when I know how much gain could come about.

A few weeks ago I worked with a team of people who are managing a forest district. These nine men have been in unnecessary competition with each other for years and it's so tragic because they're such beautiful, potentially powerful people, who have so much in common and so much to work on together. I had a strong feeling of remorse about that. When they started turning that around, getting with each other, cooperating, the richness of what started happening between them was a real joy; a joy for them and for me. These people who had not really communicated with each other for two years, within an evening were really talking with each other and within two days had started working *together*. They can be far more productive, far more happier in their work, more relaxed in their physical being and in their spiritual being, just by moving from competing to cooperating.

I want to be careful about putting down competition entirely though. Maybe it's natural human process to compete. When it comes to basic, raw survival, it's possible that that competition has to come to the front. It's that viciousness in me that rises up when I think I'm in a fight and it's to the death. I may feel I've got to kill or get killed. But I think we let that permeate through to other situations in an affluent, civilized society when we don't need to. When we are worried about our survival, in any numbers of ways, may be when we compete the most.

Earl Burrows

For me to be competitive means to enter into a physical contest or verbal exchange in which those who perform according to some outside criteria are going to win and some are going to lose. There is some reward inherent in that. And I feel like the shift came in me from having the focus on winning—to other things I feel are beneficial for me.

Somehow competition has something to do with having my space intruded on. That gets to be a very personal thing and at a time like that I do become very competitive and act that out. If it's really not affecting me in a personal way, I would tend not to do much.

I have to go back a ways to get into any competitive feelings. I can remember that in all the sports I've taken part in—and that's been a very big part of my life—there has always been a big push for winning. I remember being really into that thing of pushing, beating, winning— winning no matter what, no matter what happened to the other guy.

I remember when that changed for me too. I had been out of competitive sports for about five years and then I got onto a recreation league basketball team in Boulder. I was in my mid-thirties, I guess, and I found out quickly that all that stuff that used to be there—the spring in my legs, the drive, the endurance—wasn't there any more. And my attitude toward competition changed. It became okay for me to go and play for the exercise, for the fun of it, and winning was not so important any more.

I think what I was doing for a long time was proving myself. I had to prove my worth in sports just as I did in a lot of other things I did, with women, grades, whatever. That seems to me the whole basis of competition, to prove your worth. I *have* to do certain things as expected so I can prove my value. If I do not value myself I have to act it out in a lot of ways that come out as competition. And at that time in my life I still hadn't started to look at myself as a worthwhile human being.

But as I got older I realized that I didn't have the strength or the endurance to go head to head with younger guys and win. I knew I was going to come up short. So in a sense it was partly backing away from competition, but more realizing there was something different to get out of what I was doing, something more important. I couldn't have it focused so much on the winning because I was going to come up losing too much; it became a recognition of my own limitations and a realization that there was a hell of a lot more to sports than winning.

Now I notice in me a resistance to put myself in competition, into competitive situations. When those things come up, when people start trying to outdo each other, to prove that they are better than I am or somebody else is, I just back off and say "I don't need to do that. I don't want to compete." Part of the reason for that is I get what I want without competing.

It's a matter too of shifting values. Things that used to be important aren't. That holds true physically, financially, emotionally. It seems now that I value myself much more and not the external things like money, winning, beating someone else, possessions. And I notice a great deal of difference in what it does to me inside to stop striving for those things.

In a competitive situation, one way or another, it seems like someone else has to tell you you did well; someone else gives you the reward, whether it's the roar of the crowd, the scoreboard, the good grade, the job. Someone else validates you.

Considering myself a significant human being is the thing that frees me from having to prove myself in so many ways to other people, often through competition.

John Wood

I woke up thinking about competition this morning and I had a strong sense of ownership, of possessiveness, in competitive situations. I *have* something and someone else is *apparently* trying to take it away from me; he or she is going to be better than I am at whatever it is and rob me of something.

What that something is that's at stake is not always clear. When it's an athletic contest, the competition and the rewards seem out front. When it's me and someone else feeling competitive about a woman sometimes that takes a little longer to surface. But in either case, there is that same sense of ownership. I want to *have* a victory in a race, just as I want to *have* the woman we're competing for.

The better I'm able to shed that sense of possession and know that, in a real sense, I can have neither the victory or the woman, the better I'm able to get out from under the competitive (defensive) feelings that come up.

It seems that the more things I think I own, the more I have to puff out my chest, straighten my back and defend those things from all the forces, seen and unseen, which will take them from me. And that makes me think about all the people in this country who have so many material, external things that they "own." As I get older and more self-possessed, I see myself caring less and less about those things. I wonder how many people think they own their spouse or their children or their employees.

One of my struggles has been to know the difference, then, between the things I can have and the things that I cannot. I don't want to own another person; it's a false hope. In the end, they must own themselves. I don't really want to own superiority over another person, though I do want to acknowledge my differences and do the best I can at the moment (I think about athletic contests).

With competition, I am coming to a sense that feels like aikido, the oriental art of self defense, where instead of stiffly resisting another, you help take him where he wants to go. It is like becoming cooperative, to help you do what you want to do and realize that it doesn't threaten me.

In a real sense, to be competitive is to be other-directed. I am oriented to your goal, your strength, your threat, instead of myself. If we are competing over a woman, the reward is her validation of one or the other of us, not our own value of ourselves. The way I want to be in the world is aware of you, accepting of you, but centered in myself.

That has very much to do with my sense of uniqueness. I notice that the men I feel most competitive with are those that seem most like me . . . their looks, the things they do, their values. They threaten my sense of uniqueness. If they are who I am and better at it, where does that leave me? This tells me the more I know my own unique qualities, the more special I'll feel, the more significant I'll believe I am and the more I'll be able to allow you your own space in my life.

CONFUSED

In the middle of the journey of our life I came to myself
within a dark wood where the straight way was lost.

Dante Alighieri

ununun

Doug Land

I don't know exactly what confusion is. I think of myself as a reductionist; that is I tend to want to put everything together and see it all as one and so when I hear a word like confusion, I think of it as a term people use to separate out some feelings. But, for me, confusion, fear, anxiety, all are wrapped up together, all facets of the same thing. For the sake of discussion they can be separated, but I don't think people are that way; it's very hard for me to see any one of these feelings as separate and discreet.

I tend to react to confusion as I do to anxiety and fear, which is to feel impotent. There seem to be so many inputs being made that it's impossible to sort them out and arrive at any unity or direction.

Some people, I'm sure, in the face of that confusion, strike out and start doing things, just anything, to try and resolve it. They don't know what to do. I don't know what to do. I think some people try doing something and others do nothing. I tend to withdraw and look at things and keep looking at them. My battles with my confusion are all internal.

I get confused when something happens to me over which I have no control or when somebody does something to me for a reason I can't fathom or understand. Then I can't see the purpose in things. Most of the time I seem pretty well grounded, purposeful, and having a direction, and when I get the most confused is when that internal compass goes awry.

When the compass is right, I know where north is and where I'm going even if I can't articulate it. When I get confused the compass starts spinning and I just shrink in, withdraw, and watch.

In the past I have used certain devices to try and get out of that confusion, but the devices are not in anyway directed to external circumstances. For instance, in the past, I might have prayed all night, just to pray, which is another way of saying I wondered internally about what was happening around me or pleaded with myself or with some kind of metaphysical force to try and get right again. By right, I mean having some perspective and meaning for me.

I think it probably works out the same for people who do things out of their confusion and people who don't do things. For me it usually clears up and I can look back and say I may not really know what went on, but I have some kind of schematic for myself and now I know my direction again.

I think it's true of me what Daniel Boone said once when somebody asked if he'd ever been lost in the woods. He answered: "No, I was never lost, but I was bewildered for a few days." That's the way I look at myself looking back; in the middle of it, it seems much more confused than that.

Confusion is different from being lost. I seem confused on several levels all the time. I can't fathom what's going on in the world. I can't understand why people act the ways they do, in mob ways, in nationalistic ways. I'm confused. And it seems symptomatic of our times. My reaction to being confused has been to gradually step back and draw my borders a little bit closer to myself, until I'm involved in a very individualistic philosophy. I think that's what's happening in the world; that's what is at the same time a source of despair and romanticism, that individualistic feeling of: "I don't know what anyone else is doing, but I know what I'm going to do for myself."

Actually being confused is satisfying in some ways. I don't mind being confused in that Daniel Boone way; that's a kind of confusion I sometimes like. I like putting myself in a position where I'm going to be confused for a while because I have confidence that out of the confusion and chaos is going to come some unity and some design and that's going to be very satisfying for me and others to work that out. That's instead of the kind of confusion where something external happens to me and distracts me from myself and the others around me.

For instance, confusion happens all the time in a family, where every one is going in different directions and you're trying to get some order out of it sometimes, like you have to be a certain place at a certain time. And I don't like to say, "All right, dammit, get up and get a move on." I really don't like that. I'd rather we work with the confusion in a way where all of us are doing something and each of us is doing something about it, is reaching our own solution and it turns out to be the solution that all of us wanted anyway. But sometimes you just don't have time for that. At that point, it seems that whoever is the strongest steps in and says "Do it or I'm going to kick your ass!" and I don't like being that way.

The way I feel about my confusion is a kind of ambivalence, the ambivalence I seem to feel for almost all things. I'd like to work out a middle way for myself between sitting and waiting for something to happen, for it to work itself out, and my having to aggressively force unity on a world that isn't actually unified. Mostly I think I'm too passive. What I want, what is difficult for me, is to "take arms against a sea of troubles" but not to overcome them, not to have to step on the situation to get past it but rather to work through it. My way seems to be to ease toward it slowly, mostly too slowly, allowing too much to go on, withholding too much of myself from the situation. It's a hard thing; as I look around the world, if I want to err in any direction, I want to err in the direction I'm erring in.

Carol Ahearn

At one time in my life the state of affairs that I lived in most of the time was one of confusion . . . I felt like things were overwhelming . . . so much content in colors, objects, and shapes . . . so much sensory input . . . so many things going on in my life. I felt like I had to censor myself, to dull myself, to wear blinders.

I don't think I live that way anymore and it seemed to be a way of exaggerating things for myself. There were so many things going on and I couldn't possibly respond to them all, so I retreated and thought of myself as dumb and scatterbrained. It was a way of staying stupid. The things around me were much too powerful and impending; it seems to me a bit like breathing hard and fast until you become hyperventilated.

When I get that way I become very stubborn in a way. Someone is trying to explain something to me and I look like I'm listening and try to look like I know what they're talking about and all the while I'm putting all my energy into *not* knowing what they're talking about, sort of scattering it so I won't have to know what they're talking about. It's like being a scared little girl. Being confused, is easier, safer than knowing what's going on and deciding what to do about it. I think that was an efficient way for me to be . . . impassive, helpless.

Now I don't think I let myself get into that corner, where I decide that everything is just too disorganized for me to handle. Now I think of myself as a more responsible person than I ever have been and now I get confused when I try to make everything clear and it isn't. Now that I've decided to have things clear to me instead of avoiding them, it's frustrating when I can't make everything clear. It's like I would like to be able to direct what's happening and it's confusing and frustrating when I can't. In almost all the instances I can think of, it's a case of deciding the way things are and then being thoroughly confused when I find out they're not that way at all. It doesn't do me any good to decide "the way things are."

Simply, I used to want to play dumb and I could be easily confused and achieve that. Now I want to play smart and pretend I know how things should be. Since there's no way to do that, I still get myself confused.

Also, if I see something that frightens me, I can retreat into confusion. Fear is very close to confusion for me. I can say "Jesus, that's so frightening, I can't understand it" and then not make sense out of anything else. I don't know what to do, it doesn't compute and I'm not going to respond. It's a safe place.

I seem to know now that what I fear, at first glance, isn't always that fearful and I'm willing to look twice before turning away.

What I usually want when I'm confused is for something to break it, something from the outside or from within me to break into it and change it. I may stay confused, but I'd rather change the confusion somehow than stay stuck. I usually remind myself of something someone said: "There are far worse states of mind than confusion." So many times I'd be happy to just ride it through and perhaps it will turn out to be fruitful.

Some days I am just not feeling weak and I have other resources at my disposal so I can fall back, admit to myself that I'm confused, look at it without getting hysterical and just let it be. Somedays I just have the confidence that whatever I do, it's going to be okay. And when I stop struggling with my confusion so much and let it go, something changes. It doesn't last forever. But when you're confused it's difficult to see all that.

Pat Rice

When I'm confused sometimes I get a little light-headed, depending on the intensity of the confusion. If my confusion is concerned with my relationship with someone I care about, I can get very panicky about it and get short-winded and my stomach will knot up; fear then becomes a part of it. Sometimes it's a fear of rejection or of criticism or of attack. If I'm not sure of where I stand in relationship sometimes in my confusion I'll withdraw and pull myself out of the situation rather than going in and opening up all my confusion to the other person. I tend to be confused privately and put on a public show that everything's cool.

I don't know where my biggest confusion comes from. Under stress or in situations where there's physical confusion, I seem to do well. But I get more confused when it has to do with interpersonal things . . . me in relationship to others. If I'm threatened in a personal way, my mind starts to race, my heart pumps, the adrenalin starts going and I feel vulnerable and confused. That always incapacitates me. Some people seem to be able to figure out what to do, to develop strategies, but I just fold up.

Sometimes in Center staff meetings I get confused, or maybe I get threatened and then confusion comes. That seems to depend on what my needs are at the time and how I'm feeling about my relationship to the group. I went through a period a while back where I really felt inadequate and unproductive, just a zero. And I remember a staff meeting where there was considerable stress on the point of people giving themselves permission to speak and say what they needed to and I realized to myself, "Oh shit, I can't do that; I can't get in." At a time like that, confusion overcomes me and I lose touch with my resources and how to get what I want. I can't think clearly.

I might do one of two things then. I might shut up completely. Or I might look for the first open door in the conversation to jump into. If someone else opens up and gives me an opening to respond to in a way that's comfortable to me, I'll really try and come in because I really want to be a part of the group. It's very hard—practically impossible for me to say "I'm just really confused and I need someone to tend to me."

If I were in a "medium" stage of confusion I might be able to say what I want, but in the stage I sometimes get to, I don't even have the resources, I can't think clearly enough to do that. That's when I really want help. And the bad part is I don't know exactly what it is I want; I just know I need something . . . reinforcement, support, response.

There's another way I get confused. That's when I don't know where I stand with another person, particularly a woman. We maybe haven't discussed things, got things out in the open so I don't know whether they want more or less from me or what they want. Then I tend to get quiet and withdraw. I can really get confused about what I want and whether or not I should move closer or keep my distance. Then I wonder what they want and I can get into a real negative trip about the whole thing. The confusion and the fear seems to come from not talking about what we need from each other. Then sometimes by not doing anything or saying anything, the wrong messages get sent and the distance between us remains.

There's some confusion I suppose that it's good to live with, not to get rid of too fast. I'd like to feel secure enough to let that ride sometimes. It would be good to be freer about that . . . to either own it or sit with it—or both.

Confusion sometimes comes from my need to be accepted, my need to be included and if I didn't have those needs so strongly, I could be straighter about where I really am. But having that need, that fear of rejection, I sometimes won't be straight about where I am and I find myself in a confused relationship again.

I really would like to be able to own my confusion and be open enough about it so I don't have to get into my withdrawal thing. That tends to leave the responsibility for the relationship all on the other person; they have to take the initiative. But I'd like to take my own responsibility. I'd like to be able to just go ahead and talk about the confusion, not try to talk my way out of it, but bring it right into the open.

John Wood

Sometimes it seems I live my life in a perpetual state of confusion. Things change within me . . . my values, my actions. Things change in the world around me . . . some close to me, some more distant, but all saying "There is no harmony among men. Confusion reigns. What is true today will surely not be true tomorrow."

Some days it seems terribly hard to move, with any sense of peace in myself, through a world I see as so complicated and crazy.

I am confused today. I am sitting, shaking my head, looking off in the distance and saying to myself: "I don't understand. I just don't understand." I have a sense of despair about myself and others close to me. Things I thought were true are not. People I believed cared about me act like they don't. I feel sad, hurt, untrusting, and confused. I don't know what I want for myself today or what I want to do about the state I'm in.

This seems to be the worst kind of confusion for me, when things inside—basic, important things—are tossed up in the air and I don't know where, or when, they'll come down.

More, I seem to be fighting a battle of things controlling me or taking control of my own life; more like walking a tightrope. And when it feels like I will go to the side of taking control of my own life, in this state, I will withdraw, isolate myself for a while. As if I need to pull back from the confusion and hurt to gain a sense of my own center.

In my confused state it seems if I give up control to people or situations around me, I will be hurt again. I will be tested, changed, spun around and up in the air again.

So for now I retreat . . . a little, I hope. I admit my confusion to others, but I don't take any real risks. It seems best to think, be with myself, listen and look. Perhaps tomorrow I can take a step out of my confusion.

Sometimes confusion can be a way to avoid making a decision. I can step back, rub my forehead and say: "I just don't know what to do; I'll leave it up to you." That seems to be leaving the responsibility for a decision of mine up to someone else. I don't like it when I do that. At those times I wish I could make a decision for myself, about myself and own it. On the other hand, I don't want to force a decision out just to satisfy someone else who needs one. As you can see, it can be confusing.

I realize that another kind of confusion is not so painful for me. It is when I feel a real sense of myself and the people around me or the world in general seems in chaos. I am able to let that go and trust that some sense of order, even if it's only temporary, will come out of it. Even though people I care about may be confused, I do not want to find an answer for them. I do want to let them know I am there, that I care and that it's all right for them to be totally confused.

It used to be that even that kind of external confusion disarmed me and I thought that I somehow had to set the world in order again. It seems much more comfortable now to let the world go on turning and trust that the sun will come up tomorrow.

I have a vision of two ways to be in the world that has to do with confusion and fear. One is to feel afraid and abandoned, like a lost child; I don't know where I am and clutch up at the thought of being lost and forgotten. The other way is to adopt the posture of being a "citizen of the world" and believe that, wherever I am physically or psychologically, I can be at home with myself and that a path to travel will make itself known before too long.

As I write about that I am finding courage to be that way with my own self today.

DEFENSIVE

Simply by being compelled to keep constantly on his guard, a man may grow so weak as to be unable any longer to defend himself.

Friedrich Nietzsche

Bill Stillwell

I know that I'm getting defensive when I have the fleeting sensation that whatever feeling or idea I am presenting is not all there is in me, that it's not the totality of the way I am about that particular thing. There is something more there that's not coming out.

I feel defensive when I am "called" on something, when someone challenges me. It could be something that we have agreed on that I would do, contracts we have made between us and somehow I haven't lived up to my end of it. I begin to get very defensive when I start to realize that that is indeed true. It makes me frightened. I want to protect myself and at the same time attack back; I see whatever is in the air as an attack on me. I tend to try and lunge back and justify what I've done rather than withdraw.

Trapped is a word that comes to mind. Sometimes I get trapped in the incongruity between what I want to be and what I am. I realize it myself, it's not just what someone else says about me. I think the attack, the accusation is true too. I seem somehow to recognize that I have not done exactly what I wanted to, that I have not lived up to the expectations that others have put on me and that I have put on myself. Sometimes it's a case of my taking on other peoples' expectations and they turn out not to be mine. Then I get defensive about not meeting them when I shouldn't have taken them on in the first place.

Sometimes the image I have is of protecting my perfect, congruent self. In other words, I think I have to protect a picture of myself as a competent, "good" person or consultant or whatever. When that perfection is flawed, whether it's through someone else's eyes or my own, I feel I have to defend, to protect my image. Mostly I think I get more defensive if someone else points out my incongruities than if I admit them myself.

When I'm with people who are always sure of themselves I can get pretty defensive. I'm not sure of myself. And I don't particularly care to be sure of myself all the time; I like to be seeking rather than knowing.

When I'm in situations that I'm not sure of, I can get defensive. If

I think I've gotten in over my head and am doing something I'm not competent in, I'm susceptible to that. It's funny, I moved toward a position of knowledge of being in control, but I also want to be with people in situations where they have a part of the knowledge and control too. Then neither of us has reason to be defensive. The inequality, the one-upsmanship, the competitive feelings are the things that bring out my defenses. I'm most comfortable not being defensive and taking care not to force others into defensiveness.

Sometimes being defensive is a way of being which serves me. It seems to come from my feeling of inadequacy in a situation; I can admit those feelings to myself and others or choose not to. Sometimes that is good, sometimes not. But I also have strong feelings of wanting to be adequate to that situation and my defensiveness is a way of saying, "I really was adequate; they just saw it wrong." Sometimes I'm not adequate enough and I don't want to admit it; then I defend.

Mostly, I don't want to go through the world being defensive. I think about two things in kind of a long range view. One is to keep trying to perfect myself, to improve, to grow and move toward the things I want for myself. Then it happens that I have to be less defensive about parts of myself. The other is kind of the opposite; it's to know and to admit where I'm not that good, not that effective and to accept that in myself. The things I want the most for myself and am not making much progress on are the things I get the most defensive about.

Betty Meador

I think defensive for me is a mind set or a state of being, not just a reaction to something specific or something I go in and out of quickly.

I am often defensive when I'm in a relationship where it seems as if the other person knows more than me. And it means somehow that I can't stand behind who I am; I can't be myself comfortably. It's as though the state of being myself and feeling good, comfortable and strong, disappears. It doesn't seem so much like I'm defending myself, but more like myself is gone and there is nothing to defend.

When I get into that, I tend to try to please the other person. I start to say things like "Yeh, I'll do it your way. You're right."

In its extreme form, my defensiveness gets into a state where I want to become the other person. It's a case of completely identifying with him; I take on all of his values, do what he's doing . . . I just lose all sense of myself. It's as though I'm saying, the only way to be in a relationship with him is to be like him completely. I'm not sure that that's defensiveness, but it comes out of a sense of myself being driven away by another's standards and judgments.

I'm thinking of a specific situation about being defensive . . . I've been going to this psychiatrist to consult with him on how to handle a patient I have. I tell him as much as I can about how I've been dealing with her and what's been happening and he comments on it. And it's gotten to the point where I don't think I can do anything right; he just keeps pointing out more things or different things I should have done. It's made me very defensive with him and I go in expecting to be proven wrong. It seems like a set-up situation to me—I am not sure what I'm doing, but I want to appear smart; I want him to think of me as a capable therapist. Maybe it's not so much that I want him to think of me as a good therapist, but that I want to think of myself as good and his constant downgrading shakes my faith in myself.

I think my defensiveness would change for the better if he gave me some indication that he thought I was doing a good job. Or if he were to say sometimes that he isn't so sure of himself either. He doesn't have to be defensive when he's "right" all the time.

Sometimes I feel some anger with defensiveness; I want to strike back at the other person. But I usually don't do that; I get into pleasing the other person and I'm left sitting on a lot of angry feelings. It sometimes seems like a child-father relationship and I'm the child. I couldn't argue with my father; I felt helpless in trying to fight him or prove him wrong. That seems to me like a typical child-father relationship. And I can't be loved by being mad at him so I'm going to be loved by pleasing him. I feel like I have to go along with him. But all this is in a situation where I feel smaller and weaker than the other person. At those times, my self is gone and I just do what the other person wants.

What I'm discovering is that the surer I feel about myself, the fewer people there are that I feel defensive with. I seem to be getting more of a hold on that child-parent thing, the stronger-weaker thing, and recognizing it for what it is. I seem to be not so quick to assume that people are better or smarter than I am.

Also talking about my defensiveness is an option, but sometimes I'm too scared to do that. I guess I feel like that puts me in a more "down" position, to admit that I'm being closed and protected.

It really helps when someone admits their vulnerability to me. Somehow they say "I'm not perfect; I make mistakes too." Praise works for me too; it helps me relax and not feel like I'm getting a barrage of criticism. That makes the criticism, when it comes, not so hard to take.   ↰

John Wood

Being defensive is a very important concept to me. I see a lot of people for whom it is a way of life; it's their way of relating to the world.

In me, it has an awful lot to do with my growth. I don't think I can grow and be open to change when I am being protective.

When I am defensive I am afraid. It could be afraid of being hurt, rejected or unloved. Sometimes I recognize myself saying, "Oh oh, someone is about to discover something bad in me. They're about to find out something I don't want them to know." There is a feeling of girding myself, of setting up smokescreens and barriers to protect that sore spot.

I get quiet and withdrawn. I avoid contact with people and if I do talk, I will try to manipulate the conversation around to unimportant matters. The closer someone gets in conversation to the weak or evil thing I'm protecting, the higher I build the barriers, the more veiled I become.

There are certain kinds of people who will make me feel defensive and withdraw. Someone who seems certain about everything has that effect on me; someone who is sure of where he is and where he's going, know's what's right and wrong with the world and seems like he know's what's right and wrong for me. Someone like that can make me unsure of myself and protective of the things I think he will judge. Also I am defensive if I'm with someone who has much higher standards than I do and he or she expects me to live up to them . . . and I think I have to live up to them too. In those cases, it often feels like I want the other person's praise and that praise is withheld until I come up to their standards. I don't know why I give all that power to someone else.

I seem to get the most defensive when I think something I have done is "bad." The judgment as to what is bad is a judgment of mine as well as others around me. It cuts the most when someone else's judgment of me agrees with my own bad impression of myself. I seem very susceptible to a "bad boy" thing. I can get pouty and withdraw just like a bad boy would. When I get that way or get an impression of someone reacting to me in that way, I quickly blame them for being judgmental and not understanding me. I begin to feel misunderstood, unloved, unknown and alone.

There are particular things in my life that I tend to judge myself for and so feel sensitive about . . . being over-sexual, selfish, indecisive, cool, aloof, and critical. When someone taps into one of these areas I don't like about myself, I can get very defensive, tight as a drum. That seems to be a case of me protecting an "evil truth" in myself.

Perhaps the way out of that is through self-acceptance. Today I can see clearly and say to myself that I am not a bad person and even those bad traits I think I have are not present in me all the time. Though sometimes I am aloof, critical and cool, there are at least an equal number of times when I am really present with people, accepting, affectionate and warm. Why can't I see that in myself more clearly and allow my "lapses." Must I be perfect?

An important part of this has to do with two images . . . of a core of myself and a shell. When I feel the central core of myself, when I know what I'm about and can present that to the situation, I rarely have a need to defend. I feel myself "filled out" in a sense and there is nothing to hide. Another way to feel, perhaps the opposite, is to sense that I am just a shell, thinly disguising an empty person inside. My core has vanished . . . I don't know myself or have any faith in what's inside of me. That shell is crusty, hard and brittle; surely I must protect myself because the inside is dark and vacuous. I am very vulnerable.   ↰

Bob Kavanaugh

I am an extremely defensive person. I think that has come partly from my rearing, but now, more and more, it is by choice. I have at times been almost totally open, without fences, but I found it too painful a way to live. I found some important people needed my fences and I tried to build my fences with gates they could open. I found that civility and civilization require some defenses . . . some fences, some gates.

When I feel defensive my tummy tightens, I begin to talk a bit faster, my blood flows faster and I blush a little.

My most successful defense is to hide behind my openness. In group settings, I lead with intimate material that helps feign openness, that seems to open others, but it really helps keep people away from my well-guarded spots. With individuals I find myself "pre-admitting" mistakes I might have made to protect myself from hearing them from anyone else. My lips speak criticism of myself so much easier than my ears listen to it.

My ideal is to be as open and unguarded as I choose with anyone that I meet, but I find this is a distant star to follow. My shyness, fear of looking foolish, fear of looking lecherous and my fear of rejection are like tiny pixies that keep me far from my ideal. This is sometimes frustrating, but more and more I treasure the pixies; they are my unique part in my culture, my rearing, my own painfully enduring set of foibles that makes me what I want most to be—just a plain human being.

DISAPPOINTED

こ~こ~こ~

Howard Saunders

The first thing disappointment makes me think about is a situation I get myself into often. I easily get hyped up about things, the possibility of things happening. I gain a lot out of that excitement. But then maybe several months go by and I've told a lot of people about this thing happening and it doesn't happen. Then people ask: "God, aren't you disappointed?" and I have to say no. The most recent example is the trip to Europe I was planning. I was really excited about it in the beginning, in the planning stages, but by the time the point rolled around to make up my mind to really go, I was in a different place. I didn't really want to do it. I wasn't disappointed—I had changed, I guess, and no longer wanted the same thing. I think it's good I can accept that.

If I fall in love with someone and they don't love me, I am disappointed for a while. What I had hoped would happen didn't happen, but after that initial disappointment it seems to fade easily. I have the expectations, there's a situation, a scene set up somehow, I don't get what I want and I'm disappointed. And then it's gone. I just don't hold on to disappointment. But I do need a release of some kind from the expectation. For instance, if I really care about a woman and I want something from her . . . loving, a relationship, something . . . and I don't get it, I'm disappointed. But it's important for me to face it and release it . . . somehow I get to confront the object of my expectations and release my emotions. Then I can get rid of it. I just don't think disappointment is a big deal.

The last big disappointment I felt was when I saw the illustrations I had done for Saturday Review in print. I was really disappointed that they had abused my illustrations; they hadn't designed them into the magazine the way I'd hoped they would and I felt like I was given a bad deal. They didn't meet my expectations. I had such an investment in those and they just didn't make. I was disappointed. I bitched about it. But it's funny, I got confused about them. I thought "Maybe they're not as good as I thought they were; maybe they didn't deserve any more play." I didn't have much faith in them. But then I decided I liked them; I really had a fight with myself. It was like their treatment of them didn't match up with what I thought of them, and it disappointed me and kind of shook my faith in my work.

But disappointment for me is so fleeting. I'd like to make a case for it, but I can't. It's so fleeting. I can care passionately for things but I don't have to get fucked up about it.

It seems today like I have a lot of energy. I have a lot of hopes for myself and a lot of ways to express myself. If I only had one hope perhaps my disappointments would be bigger. Instead I seem to have smaller ones that pass quickly.

I do expect a lot of other people. After I've sized them up and think I know them and know what they're capable of, I expect them to do those things I think they're capable of. And I think that's because I expect the same of me. And when I get into that set, I get angry at those people I'm expecting something from, saying to myself, and them: "Dammit, I want you to live up to what you're capable of." That's a pressure I can put on people. I don't think I give people much room to fuck up.

Andre Auw

When I'm aware of my disappointment, I'm aware of a kind of sadness, a hurt. I don't experience much of a physical reaction, partly because I think disappointment is a rather low key thing.

I seem most susceptible to disappointments that arise out of expectations in personal relationships. I am expecting something from you, that's not realized and I suffer disappointment. Frequently that comes out of a misunderstanding. I am very sensitive to being let down and if I understand you are going to do or we're going to do something together and it doesn't happen I can easily go from disappointment to hurt to anger.

One thing I recognize is that my expectations are fairly specific. I don't seem to get into high expectations of a general nature, of wanting you to be a certain way, therefore it seems easier to deal with my disappointments because they come from a specific action, or lack of it.

A lot of growth I've experienced in the last five or so years seems to be in the area of accepting people where they are and not to put those expectations on them of ways I want them to be. Of course it's hardest when it counts the most, when it's a relationship you really count on. I have a sister, for instance, that has been somewhat difficult for me to deal with. I could accept eccentricities in all sorts of other people but couldn't in her. Finally I became aware of what was going on, what I was nourishing and perpetuating . . . that a lack of acceptance in me perpetuated the problems. I demanded that she accept me the way I was but I was not willing to accept her. When I could accept her with her own specific needs, I could then deal with those needs. Now that that's out in the open, oddly enough, I can meet some of her needs and openly say no to others. And she can accept that now. A real tenseness we had is gone.

To connect that with disappointment, I expected her to treat me adult-to-adult, not as mother-to-child, as she sometimes needed to. But there is a part of her that has to be a mother to me—there's a part that can be an adult to my adult too—and she has to get those mothering needs met. So when I could take away my demands that she just be a mature adult all the time and accept her as she is, a lot of pressure was taken off. Then I didn't expect her to be just what I needed, then I wasn't disappointed. I could deal with her in a straight-forward, caring way.

That touches on the way I handle disappointment now, which is better for me. What I used to say was "You have really let me down, you have really disappointed me. And I blame you for it." What I try and do now, as soon as I experience disappointment, is look for what I've been doing to set that up. I look at my expectations, assumptions and fantasies to see how I've done that to myself. Now, instead of blaming you, I try and accept responsibility for my own disappointment.

What I hope is I'll continue to have that bell ring when I feel disappointment coming on and be able to ask myself: "Okay, what is it that I'm doing to disappoint myself?" I hope that comes more easily and more naturally than it has been; sometimes it takes a while. Sometimes I need to nourish that disappointment for a while, play a little bit of the martyr.

Now I want that bell to start ringing sooner. I can get a warning when I see I'm not taking care of myself. I don't feel comfortable, a little funny in the situation—I just know when I'm not taking good care of myself. So I say, "Okay, what do I need to do for myself to make things right?"

There is a great deal of power and energy that comes from being able to own my own truth and when I have been deceitful, it bothers me. When I'm able to admit that, to say I have deceived myself, just being able to admit that has a kind of energizing effect on me. Then I recognize what I've been doing. Part of the deceit has been blaming the other guy for everything wrong that went on, as if I'm the poor, innocent, injured party and this mean son-of-a-bitch comes in and screws my life up. When I recognize that I feel better and can start taking better care of myself right now. I can admit to myself and others what has happened and learn something for the next time.

Usually at the root of that disappointment is my expectation and I see that I have been lazy and irresponsible about checking it out. I set myself up for it. In the past, I would feel "good" about blaming the other guy; today I feel a lot better about accepting my own part in it. ↶

Roger Ledbetter

I seem to have experienced as much disappointment as anyone. Disappointment never feels good to me. Inside it feels like nausea, anxiety, a real letdown, a sagging.

If I'm disappointed, I've had a fantasy about reality. I've created a set of expectations in my head that fills some kind of need for me and when I feel disappointed, I feel a different reality setting in, super-imposing itself over the "reality" I had dreamed up. When it's bad, it's a feeling of utter aloneness. It sometimes scares me because it makes me wonder about all the rest of my fantasies and dreams and how reality will treat them.

For so much of my life disappointment has hit me really hard. I could get disappointed easily and a whole set of defense mechanisms would come in . . . rationalization, avoidance, withdrawal. I would say, "Aw, it really didn't matter that much anyway." It seemed like I could get into the pain of disappointment much easier than I could experience joy. I could take on the pain of the world; I seem to have a lot of outlets for pain. So many disappointments, so many pains, and I built up an elaborate set of mechanisms for dealing with it. I got to the point where I was waiting for the next disappointment to come along so I could show myself how well I could take it on . . . always creating these great expectations and having reality hit me hard and cold. It started to make me very cynical.

But the big part of me that's the idealist keeps coming through. I still want me and the world to be perfect. I still throw up that grid of high expectations and though that's still a part of me, I am beginning to free myself from that. Part of that is a lot of my fantasies for myself are starting to come true—or I'm starting to make them come true. More, I am moving myself away from having such great expectations. I still have a set of ideals, but am getting much better at doing away with specific, day-to-day expectations.

I guess the biggest thing I want for myself is to be like a child in the universe, to have a sense of wonder about everything, even the most mundane things. Everything is new; there are no etched-in categories for everything. Those categories, those boxes, keep us from experiencing things as totally new. That's my ideal, to be in that child-like state.

Sometimes I look at my life and I see the same mistakes over and over again. The hopes and the disappointments repeating themselves. The pain that I have to swallow. I see it trying to teach me something each time, but there is so much dissonance and diversion that I can't see the lessons clearly. The "why" of my hurts and my high expectations does not come through. I get myself into a situation where I want something, expect something to happen, and because I'm in a hurry or in two places at once, I don't get into it. I put 10 percent of myself into it and then 100 percent of myself reacts violently to the mistakes, to the fact that it doesn't come off like I wanted it to.

So instead of embracing the energy that the disappointment and pain represent, I just say "screw it" and move on to the same situation again and again. What I'd like to do is let myself go into the disappointment, the pain and really learn from it. I need to own it and fully realize how it happened and what my part in it was. I probably only need to do that once. But what I do is to move on quickly to something else, so the significance is lost. I need to learn more from myself.

John Wood

It seems as if I have a lot to say about disappointment. Is that because I have been disappointed a lot? Perhaps not. Perhaps it is because I think about it and do a fair job of avoiding it.

Disappointment gives me a sinking feeling, thinking about specific instances. It feels like something is sinking inside me (my heart sinks in my chest?). It's almost like there was a big barrel in there waiting to be filled, hoping so much to be filled, knowing that it would be filled and then, a sudden realization, it's not going to be filled. It seems to make it all the more empty.

I think of several kinds of disappointment . . . in myself, with others and with events or situations that are coming up in my future. I have been disappointed in myself lately for not working on this book more. I have set up a schedule for myself and have not been keeping up with it. I have a thousand avoidance games that I play, things I can find to do instead of setting down at the typewriter and writing. This is an old game with writers. But the disappointment begins to get to me. As time goes on and I don't do the work I expect myself to do, my disappointment in myself grows, my opinion of myself gets less and less. I need a way out of that, not just today but on many days, because the disappointment and the low opinion of myself cripples me.

Here I am disappointed in me again. Lower. Lowering. It is a lowering thing. By telling myself I continually have to do more, to be better, I am constantly downgrading myself. Hell, I do that more to me than I do it to others or than others do it to me. I am reminding my children always to have a high opinion of themselves, to accept what they are. Can I not do that for myself?

It's as if I have a picture of what I want to be (should be?) and when I live up to that picture I like me. When I don't do the tasks, be the ways my image would have me, I don't like me. It seems so simple saying it. What I wish is that I will love myself through thick and thin and loving myself in my "bad" moments will make me feel all that much better and the sooner I will get back to doing the things I really want to do. And I trust the things I want. The disliking myself, the "poor" me, bad guy, martyr thing is a way of perpetuating my down moods. It's lazy and irresponsible.

I can apply those same notions to others and what I expect of them.

There is another disappointed feeling that seems a little more complex. It has to do with relationships, situations, occasions or groups of people. Perhaps the root is the same, but it comes out now in different words. I think it springs from my needs. I have needs for affection, undertsanding, acceptance, camaraderie and a host of others we all experience. And I cast about for people, groups and occasions to satisfy those needs. I have a way of saying to "Yeh, you're great; you meet a lot of my needs and while you're at it, take care of these too." Then I drop that in their lap and expect them to regularly meet my needs without much effort from me. Invariably I'm disappointed when I do that. I withdraw, pout, feel unloved, and give ample portions of blame out to almost anyone around.

How to change that? I want to speak out clearly and openly for what I need. I want to try and get what I need when and if it feels right with my partner or others I'm with. If I don't get what I need and it's important to me, there are other stores open somewhere. To suppress what I need is a cancer inside of me. To expect others to meet my needs when they're not clearly expressed *or* when they can't or don't want to is a sure source of disappointment, resentment and bitterness. ↰

Bob Kavanaugh

Right now I am disappointed. Something I wanted very much was snatched away from me—fairly, but this does not ease my pain. I feel sad. I feel angry without a scapegoat, frustrated without a hope. I even feel vindictive—secretly (so secretly) wishing that the "culprits" who were the unwitting occasion of my disappointment will lose the thing I wanted and perhaps I can gain through their loss.

I find my greatest disappointments come from the loss of my own expectations. A plan, a hope, an ambition—they are like people to me, my own creations, and when my expectations are dashed I begin to grieve inside, to act out my grief in mourning behavior . . . sullenness, rage, hardening of my heart, fear of expecting again. But I also experience a kind of relief which I rarely confess; each of my expectations demanded of me some commitment and when I am relieved of my responsibility a weight is removed, I feel a freedom that in the midst of my expectations I could never feel.

I've been trying to handle my disappointments in a new way. I sit and let myself feel the full scope of my reaction, trying to find out my primary feelings below the surface. My glorious dreams and expectations are usually accompanied by a feeling, or wishing for, omnipotence— a need to control and run the universe, inside my head and occasionally outside it too. All this seems to cover up a deep fear of impotence and failure.

It is so tempting now to reduce my hopes and expectations so as not to be disappointed again. Even when I therapeutically grieve and fully experience those sadnesses, I still feel my loss deeply. It seems as if new expectations, new dreams, can only grow well if I plant them side by side with my disappointments. My real losses are never totally uprooted, but are overshadowed by my new dreams that begin to flourish.

More and more I find myself tempted to hedge all my dreams behind some anticipatory grief—to protect myself in case of disappointment or failure. The wisdom for me in this is to always keep enough perspective on every expectation so that disappointment is "manageable" and does not result in a cynical resistance to trying again.

FREE

All I ask of living is to have no chains on me.
Blood, Sweat and Tears

⌣⌣⌣

Jack Bowen

Free is something I want to feel more often. I think about flying, surfing, sailing, nude in the warm sun, touching someone I love, making music, being quiet, working with my hands . . . those are freeing things for me.

I feel full of energy, whole, unfragmented, when I'm free. Sometimes I think I get free by moving away from people. Getting rid of my financial obligations would make me freer.

I think about living exactly the way I want to live . . . not worrying about clients, not worrying about making money, not worrying about my house, not going anywhere I didn't want to go. I have been without those things in the past . . . a business, a family, a home . . . but I gathered them around me because I wanted them and believed they would make me happy. Also it seems like something I was supposed to do. Owning a home is *supposed* to make you happier than renting a house. Having a family is supposed to make you happier than not having a family. Making investments is supposed to make you happier, safer from the threat of financial doom, than just spending your money. Having money is supposed to make you happier than not having money.

I think being free has almost nothing to do with the physical realities around you, but that it's a state of mind. It's a way of living your life by taking risks and being able to take the consequences. It has much to do with having the courage to live my life the way I want to.

Having Maria and Andy out of my life would make me freer, but I don't know if I want that freedom. There's a kind of bondage there, without comment, and I would not let myself live without them even though they take a certain amount of freedom away. Not to be special to them is something I don't want right now, that emptiness seems too great. There are times, however, when I would like to be away from them, to have quiet time to myself. I can grab little bits of freedom that way.

Sometimes I think about Fromm's notion of escaping from freedom. I tend to bind myself up in situations to keep from being free, to keep from facing the consequences of my freedom. An example is the thing I went through lately about wanting to do some work in the gay community. I've really wanted to do that; that would be pursuing my own freedom not freedom to do nothing, but to do what I want to do. The threat of the consequences . . . what people would think of me, financial reversals perhaps . . . was what was holding me back. I wanted to be sure to maintain my security, but that meant I was trading my freedom.

In the same way, to stay in a relationship that is no longer meeting my needs because I'm afraid I might not find another relationship is a heavy trade-off. What are the things I really buy in exchange for my freedom? In a relationship, there is somebody there to take care of me when I want that and somebody for me to take care of. There's somebody that I know will affirm me. There's somebody there who will contribute to the upkeep of my household. Those are things I want and am willing to trade for.

Most every time I test my freedom, I find that the boundary is mine, the restriction is my own and not one that is in my environment or that someone else is putting on me. That knowledge, in a sense, makes me free and my freedom is limited only by my fear of risking. My freedom is change; I can't do what I want to do and have things stay the same."

The most important thing I've learned about my freedom is learning where my non-freedom lies. I think I'm a very fortunate man and in many ways a great deal freer than many people I know. For the most part, my freedom lies in me. The opposite of my freedom is fear and I maintain that non-freedom by failing to challenge my fear.

Tony Rose

It seems like I have had tremendous opportunities for freedom in my life. Looking back on my recent past, I see how much freedom I've had. I had five years of graduate fellowships and I could do whatever I wanted within a very broad range and was mostly responsible for myself. My financial obligations were taken care of for the most part and I was free to explore whatever my nose led me to.

I came down here to WBSI, on a two-year fellowship, and could do anything I wanted to—not just anything within the realm of a graduate school of psychology, but anything in the world. That was scary, liberating, crazy. I fell in love, I made mistakes, I went crazy, I learned, I raced all over a bigger world then I had known, I experienced people in a new way. One of the most important things was to experiment with myself, to jump into new things and experience them as fully as I could. I felt like I was constantly stretching my limits. I took that message of freedom seriously and I was conscious about pushing myself out to learn. It was not a freedom to loaf, as I expected it might be.

I think I have found that I can tolerate just so much freedom. I think it is more than most people I see—but there does seem to be a limit. Every day I sense moments of freedom . . . relief, in a way.

Sometimes I am free by tying up some loose ends, by providing a little bit of structure for myself. Like planning out my schedule for the next couple of weeks—travel arrangements, transition points between jobs and cities—giving myself a broad outline so that I can feel more free and more open to what happens as I move through that schedule. What I think I need is some aids, some bridging between experiences. I feel like I'm operating as a businessman now, in business for myself. I'm traveling and working with three different projects in the next month and I can free myself up by getting it lined out ahead of time. Then I know that at each of those projects, I can relax and do whatever I want. It frees me from planning, once I do the little bit of planning I need.

I also like to be free from worry about financial needs, but that seems to be a receding horizon for me. There are people who worry about having enough money for the next five years, or longer I suppose, but I worry about the next five months. Even that creeps back to four, three months. Hell, hunters and gatherers used to worry about survival needs from day to day. There's a real freedom about being that way, being free to hunt and gather in everything that happens to me in a moment, in a day. The more time in my future I'm worried about, the less free I seem to be.

I think there's that hunter in each of us, that day-to-day survival primate. That's an animal that is really free, who is really living in the moment. I get into that feeling and sometimes spend days feeling like that. It's one of my supreme ecstasies. It's a setting free of an essential me. In our society there are certain parts, overlays of myself, that are not "allowed" to be free. Every moment I can get in touch with one of these essential, basic parts of myself and let it go, I feel very, very good. To squelch those parts is to squelch a whole human aspect of myself, my aliveness. That makes me think that to be free, to be whole, is when some new aspect of myself pops into being, or when an old one is reborn, and I am *free* to let that happen.

I think about the statement "He travels fastest who travels alone" and I think that's true. I'm trading my restrictions for speed, for freedom and I'm letting go of security. I think of myself as very much alone and that's come to be okay. When I think of the range of emotions that will be expressed in this book and experimenting with them—that I *am* them and more—you're damn right I'll be alone. When I take the freedom to go into all those dimensions of myself, there aren't going to be many people around. Even if there's someone in the next room or next to me in bed, the probabilities are very low that we'll be in the same place at the same time, when they're living the same range of emotions that I am. Yeh, freedom takes me into alone-ness. If I don't want that, I can get together with someone, give up some of my freedom, my experimenting, and see if we can work together. I sense a continual going back and forth between the two in me, like tides. I've come to accept that. ⤸

Bill Coulson

When I feel free I feel un-mindful. It's a devil-may-care attitude. When I really feel free I don't care about the consequences and also realize that I don't need to worry about them. It's a little like being drunk; everything seems more simple.

When I want to act free and don't, I think what keeps me from it is not wanting to be seen as irresponsible. Probably I am more worried about how it appears than how it really is. I don't think I worry much about *being* irresponsible, I worry about *appearing* irresponsible.

That's in thinking about it. When I *feel* free, I don't even worry about that. It seems the way I ought be and the way everybody ought be and the way I want to be more often. Maybe if I were more familiar with my own freedom, I would follow it more often and have that sense of assurance that it would be right.

I can't think of myself as a free spirit. That sense of responsibility, not wanting to hurt people's feelings, not wanting to be misunderstood, my sense of courtesy . . . those are the things that keep me from being more free. When I am being free, I worry that other people are going to misunderstand me and think my actions are against them somehow. I want to realize that it isn't against anybody; it's for me and for everybody. But in more guarded times, I worry about others not knowing that.

Sometimes I think I act free because it's going to work. I mean it's going to impress people. They will say, "Look at him, how delightfully free, or silly or creative he is." I'm suspicious of that, because it ought to be just for my sake alone. When I sense myself predicting others reactions, one way or another, I know that's not really freedom. It's just a subtle kind of charm.

It's funny. I don't have a goal to be more free. That seems contradictory, kind of like a program. If I stumble into situations where I feel free, good, if it doesn't have bad consequences. I have done things where I felt free in the moment and later they have come back to haunt me. Then I wasn't sure whether I was acting free or just being uncautious and inappropriate. I don't want to be inappropriate. I'd like to be the kind of free that would win me friends, please myself and make me a good citizen. I wouldn't want to give up my personal freedom to be those things, but I don't have a big freedom program going.

I do know that I am difficult to control, that at this point in my life I couldn't work for anyone. I like having my freedom in that way, but having my freedom is not like feeling free. Having my freedom is a pretty painful thing at times. It's like when you're writing a book and having to make yourself work; that's not very free at all. But it's the price of having freedom and I wouldn't give that up. Maybe people who have this are not permitted the luxury of feeling free as often as they might if they had more conventional jobs and structures. Decisions would be made for them and they could rebel against authority. I don't have any authority to rebel against; I have to give myself orders.

While it doesn't feel free, this self-employed, self-disciplined life does feel good. It also might make a man out of me, because I have to do something or I won't work and that something has to come out of me. I can't put it off on anybody else. There is nobody else to blame. But I wouldn't trade it; I'm doing it my own way.

Sometimes I think freedom is more likely to be found within a framework of constraints that it is in complete abandon or drunkenness. So if I'm in a somewhat constraining situation, it might occur to me, on the positive side, to explore how I could still be free within those constraints. How can I be free without escaping or drastically altering the situation I'm in? I think that's an important, relevant question for most of us in everyday situations.

When I'm in a tight spot, I want to understand and love the situation I'm in rather than escape it or turn it around completely. It's something about respecting the integrity of everyday, rotten experience.

I wonder if we can learn to love the situations we are in rather than always moving on to greener pastures. It's not as though I'm resisting freedom, but I don't want to be seduced by it. I don't want to gain freedom and lose myself.

FRUSTRATED

You must become a chaos ... to give birth to a dancing star.

Picasso

〜〜〜

Marcia Jaffe

My frustration is a burning desire for change. I am first aware of it when I become dissatisfied. I have the feeling of wanting to change and not yet knowing how or what I want changed. I'm usually into my thoughts of how I would like things to be . . . I know where I'm not, but *not* sure how to get where I want to be. I am aware of my inability to produce what I want: usually an abstract idea of a future goal, a new way of being, a new environment.

When I am frustrated it feels like lots of energy is being blocked. I become anxious and feel confined. The more frustrated I become, the more I start moving towards my change. I feel knotted inside, as though I want to burst out of the chains I've wrapped myself in. I feel angry (though this anger is nonspecific and is usually at myself.)

An instant frustration for me is picking up the newspaper or watching the news on TV. Many of the directions this country and this world are moving towards cause my frustration . . . which often comes out as anger. But when I examine the feeling more closely, most of this anger is at myself for not being more involved with working to change what I dislike, worry about or deeply believe in.

It is difficult to be around my friends, though I find that speaking about my frustrations to others seems to lessen my immediate tenseness. It is often hard to give to others when I'm frustrated because I am entangled within myself. I get angry sometimes over small things that I am later sorry for.

I feel compelled to move out of this state of being. There is value in my frustration because as if worsens, as the chains grow unbearable, I am forced to change, to reach out for something new, something meaningful and fulfilling. I move from this feeling when I allow my energies to go in some direction outside myself, whether this be in painting a picture, writing a poem, seeking out a new environment or even playing a hard game of tennis. If this doesn't satisfy me, the next gush of frustration descends upon me with more pressure to change my life. Often it seems the real change I want will not be brought about until I discover a new life-style, a way of using my energies to fulfill my special desires and dreams.

My frustration is the rumbling of my inner self for new outlets of expression and exploration.   ⤻

Bob Kavanaugh

I waited until I was frustrated to write this—until I thoroughly experienced the signals of frustration—tightening in my gut, a general lassitude of spirit, and a kind of diffused depression.

My frustration is a breeding ground for ancillary feelings: self-pity, an ease to anger, a proneness to lash out at easy targets, to pick on well-put-together people, to cause trouble at meetings by sharing my frustration and causing it in others. This posture causes pain later, spinning off to me and others from the dual image I reflect—the frustrated me and the confident, secure me.

When I'm frustrated I try not talking in groups, but even my silence seems to speak—and the contrast between the two selves is noticeable and influential in controlling others. If frustrated prior to doing counseling, I now "indulge" in a few minutes of co-counseling—hopefully preventing my feelings from unduly interfering with the counseling process.

My frustration is best worked through in two ways: (1) talking to self or others, sorting and concentrating on confidence-inducing aspects of my life; or (2) with deeper existential frustration flowing from my quest for meaning and purpose—I simply let it be, let it rummage about inside—avoiding pat answers or easy evasions. Gradually, I feel myself letting go of some of the terrible demands and expectations I put on myself, allowing a modicum of self-pity, concentrating on my self-worth, my contributions, my value as a human being, until my vision grows clearer. I guess in retrospect (I no longer feel frustrated) I am getting a lot out of my frustration. It gives me permission to avoid much of what I want (partially) to do. It softens my desire to be committed—to do my human best instead of sitting around sadly wishing I were more like some kind of God.   ⤻

John Wood

Frustration often comes out of boredom for me. It's a feeling of wanting to do something, not knowing what that something is, and of course, not being able to start. This type of frustration seems more important to me now than the frustration of knowing specifically something I want to get done and not being able to do it. I think the first seems to be a self-directed frustration while, at least some of the time, the latter is directed at others.

It's often hard for me to figure out specifically what's frustrating me. That vagueness then can lead me into a circle of more frustration. Lately I have become better at knowing and accepting the difference between the things I can change and the things I cannot and not becoming hung up over the things I can't do anything about. This has a lot to do with being responsible for myself and not for others—and with accepting my imperfection.

Sometimes there's a very "spoiled-kid" thing working when I'm frustrated . . . "I want this. Why can't I have it?" "I know you can do it. Why won't you?" And the question "Why?" comes up a lot too— as if I have to know from myself or others, the "Why not?" of what's frustrating me. Frustration surely leads to anger in me if it is not expressed—openly and directly to the object of my frustration—be it myself or others. (I can talk to myself or ask others to help me talk about the me that's the object of my frustration.)

Frustration is also a result of setting goals for myself that I want to fulfill too badly or too quickly. When the goal or task I have set becomes controlling—more important than what I am doing with/to myself—that's a danger signal for me.

Steve Doyne

How do I know frustration? When I want to say something but the words don't come out; when I move my arms up and down as if I were talking, but I'm not talking, just thinking about what it is that I so much want to say and want to be understood by others. When my stomach tightens and tenses until I can feel the muscles in my abdomen draw me tighter together. What do I do about frustration? I talk, act; rarely scream or yell. Sometimes I quit what is frustrating to me and do something entirely different (like go run on the beach). Sometimes I talk to my wife about the frustrations I feel, which don't necessarily relate to her—but I end up "bringing them home" anyhow. Sometimes I debate what way is best to relieve the frustration with myself alone. If I'm very, very frustrated I get angry, and defensive, and moody, and distant, all at once. That doesn't end my frustration usually but makes it hard for me to be with others. Frustrations for me rarely go away by themselves—I have to act, think, or "do" them away.

GUILTY

❧❧❧

John Wood

Feeling guilty is a diminishing, belittling, unworthy kind of feeling for me that always makes me think less of myself. Somehow I am smaller and the rest of the world is bigger than me, looking down on me. I have this picture of myself crouching down with hunched shoulders amidst a circle of a dozen or so giant people, scowls on their faces, pointing their fingers at me.

I can't get past the idea that by thinking less of myself like that, it is elevating someone or lots of someones to a higher, more important position. It may be that the state of California and its laws are more important than I am, that the woman in my life is more important than I am, that my parents' ideas about moral behavior are more important than mine or that the rules of an organization are more important than my own standards. This leads me to the whole notion or rules, contracts and obligations and how they tie in with guilt.

When I enter into a relationship with a person or an organization, certain contracts are set up. Sometimes they are formal, legalized contracts . . . marriage, a professional salary for duties performed, an agreement to abide by rules in order to be a member and so on. At other times, I enter into relationships with people and groups and the contracts or obligations are assumed. What is "normal" or expected in our culture somehow becomes an informal contract. The more intimate the relationship, the greater the sense of obligation, the more guides to conduct and, hence, I feel a greater possibility for feeling guilty about not living up to all that.

The movement in my life lately has been away from contracts and obligations and toward more individual freedom and responsibility just for myself. That seems to be good and bad. On one hand I have more freedom and power over my own life and on the other I see that some of those choices are taking me away from intimacy and long-term enriching relationships.

Lately I am careful about the contracts I make with people. I want to fully realize what I am saying when I say "yes" or "no" to another human being and to be able to live up to that. I have a strong sense within me of doing the things I say I'm going to do and it has made life simpler for me lately to cut down the number of those "contracts." That has taken me away from a lot of guilt because the things I choose to do are the things I want to do and that I have a real commitment and enthusiasm about. They are not things I have agreed to out of pressure from an outside source or another person. They are not things I think I *should* do.

The idea of "shoulds" is important to me. I should work on the car today with my father; he expects me to, it's what a "good" son would do. But the fact is, I don't want to. I have several other things I want to do and I don't know anything about cars and have no particular love for working on them. In that case, for me, choosing to work on the car with my dad could be filled with resentment and impatience. On the other hand, I could feel really guilty about not doing it unless I straighten out with my father my feelings—and his—about this particular incident and, in general, the contracts we have in our relationship. This seems like a lot of work sometimes and I can get lazy about all the work good relationships take.

In this case, and in many others, my guilt comes from an outside evaluation of myself, whether it be my father's opinion of me or what I feel about how the world sees me. It seems easy to be diminished and belittled when most of the opinions about myself are coming from outside me. If I continue to depend on those evaluations instead of my own, good or bad, I continue to give up power and creativity.

My guilt is essentially feeling bad about myself because of some offense—real or imagined—that I have committed. Often that "offense" is not being what others expect of me. The more I am able to move those standards, evaluations and rewards about my behavior from "out there" to inside myself, the more potent and creative I become.

I want to be responsive and cooperative and helpful and I want to enter into relationships that carry obligations . . . I don't want to escape that. I think moving more toward my own center will make me more responsible to those kinds of things not less. But I don't want to have to live up to your expectations of me, or the Center's, or the university's, or the state's, or the Supreme Court's. My own expectations for myself are plenty, thank you.

Bob Kavanaugh

I used to be more of an expert here than I am now. Maybe I block more or maybe, hopefully, I have learned to disbelieve the myriad of voices that haunts my superego. The voices are still there, not stilled yet, but not so loud as they used to be. They seem more diffused, less raucous and not nearly so painfully punitive when resisted.

My guilt, when "rationally" analyzed, was tied into the broadest possible Catholic mythology with sanctity and the imitation of Christ as the pinnacle and every law and clerical demand as the limits. Each breath, each thought, each tingle, deed, and interaction had meaning and purpose, rules and models. The ideal became the law and there was little room to be ordinary. No mistakes were allowed for growth; no room for youthful goofs. All was perfection or sin. A horrible sense of human unworthiness pervaded this growing lad; only God was really good. My life seemed to include obedience, helping others, saving souls, sexual ignorance and, at best at the end, ending up in purgatory for more years than most.

This was, or is, my rational analysis.

Now I see that my guilt was explained in a myth, that, if resolved, my guilt would have had another myth—or at least it would have been just as severe without a myth. The roots of my guilt are seemingly rooted in the general lack of self-worth imbibed in early environment, in my projected fear of being hurt, in my existential feelings of impotence and tiny-ness measured against my desires to be omnipotent and eternal.

I deal with my guilt now by trying to do the things for which I might feel irrationally guilty, then feeling it, working through it, past it to the feelings on the other side. I have become to myself the more permissive parent I never had, the loving father I always wanted God to be, the stumbling child who became too responsible too early, the forgiver I sought formerly in confession and my own assigner of penances to repair any real harm or hurt I may cause.

My problems now are with self-deception . . . being too often judge, jury, prosecutor, defense and convict in my own case. My new struggle is to deal with the guilt I feel about possibly overreacting to my early excess responsibility, a kind of pendulum effect. Perhaps it's a cop-out on being as genuinely responsible, loyal and trustworthy as I want to be. Maybe I need more ideals as guides, if not as laws. Maybe . . . maybe . . . but for now I hope only to test the pendulum effect, to move back closer to the center between my old mythology and my new self-governing permissiveness.

Howard Saunders

I spend a disproportionate amount of my time and energy trying not to feel guilty. It just seems intrinsic as it can possibly be; guilt is so built into my system that I am susceptible to feeling guilty about anything, *anything*. I really can't go through a day without feeling guilty about something.

Sometimes I think guilt is biological. I swear, sometimes I think there are guilt chromosomes or genes built into human beings, especially human beings of eastern European Jewish descent.

When I feel guilty, I feel like shit; I feel awful. It's a physically heavy, weighed down feeling. I can feel myself moving slower, plodding, walking into a 50-mile-an-hour wind with my head down and it's raining. And I have these little tricks I do to try and get rid of that feeling; one is to shake my head very hard back and forth to try and make everything go away. It just feels awful.

There are things I think about that typically make me feel guilty . . . old friends that I haven't called or written in a long time is one example. And the longer I don't call them, the guiltier I feel and the guiltier I feel the less prone I am to call. That goes back to my mother. As soon as I went away from home I was supposed to call her. If I didn't call the first week, I got worried about the shit I was going to catch for not calling so by the end of the second week I certainly didn't call. Then it becomes eight times harder to call. Then, always, after I've worked through enough of this, eight seconds before I'm about to call my mother, my mother calls me and lays this big trip on me. And I feel guilty and she intends for me to feel guilty—so I wouldn't do it again.

That seems to me what guilt is all about, when someone tries to instill that fear in another person, it's a control device to make sure you'll do what they want you to. They even warn you ahead of time that if you do what you did to them again, you're gonna catch hell. For me then it becomes an impossible situation: I fight not to be controlled by them, but I am controlled in another way, by my own feelings of guilt. I'm on the hook. I'm in debt and I seem to live on it.

There seems to be a "they" out there—there's always a "they" isn't there?—and I am obligated to them in some emotional way. I owe. Responsibility. I am responsible for my mother's life. This is something that is very Jewish—and I don't want to speak for all Jews, but it seems so deep in us—a Jewish boy grows up with the thing that when his father dies, as he surely will, the son will take care of his mother. It was at a very early age that I knew this; I was acutely aware of it. I lived in fear of my father dying and when he died, I didn't cry so much as I was in shell shock. All that responsibility came down on me and I had to live up to it.

When I think about this in logical terms, it seems the only way to get off the hook, to get rid of those obligations I feel, is to cut the line. But then I think if I'm going to be a responsive, sensitive human being then I'm going to be responsive to the people I care about and I do assume some responsibility for them. And while I can intellectualize the differences between "responsiveness" and "responsible" I get easily confused about that when it's happening. Sometimes I feel very sensitive to where people are with me and how they're affected by my actions; I can say, "well, that's just their trip," but I don't feel it. I seem to take responsibility for causing their feelings. I don't know how to get out of that. Sometimes I feel somehow responsible for every human being I rub up against, whether it's a personal contact or a contact through my art or the message I'm conveying through the media. It seems that responsibility is so deep-seated in me that I don't think I'll ever get rid of guilt.

When I feel guilty these days I get uptight and defensive and in a lot of little ways I try to say, "leave me alone." I think that's trying to say to the other person; "You haven't got me by the balls." When in fact they do. Sometimes the harder I try to get out of that control, the more I get into it. It maddens me to see how much I can get under someone else's control. I have accepted the guilt they want to hand out.

My situation now as far as work is concerned seems typical. I have an agreement with these people that I will spend 20 hours a week there for X amount of dollars. Now I know that they would like to have me at their beck and call; I know that. They can say that it's not true but it's coming out of the corner of their mouth. When pushed on it, they'll admit they want more of me, but that they can't expect me to be there all the time and we get into this whole number. I get to feeling guilty when I'm not there as much as I think they want me, when I'm not meeting the expectations they have. In one reality, I've said to them, "I'm only giving you this much time" and they've said "Okay, we're willing to go along with that." But then I feel guilty for doing that. By God, today I'm going to go in there until noon and say "Up yours" after that.

I was reading *Journey to Ixtlan* last week and Don Juan was say-to Castaneda how he blamed everyone else for what's happening to him, when in fact it's not taking responsibility for his own actions that gets him into that confused, poor-me place. I think I'm that way too. Starting to take responsibility for myself seems to be a way out of so much guilt.

Bill McGaw

I notice that when I feel guilty I have kind of a tightening sensation around my eyes, my mouth dries up and feels little cottony inside, depending on the severity of the guilt. If its particularly intense and I feel particularly vulnerable in the situation, my sphincter muscles tighten.

The usual thing that makes me feel guilty is procrastination . . . I know I'm not doing stuff I should be doing; I just keep putting it off. The "should" is both society's and mine and most of the time it has to do with economic things, things that will make money—responsibility to hustle for work, things like that. That particularly gets on me being self-employed. When Audrey gets nervous about income, I can sense it, even though she squelches the tendency to get on me about getting off my duff. I can feel guilty without anyone reminding me.

Procrastination seems to be the main thing. When I was a kid, I used to lie and steal and feel really guilty about it. Now it just seems to be the way I feel about myself and the things I ought to be doing.

More often than not when I begin to feel guilty, I withdraw. Then there's a funny kind of artificial bouyancy, a lightness that kind of changes the subject . . . "Well, what's for dinner tonight?" or "Anyone feel like going to a movie?" It's a distracting sort of tactic. It's hard to do that with my woman because she deals so directly with this kind of thing. So I don't get away with it very often and I appreciate that. So I can go through those kind of rituals that I do, but if it's warranted we really do talk directly about the stuff that's making me feel guilty.

I let people down, I think, and occasionally, I feel guilty about that. I don't write to friends and relatives enough. I don't call my mother or keep in touch with her enough and that nags at me once in a while. I don't take enough time with my children . . . other things, not following through . . .

It's funny, I would expect my reaction to those things would be to act over-solicitious to those people when I see them, but usually I don't. I seem to just ease off and let it go away. I don't think I take much direct action when I feel guilty. But maybe that's because I don't feel really guilty very often. I guess when it gets to an intense level in me, I do something to take care of it—I follow through with the people I've been thinking about, I knuckle down and do some work, whatever.

I don't think of myself as a wallower in guilt, the way I see some people. Some just buy themselves more guilt and it's somehow useful to them to keep them in their miserable, inadequate bag; they don't have to raise the level of their performance, they don't have to accept the news that they are capable of performing on a much higher order— that's scary. Guilt is a way to maintain that helpless, inadequate, failure thing.

Sometimes I wish I were more able to energize myself, to do the things I want to at the moment, on the spot and not to procrastinate so long. But sometimes I don't want that; I feel quite comfortable with my laziness. At times I think it's cyclic . . . I go into periods of laziness and procrastination and I start liking myself less and finally it gets to a point when I get energized and tear around getting a lot of things done that I want to. I don't know how to change that, or if I want to.

In extreme cases though, I want to be able to fully face the situation I feel guilty about, to admit the bad feelings I have and to become responsible for myself in that situation.

Andre Auw

I feel really good about the way I handle guilt now, in contrast to the way I used to. But, I don't think I experience much guilt now . . . or the guilt I experience is in quite different areas than it was. I am much more aware of feeling guilt in interpersonal relationships—when I hurt someone or ignore their feelings. Before, my guilt was related to what might be called infractions of the law, the laws of the church or the laws of society.

When I was in that period of my life, as a teenager and young man, guilt was a much different thing for me. Because the penalties were so great, the guilt was correspondingly great. I mean Hell or eternal damnation is a pretty heavy thing. As I grew older, though, I began to question those laws and those penalties; they began not to make sense. So that changed. I began to doubt all that. I began experiencing things that would have formerly produced guilt and gradually they did not produce that much guilt.

It's interesting, at that time I was much more concerned with observing the laws that had been set down for me and not so interested in what I was doing to other people. Now, that's reversed. I experience more guilt now when something goes sour in a relationship and I feel responsible for that. At those times I get angry with myself, unhappy, depressed, and generally unsettled until I can somehow correct what's happened.

I think I know myself and when I do things that make me feel guilty, I have a sense of disappointment in myself that I have conned myself into something that I know is much less than I want to be. It's like I have let myself go and really made a mess of something and I know I'm better than that.

It's fear. That's what it is. It's fear that comes as a result of some "should"—I don't always know where the "should" is coming from— but I experience a real fear of what's going to happen to me if I don't meet that "should." That ties in with how my feelings about my own guilt have changed. I don't have as many "shoulds" as I used to and the ones I have are more my own than they are from other people or institutions. It's like some authority is telling me unless I do what I should, I will suffer and I'm afraid of suffering. So that becomes a real weapon. The funny thing is, our fear is sometimes so great that we never test it out to see if that great catastrophe will happen.

My "shoulds" come from classic sources . . . the church, my parents, peer pressure to perform, what my friends expected me to do or be, societal norms . . . this is what good boys do, this is what an honest Christian does, this is what a clean living American does . . . all those.

I have been toying around with something in my head about resentment because resentment is so often tied up with guilt. I think, in a sense, resentment is a salvation, or the beginning of one, from guilt. I think resentment is that sense within us that says "this is unfair" and that builds to a point where I say to myself that it is too unfair and I resent it too much and I am going to do something to change it. My resentment, my sense of unfairness finally allows me to question and challenge the source of my guilt. I finally just say "I don't need to put up with this."

What I generally do with my feelings of guilt now is let my feelings go and experience that guilty feeling until I come through to some awareness of where my area of responsibility is. Then somehow that begins to change and I sense not so much that I have done something that I'm going to be punished for and can change or try to change. Then I start thinking of ways that I can repair or correct what I need to.

But sometimes guilt is really hard to get out of; for some it is a pattern of living. With clients of mine, what I try to do is guide them into experiences that formerly they might have felt guilty about but can now feel okay about. I don't think guilt is something you can talk your way out of, but we all seem to try and do that. For me it's more a question of experiencing things and feeling good about them instead of living in fear. Too many of us live in that powerless limbo and think that we can't do anything about it. When we experience some things that make us feel a little strength to change our own situation, a lot of that fear and guilt starts to go away.

In a sense, we give other people the right and the power to make us feel guilty. What I want to do is claim as much of that power as I can, as much as is rightfully mine. I want to take back the power that I've given to other people. What they think of me is not so important and the things they say will happen to me, I don't believe any more. This sounds ideal to me—I'm not always this secure—but generally, I'm just not afraid of what other people or institutions will do to me. If I'm not afraid of the punishment, I can't feel the guilt.

One of the big things now, when those feelings of guilt come up in me, is that I recognize I am feeling a little down on myself, a little depressed and I have to do some good things for me. I have to treat myself in a sense. I have to take good care of myself and I know how to do that a lot better than I used to.

HOPEFUL

Hope is a good breakfast, but it is a bad supper.
Francis Bacon

↜ ↜ ↜

John Wood

I am afraid to hope. I am afraid that I won't hope.

In that paradox is so much of my life. Hoping for so much yet being afraid to fully admit my deep hopes to myself and therefore admit my responsibility, my obligation to do something about my own hopes.

I know that being hopeful is an exciting thing for me. The expression "getting your hopes up" seems literally true; it seems as if something is rising within my body. I can almost feel myself being lifted up and out, leaning forward. That is an exhilarating kind of feeling and a vulnerable one too. Getting my hopes up and out means that they might be satisfied or that they might fall flat on their face.

I remember how hopeful I was about my second marriage. So much of my hopes for myself and my fantasies about the kind of relationship I would like to live within were tied up in that. Then as that relationship began to change and we grew apart and lived apart, I realized that one of the things that hurt the most was how much I'd hoped for and how close we'd come to it. It seemed like a wide, expansive, open kind of hoping and it was so large it carved out plenty of room for the hurt. Perhaps if we had not hoped for so much and we had not come so close to realizing that, it wouldn't have hurt so much. But I always have thought of myself as a gambler. I hope I can remain that way.

I have hopes for myself, by myself, and I have hopes for others in my life. I have hopes for my children and for others that I love; it is these hopes that lead to a lot of disappointment for me. It's the hopes for others that I don't have much control over. Sometimes I feel like I just have to stand back helpless and watch loved ones make mistakes, hurt themselves and others and I can't be a real force in that. Even if I was, who's to say that my hopes for someone else are their own hopes. There is nothing so meddlesome as someone pushing me into what they hope for me. On the other hand, I want the people I care about to know what I hope for them and that somehow I stand ready to help them reach toward those if that's what they want. It seems the best thing I can be is a source of support when someone takes the risk of throwing their hopes out into the world and going after them.

My own hopes for myself are something else again. I do have a large measure of control over what I want for myself and the things I do, or don't do, to go about meeting those hopes. The first thing that is important to me is to know what my hopes are . . . to have them out there on the table in front of me instead of buried inside, covered up by obligations, circumstances of life or fear. I would prefer them out there, staring me in the face, saying "This is what you want to be." Then I have the choice of doing something about them, at my own speed, or acknowledging that I don't want to pay the price it would take to get them.

As I start to travel down the road toward my hopes, small successes help. It's a mistake for me to want everything at once. In fact, I can sometimes provide myself with small success experiences to encourage myself and gain confidence.

As I grow older I realize that the hopes that I talk about and do nothing about are only hollow symbols bouncing off the walls around me. They are empty promises to myself. This doesn't mean that I can't talk about my hopes or let them rumble around inside for a while, but being hopeful has a lot to do with potentials becoming reality. That's become a code for me for being happier and more creative.

I guess hope for me is like an oversized suit that I want to grow into. I'm thankful that I'm still growing.

Pat Rice

I have always had a kind of optimistic, hopeful attitude in general. I can remember when I was younger I would sort of play with it. I was afraid to really hope or believe that something good was going to happen, so I wouldn't attend to that directly. I wanted it, but I was afraid to openly hope for it. I can remember moments of being excited, believing that something really could happen, but I wasn't willing to invest a lot in it.

When I first became interested in learning to fly, I really wanted to become a pilot, but I couldn't put my whole heart into it. Instead I kind of let it happen and edged into it.

One of the things that caused me not to be completely up front about my hopes is that it seemed kind of embarrassing and a failure not to achieve them and I would have hated to have that become public. If there was a failure and a disappointment, it had to be hidden from the public. So keeping my hopes down kept me from being terribly disappointed and publicly disappointed, embarrassed, and humiliated.

Sometimes I seem to have a kind of passivity about certain things. A lot of good things have happened to me and I've put myself in places where they could happen, but I haven't gone out and aggressively gone after them. I think there are things I could have had or goals I could have achieved if I'd really driven out after them. It seems like a basic difference between people—those who wait and make themselves available to things and those who are active about going out and getting what they want. I've changed a bit; I am more aggressive now in going after what I want and that's gone along with a whole change in me. I feel like I can stand failure a lot more than I could. I don't need to succeed all the time; it's not as devastating to me if I don't. That allows me to risk more. And I've learned things from other people too. I've learned by example how to go after what I want and to be a little more aggressive. That can get into a winner-loser thing for me. A winner is an achiever who goes out and gets what he wants and a loser just sets back and lets things happen to him. But I have that in better perspective now.

For me being hopeful really makes a difference in the speed and way in which growth happens in people. Some people I see are pretty hopeless and if I can show them some hope a lot of things happen for them . . . if they find out they can talk about and explore some of their problems and pain, if some of those things begin to make sense and they see that it's okay to have problems, to be anxious, to be hung-up . . . they can kind of breathe deeply and see that there's some hope for them. They can see that there is a way to make things better. When that's not there, I get very pessimistic about people changing very much; they stay locked into a self-defeating attitude. I think that's a critical factor in therapy, that point where they believe things can change and they start to feel better about themselves, manage their lives better and make better choices for themselves. I spend a lot of time with people just being with them in their hopelessness. Sometimes it's a very slow process and giving them a pep talk doesn't do a damn bit of good. My view of that is that the presence, the contact, just being with people in that state, will begin to generate something in that person. But the hope has to come from them.

One of the things I hope for myself is that I can gain more confidence in myself. I think if I had more of that, there's a lot more things I'd be able to do and perhaps I wouldn't worry about security so much. That little lack of confidence, that edge of insecurity, gets in my way; it inhibits me and sometimes keeps me from making my hopes into realities. It keeps me from giving myself energetically to something I want. I guess that's why I don't do some of the things I want to, because I'm not that confident I'll be able to carry it off.

Lately it seems like a lot of things are opening up for me; there are lots of things I'm allowing myself to hope for. I don't know what's going to happen. But it feels like I have less self-defeating attitudes about myself and more of my personal energy is available to me. That

breeds success. I'm not inhibiting myself as much as I used to. That
feels good; I like that.

Maria Bowen

When I feel hopeful, my body feels full of energy; I feel alive and
moving. I breathe deeply. I can do things for long periods of time without tiring. I become excited and alert. I see much more of the things
around me and feel much more in touch with nature and more attuned
to people. It's exciting; I have a real sense of purpose and movement.

I'm remembering the last time I was full of hope; it was when I
was pregnant with Andy. I was going to have a baby, *my* baby, and going to be part of an unfolding process for somebody else from the very
beginning. It was like life was opening up in a different direction. I had
planned for it and was ready for it and was very excited about it. I felt
good about myself, my body and my future. I loved it.

I think I am very optimistic by nature. Working with people the
way I do, one has to be hopeful. With everybody that I see, I have hopes
that their life will change in good directions. Otherwise I would be miserable. There are of course disappointments that go along with high hopes
but I don't seem to experience the high hopes and the disappointment
as much as I do a feeling of helplessness. For me helplessness means that
I wanted something to happen and it's not going the direction I wanted
and I don't have any control over it.

Like when I try to lose weight. I get my hopes up for myself and
start out on a diet and then, for one reason or another, I get bogged
down and am not losing any weight and I get into this feeling of helplessness. It's like realizing that I can't accomplish as much as I wanted
to. The fear that I have is that perhaps I have wished for something beyond my capabilities. But something is stopping me at that time and
I'm not sure what it is. That usually depresses me. Then it's easy for me
to start putting myself down and I can start comparing myself to others
. . . it's a bad place.

I can get hopeful about learning to do new things; right now I'm
learning how to sew and I'm getting excited about it. I get hopeful about
relationships . . . when Jack and I get into a bad place and have to
work through that with each other there is a great deal of excitement
in getting out of that and realizing how we can grow together and the
direction our lives can take. I get hopeful about things I find out about
myself that I didn't know before. A typical example is my finding out that
I can be more assertive with people, to express myself more directly, like
calling you today and telling you about my confusion and my doubts.

In the past I was a person who couldn't say "no" to anybody. I would be a nice girl and say "yes" and end up resenting it later. I had a lot of friends, but no deep relationship with anybody because I found myself so spread around I didn't have time to develop real friendships. So it's exciting and hopeful for me to start to say "no" to people and to be more aware of the choices I make about how I spend my time. I am learning to establish limits for myself. That is a real hope for me, to choose more directly how I am spending my life.

When I am hoping for something, in the beginning it seems as if I have to make a very big effort to start down that road and it costs me a lot the first time. Then, gradually it gets easier and it becomes more and more a part of me. For instance, with saying "no" to things I don't want to do, it is almost automatic now; I can make the choice right on the spot instead of saying "yes" and then trying to find a way out of it.

Right now I am hopeful that I will use more and different parts of myself. What that means to me now is getting more in touch with my body, feeling more comfortable about it. That took a great deal of commitment to begin and a kind of readiness in myself that I don't completely understand. A lot of it was taking the step of asking somebody else for help; I thought I could do it by myself. I found out I needed the help of some other people, the encouragement of friends and besides a lot of commitment on my part. Somehow engaging other people in the process with you deepens your own involvement. It's not so easy to back out then.

Andre Auw

Hope is very, very important to me. Let me say first how I see that in other people . . . I think one of the big turning points in therapy is when people say, in one way or another, "Ah, yes, I am beginning to see some light at the end of the tunnel." At that point, things start to be different. It is an expectation that good things can happen, whereas before they have been living under a cloud of "No," powerless and trapped by their own lack of hope.

What hope means to me is moving from a negative, nothing, zero point of view into some sort of potentiality, a letting in of the good possibilities. I've always been somewhat hopeful, somewhat optimistic and have never been one to live under a cloud, no matter how bad things were. So, in that sense, I haven't had a desperate struggle to find hope for myself. But I have been in the position of not allowing myself to hope for bigger and better things for myself.

For instance, before I decided to get my Ph.D., I was sort of meandering along, not feeling terribly content or happy, feeling like there were other things I wanted to do, but thinking that I didn't quite have what it took to get there. It seemed so impossible that I didn't really consider it. Then I came down here to work on a project with Carl (Rogers) and began to get stimulated by the work and some of his remarks to me. And I began to say, hey, maybe this isn't impossible after all. Hope kind of came in and pointed out that all kinds of good things could happen that I had been saying "no" to.

It's like coming alive, being reborn. I got excited and had a real sense of delight about life. That kind of feeling is so good, it's almost too good to be true. Like, "This couldn't be happening to me, maybe somebody else, but not poor little old me," which tells you how I was feeling about myself.

This is what's important; when hope comes in, I experience power. And that's what makes the difference. That's what I was saying about people in therapy earlier, I try to help them experience power. I'm not always sure which comes first, the hope or the power. Maybe you have to feel some power first and then hope comes or maybe the suggestion of hope and things happening make me feel good and I begin to feel powerful.

Sometimes with hope, terminology gets in my way. I think there's a difference between hoping and dreaming. Fantasies and dreams are not what I mean when I talk about hope. Hope means that I am already doing something about what I want, I am active; hope means I open myself to the possibility. The "hoping" that some people talk about is saying, "I would like to be able to" or "I wish that I could;" it's a vague, subjunctive, dreamy kind of maybe-perhaps thing. But when I say that I have hope it's different than saying I have hopes or dreams. The hope means that I see the possibility of doing something about it and I experience the beginning of some energy. That's the beginning of the power I was talking about.

People that have dreams but don't do anything about them don't, as far as I'm concerned, experience hope. They just keep on saying, "You know, I've always wanted to do that." That's not hope. I think people who constantly do that are not accepting responsibility for their own hopes and doing something concrete about them. They seem to expect the fairy godmother to come down and make it happen. And it doesn't happen. They wait and expect and are disappointed. They don't feel that they have within them the power to do what they want.

I can do something about my hopes, instead of just saying I'm helpless. It so often happens that we feel powerless and we need to grab onto some feelings of strength—and we may need help with that—in order to make hope a real experience, a reality.

Cheryl Thurman

Hope seems like a way of being in the world. It's like a force that keeps me going, that makes my eyes sparkle, that makes me laugh and enjoy life.

Hope is like a flowing movement forward. It is open, expectant and alive. But I hadn't thought a great deal about it because it is such an ever-present thing in my life. It's almost as if I took it for granted. But if I didn't have that hope in me, I don't think there would be much reason for me to be alive. Faith is tied in closely with that, faith that the direction in which I'm moving is right for me.

When I get into specific hopes for myself, I get really excited and active. I become aware of my surroundings and really in tune with people around me. I love it.

I think that ever since I've been back from Minnesota and my operation, I've been in a hopeful, expectant place. It's really been good. I've been active, more able to be with people, more open to them than I have been and taking care of routine business in a better way. Things don't hassle me as much.

Openness and hope kind of go together in me. When I'm closed, I'm feeling kind of desperate and can't find real meaning to my life. I feel very tenuous. The worst of those times is feeling close to suicide, but I know, at the same time, that I'll never do that because my hope never dies. But the more desperate I become the lower my hope goes and the more closed and withdrawn I am.

The hopes I have for myself have to do with evolving and being in every day with as few expectations as possible and being open to whatever comes to me. I'd like to be more present now and less holding on to the past or grasping for the future. That's kind of a picture of myself that I hope for.

I'm taking steps toward that. One thing I'm doing is a period of meditation, I set aside for myself every day. I'm able to give myself some space to get in touch with my body and let go of all the words that are going around in my head, to let go of things, to stop and settle into myself. That's really become a nice space in my day.

I also want to learn from myself and from other people about what keeps them from getting what they want.

Hope is an awfully good feeling for me. I have more of it than I used to and I hope I get more. It's a dynamic, active, energizing feeling for me. It has to do with feeling good about myself: I like me and I hope the best for me. Sounds like a greeting card to myself, doesn't it?

HURT

Would you hurt a man keenest, strike at his self love.
Lew Wallace

╰╮╰╮╰╮

Doug Land

Hurt seems to me to be a sinking, diminishing feeling. My chest and trunk seem to be caving in. I don't think I get hurt much anymore, but it's because I don't let myself. What hurts me most is when someone I have extended myself to, become vulnerable to, either is insensitive to my feelings or ignores me. I think the thing that hurts the most is being unrecognized or unknown, just being erased. Like if there are three people in a conversation and I am doing my best to make my presence felt and they just ignore me, that really hurts me; it's like being invisible.

My reaction to that is to flee, to get out of there. On occasion I might become aggressive, insistent, become louder, to try and present more of me, but I'm more likely to retreat. I have done both and I like it better when I retreat, rather than when I insist they recognize me. It seems there is no way I can insist on being seen without taking away from myself the very thing I wanted, which was to be recognized just for me, without insisting.

I think the only people that can hurt me are the people I care about; that I acknowledge my caring about. Other people can hurt my feelings or rebuff me, but it's not the same thing to me. My family can hurt my feelings and none of them has anything against me, but sometimes it doesn't take very much at all to hurt me.

I remember just last night how sensitive I was to the kids and Elsie. I got up to go into the bedroom and Geoff asked me if I was going to bed. Yes, I was, I said, was there anything he wanted. "No, forget it," he said, so I went on. But I could see something was going on that had to do with my leaving the room. It turned out that he wanted his dog, Irish, to sleep in his room and he had assumed that I would keep him from doing that. Well, that hurt me; it seemed like I was the heavy in the situation. And I got a little paranoid about it. It was like Elsie was telling Geoff that Dad wouldn't want him to do that and I was the bad guy set against them in the situation. It got worse and I imagined the whole family plotting to do things behind the heavy's back.

I can see my own paranoia in it now and it seems silly, but at the time I was hurt and angry. I even generalized it, by saying that they always did this kind of thing to me, plotted against me. It's like they didn't love me and I really got into feeling sorry for myself. But I think that thing happens only with intimates because you expect them to love you no matter how you are.

Most of the time, my reaction is much more constructive; I'm able to say out loud, "That really hurts my feelings" and not have that much invested in winning or losing—I just want to resolve the situation. Getting my feelings out seems to at least clarify where I am and where the other person is in relation to me and I'm able to go on without getting into the delusions/paranoia thing.

John Wood

I get hurt when people judge me, without understanding me. I seem capable of so much good and bad, and am all too ready to accept their judgment of me as the truth. I think about a recent example. Carl said to me: "You are so damn self-centered; you are not invested in anything that doesn't concern you." I stopped for a second to consider and said, to myself, "Yeh, that sounds right." But then I could see that he wasn't loving me for being that way and I was hurt. I thought that others would join him in his judgment. I was beginning to feel like the bad guy for being self-centered.

Then I rallied. I said, "God-damnit, you say that from a very limited exposure to me. There are a lot of other parts of me that you don't know. I'm really pissed off at your just throwing that judgment at me." And I *was* mad. Looking back, it seems I took Carl's statement in, took it as truth and was hurt by it. I then became angry. (Is that the axiom, "the truth hurts?")

But in my good moments I know there are many versions of the truth and that I am many faceted. I can choose to believe (act on) someone else's judgment of me or I can choose to consider it then disregard it as not true for me. In this case I was hurt by Carl's statement because I do think of myself in that way sometimes. I did express my anger and my hurt to him, because he matters to me, and, later, we took the time to talk and I tried to make some other parts of myself known to him.

I think of two other times when I am hurt. I feel bad when I hurt someone else. There have been times when it really tore my guts out when I hurt someone I was in love with. It felt very much like someone was reaching their hand into my stomach, grabbing a handful of intestines and wrenching them around. I don't know what the hell to do at those times . . . if it seems as if who I am is hurting the other person. "I'm sorry" seems so damn insufficient.

I also get hurt when I disappoint someone else, especially a woman I am involved with. I seem to understand that better now. In those cases I seem to be trying to live up to what the other person wants—*even* when those wants are unexpressed. Wow!

In both these cases I ought to be doing some "homework." I want to check out in advance what someone I care about wants and needs from me. I want to know what will hurt them. I want to know what they expect . . . and for them to know those things from me. Then, going into a situation, I can choose for myself, having some kind of feeling for what the consequences will be.

I don't see any way I can avoid pain. I'm not searching for ways to avoid it. In fact, I worry that my danger is that I will live trying to avoid pain; that means not taking risks, not giving myself, not putting myself out there.

But I can avoid unnecessary pain. One way I see of doing that is to have a real openness between me and the people I care about. That's ironic, isn't it? Be open and you're open to pain. And I'm saying be open to avoid pain. Well, I know, deep down, that I cannot experience the joy, the ecstasy that I want out of life unless I am also open to the deep hurt that caring can bring. It is not a one-way street. Further, it seems like a choice of being open, caring, and susceptible to hurt or feeling that numb, closed, protected pain that some go through life with. The latter seems like death to me.

Janet Colby

My pain—when the thought of him enters my head uninvited—just shoots through my whole body. My whole chest, from my armpits to my pelvis—is tightened by a band made up of a trillion nylon filaments, tight as tight can be. I feel them together and I feel them separately; they grip me in waves of intensity and I seem to feel them cutting through every organ and membrane in me. That band just keeps working on me, tightening and stopping, then tightening further. And it keeps up and I just have to weep. I don't know what would happen if I didn't cry . . . just to let it out.

My weeping, my tears, somehow make the tiny bands get fuzzier. They soften and the pain seems to subside. It's almost as if the pain were passing out of my body with the weeping.

When I am with someone that hurts me; that is, someone says or does something that hurts me, I'm not very good at expressing that hurt. I assimilate it, take it in kind of like an amoeba and engulf it. I sponge it up and go on. Then I get protective of myself and become very verbal. Words start flowing out; that's typical. I become intellectual and start a mental sparring with whoever has hurt me.

The relationships I've had seem so swift or so surface that they've never reached a place where I could sit there and say, "hey, you're hurting me" when it really mattered. It seems like they're going to be gone anyway. But that really seems like I'm doing that to myself.

Somehow when I am able to say, "ouch, you're hurting me," I feel really clean. When I can say that plainly it's like tabling the emotion, putting the hurt out in front of me. The tight bands seem unstrung; they dissipate. That doesn't mean it's gone, but it is out in front of me for both parties to look at and somehow that feels better.   ↰

Elsie Land

The only people that hurt me are the people closest to me; it's the people I live with. And, of course, the ways they can hurt me cover a wide range of things, from turning their nose up at what I've prepared for dinner, with a "yuch," to being misunderstood when I have tried to do something to please someone . . . what I am trying to do or be to someone is not accepted or understood—that hurts.

My usual thing when I'm hurt is to dissolve into tears. It's hard for me to talk about being hurt. That just infuriates Doug; I won't talk and what he wants to do is talk. I don't operate that way, at least with him, and he's the one I operate with most of the time. For reasons that I can't put my finger on, I lose any kind of even keel and I'm not able to talk about it. The only thing I can seem to do is cry.

I don't know exactly what the tears are saying to Doug. I guess that it's just no matter how I plead my case you're going to win. Because you just have a way with words that I just don't have. You'll stick with it longer than I will and you'll be more exact than I can ever be. I've lost before I ever start. I have tried to postpone that feeling, to try and talk it out as best I can, but I usually end up all tangled up. I don't like to have to defend myself with Doug. I don't like to play games with him; he's just too good. I think that's probably why I dissolve. It's always been that way.

In recent years, when there have been more things to talk about than ever before—more things that actually bugged both of us about each other—we did have to sit down and talk it out and I'd goof it up by crying.

When I'm hurt and engulfed by tears, most of the time I want to be by myself. When something happens on the spur of the moment —someone doesn't like what I've done and it takes me by surprise—if I'm tired, I'll just start oozing tears. Usually someone comes to my defense and is very nice and in that situation, I don't want to go off by myself. It's like with the food at the dinner table, if I get the message that, "we like you but hate your food," that could be okay. If they tell me that they appreciate me despite the yucky taste, it's easier to take.

Terry Van Orshoven

When I'm hurt, I'm disappointed in myself usually. I feel foolish, like I've set myself up, putting false expectations on people around me. I set myself up to be hurt. When I'm hurt I'm usually angry at myself for failing to say what I needed or reporting that I was tired or cranky or whatever. And I get myself into an interchange where someone dumps something on me that I can't take and I typically get pretty pissed off at me for setting up the situation. It's like I suck someone else into not knowing me and help them jump in on some vulnerable spot that I haven't said anything about.

Another way I set myself up to be hurt is by expecting people to be like me, or better than me . . . to be sensitive, ethical, scrupulous, ha, even a mind reader. Like I expect people to know that I sometimes choose not to be aware of everything that is going on. Because of what I do, people expect me to be extremely aware and sensitive and when I'm not those things, that's where I get hurt, because they get hurt and strike out at me. I'm not always aware; I'm not always sensitive; I'm not always accepting. Sometimes I just want to be alone, not messed with.

I can be deeply hurt by being misunderstood. If I tell people I am one way and I keep getting picked up as another way—either because someone needs to see me that way or we're just not communicating—I get all wrapped up and frustrated and hurt. I don't mind being a sonofabitch if that's where I am at the time, but when I'm not feeling that way or seeing myself that way and someone else is reacting to me as a sonofabitch, that hurts, that really gets in my shorts.

I guess I expect so much from myself that when someone in a relationship with me gets way beyond my own expectations of me—it just drains me. I'm already working on expecting less of myself and someone is asking for more—wow, I can expect myself to be perfect, but when someone else does, whew! Sometimes I just can't reach out 9,000 miles, I reach out one foot. And when someone really close to me expects me to reach that 9,000 miles and I don't, I'm learning how to say, "Hey, I don't always do that. You might need it and scream at me, but I still might do it because I've got my own programs going."

When I am first hurt, typically I stop acting and start thinking. I wish I didn't do that so much. If I'm really hurt though I'll lash right back at somebody, just explode. But I monitor that more than I want to; I wish I could strike back more, not to hurt, but to release the stuff that's going on in me. Those are those little residuals that I have to explode with every six months or so; then I get into a sobbing, growling, screaming, shouting, air-vomiting session that just gets rid of all that shit inside me that I haven't taken care of. It just releases it.

A deeper hurt makes me really lonely. I withdraw and start talking to myself. That's when I know that it's really important to get that out and start dealing with it. But that's hard; it's a risk to put yourself out there and be vulnerable to even more hurt.

INFERIOR

No one can make you feel inferior without your consent.
Eleanor Roosevelt

ᵕᵕᵕ

Joann Justyn

Inferiority is a very easy place for me to get into. And I immediately want to go into my inferior pose: I'm crouched over and have an arm over my head and the other arm protecting my pelvic area. I get all scrunched up, tight and defensive.

I've noticed that some people, when they feel inferior, start to talk like they feel superior, they begin to brag and say in various ways how much better they are, when they're really feeling inferior. But I seem to go the other way. I won't say anything at all and I feel myself going lower. Once I get into it, I can easily go from feeling one little part of me is inferior to feeling that all of me is worse than someone else. Like I'll be with a girl who I think looks a lot better than I do and after I'm with her a while I'll start to feel inferior about the ideas she's talking about or her opinions, or the way she walks, or talks. It gets really ridiculous. It's very hard for me to get rid of that too and to be with her in any other way then to feel inferior.

When I'm feeling inferior I just won't compete with anyone in anyway. It can become so pervasive that I just throw up my hands and say, "Oh my God, I can't be as good as them in any way." And I just retreat. I withdraw completely—and feel sorry for myself.

This happens more frequently with women than it does with men. I think of myself on a different level with men and I guess I just make that kind of comparison with people that I feel on the same level with, or in the same arena with. I don't very often feel inferior to men, just different.

Typically I will feel inferior in a physical way . . . less attractive, less together, less desirable . . . and in an intellectual way . . . this person knows so much more than I do, they're more capable, they express themselves better. Sometimes I'll be talking with someone and I'll think to myself, "She just has so much more on the ball than I do; she's accomplishing so much more." At those times I think I ought to be more like them and the things I'm doing aren't worth much. Instead, I could go the other way and say what I'm doing is just as good for me or it's different and okay, but I usually can't do that at the time.

Feeling this way makes me not very friendly to the person I'm with. And I sometimes think of myself as younger than the person I feel inferior to; like saying, "Wow, you know so much more than I do." When I feel physically inferior to another woman I'll very quickly retreat and not want to be near her or talk to her at all. Sometimes, though, if I know them, I can begin to talk to them about my feelings and say the things that I really like about them and I don't feel I have in myself. I think about this with Cheryl. I'm able to share the things I feel she's better at; it's easy to talk about it with her. It's like I feel inferior but it motivates me to want to find out more from her. Perhaps that's because she's not threatening to me and with her I feel strong about myself in other ways. She is clearly different than me.

Feeling inferior and being competitive are really close for me. When I talk about feeling inferior to someone I'm also thinking about competing with them. My reaction to feeling inferior is the same as it is to competition, I just remove myself from it. If I feel equal to someone or superior, I don't need to compete.

Sometimes I get the feeling about someone and it's like saying: "You're all I am and more; I don't exist." It is really threatening to my uniqueness, my identity.

When I get that way I try and do things, think about things or be things that I know are good and strong in me. I think about gardening for instance. I have to remind myself of my strengths and kind of reinforce myself so I don't get into that "I'm-all-bad" trip. But it's something I do within myself, by myself. If I can do that, then I can be with the person I feel inferior to.

I have talked with people I felt inferior to and found they felt inferior to me. It's really strange. That happened with Wende and I. I've always felt inferior to her and we got into this conversation and it came out how she was feeling inferior to me. It was incredible. We were swapping inferiorities and many of them were about the same kinds of things.

But just being able to talk about them doesn't totally help me to get out of them. It's something I have to do inside myself.

Cheryl Thurman

When I'm feeling inferior I'm really tight, tired, lethargic and a little spaced out. I'm not very aware of my surroundings; there's a physical sensation of not being able to see very clearly and all I can see is what's directly in front of me. It's like I am completely withdrawn inside of myself. It feels like I'm really leaving my body in a way. I can still function, but it's at a low level.

Sometimes I feel inferior when I'm in a situation where I need to express a feeling but it's threatening for me to express it . . . anger, hurt. I begin to feel like I am not on equal ground with the other person and that I don't have a right to express those things. There's a definite feeling of not having rights.

Uncommunicative people make me feel that way, people who obviously keep their feelings to themselves. That doesn't encourage me to express my feelings, but it's more than that. It makes it seem like they're better than me and that I don't matter enough to be really talked to. Then there's a response in me that believes that. That's particularly reinforced when I do take a risk to express something that is threatening to me and there isn't any response or a response that negates my feelings.

It seems as if this comes and goes, like phases. It will happen to me a lot for a while and then will ease off for a while. It does happen much more with men than it does with women, particularly if I'm emotionally involved with the man.

For instance, in a recent relationship with a man, that happened to me. I was often confused about where I was with him and it seemed like I made a lot of attempts to get out of that confusion, to try and find out where he was. He would say to me, "I don't need words." My reaction was, "Wow. How neat that he doesn't need words; I need words. That must mean that I'm not as good as he is." I really got into feeling inferior to him because I had to talk; there was a constant pressure not to use too many words in the relationship.

When I feel that way I just withdraw. I don't reach out in a physical way or an emotional way. My communication moves to a very superficial level and I generally wait for the other person to initiate things.

It seems that I am coming from a funny place with the idea of being left out and not valued. It's almost as if I was handicapped; at least I feel that way sometimes.

Because of a really severe heart condition I have, I often feel like I don't have the same space in the universe as other people do. By the existence of that situation, I have less rights. I have a smaller space somehow than others. I have no right to ask that people care for me. I have no right to ask for any kind of support. I see myself as being less than fully human.

There's something terrifying about asking for those things and hearing the rejection that I know is coming. The rejection is there, inside me, but there is something too terrifying to risk hearing it. As long as I don't hear it, I have a buffer between me and the rest of the world.

What I really want to be able to do is to say exactly where I'm coming from; to risk being rejected by saying: "I've been hurt by you. I've been left out. I'm not important and I'm confused by the way you're being with me." Those are risky things to say.

I wish that I were free of any feeling of superiority or inferiority, for those words to have no meaning. I wish I could just be.

Then when I feel hurt or angry I could express it without being afraid that I wouldn't be responded to. But that has to come from me. I have to say that to myself first: "I am worth hearing; I am worth responding to." ⤸

John Wood

I think about two specific people when I think of feeling inferior. Both are journalists of considerable stature. I've worked with one of them before. The other had an opportunity to hire me when I was younger and chose not to. Whenever I come across them I seem locked into a way of behaving I don't like, a way that sheepishly acknowledges my inferiority and their superiority.

I feel smaller and younger, hesitant, careful about risking or offering strong opinions on anything. I watch carefully to see how they will react to what I say and I am conscious of trying to say things they will approve of. Then when I leave one of them, in the car on the way home, I cuss at myself for being that way; "Dammit, why can't you be at ease around him? Why do you have to slip into that routine of 'I know you don't like me very well, so I won't take up too much of your time?' Why do you perpetuate that whole thing?"

I think they think they are superior to me and I don't like them for it. I think they know I think I'm inferior to them and I want them to say something to ease that. But that's the irrational part that is not my responsibility.

When I get right down to it, I really think they are better at what they do . . . and here I pause. Are they better at what they do than I am at what *they* do? Or are they better at what they do than I am at what *I* do? Perhaps that's the point at which I begin to feel inferior, when I try and measure up to what they are or to a picture our society has of what a good journalist should be. They fit that picture; I can't always see myself fitting that picture, therefore, I am inferior.

So what? Perhaps they don't always measure up to what they want for themselves. Further, there I am in the same trouble again, measuring up to a picture I have of myself as I *should be*.

I am. I am. I am. Not inferior. Not superior. I just am. Falling into either one of those traps is a comparative, competitive thing that keeps me hidden from myself and keeps my own best resources from being available to the other person involved as well. It is self-defeating.

I think I can beat that by kicking back and listening more to myself, gaining a sense of my own center. It means coming to someone with my strengths and my weaknesses. I notice that when I feel inferior I tend to come to them with my weaknesses, the parts I think they recognize and hone in on in me. This only perpetuates the whole game.

Where are my feelings, my opinions, my strengths, when we're together? I want to be able to share those.

Maria Bowen

I start to feel inferior when I'm not doing as well as I think I should be doing. Usually that involves comparing myself to someone else I respect. When I feel that way I have a tendency to pick up in other people the things I would like to have for myself. I tend to forget the whole picture and the price I would have to pay to be the way that other person is.

If I see someone involved in some kind of activity and I say to myself, "Gee, I wish I could do that; she looks so good, so professional." And what I forget is that I don't want to work that hard, I don't want to pay the price in time and energy that it would take. I would rather be walking on the beach, playing around with Andy or just sitting with Jack. But at the moment, I'm feeling inferior I forget that aspect of it.

When I feel inferior I feel helpless. I feel like I'm not doing anything about myself or doing the things I want to be. "Here I am stuck again," is what I'm saying to myself.

At those moments I get uptight, my chest gets tighter and smaller; I feel like there isn't much space for my heart to beat. The last time I felt that way was when I visited my family in Brazil. Everybody gives a lot of importance to clothes, to being dressed up and to looking elegant. When I got there my family gave a party to welcome me and I didn't have any kind of dress that would match the party and the people there. So when I got there I felt very out of place, like I was very poorly dressed. I felt self-conscious and ashamed and tried to stay in a corner where nobody would notice me. I felt everybody looking at me . . . it was horrible.

The next day I got so pissed off at myself for being that way. I said, "What in the hell are you doing, acting like a little girl again, sitting in the corner and hiding?"

I think I feel inferior most of the time around women rather than men. I think it has to do with my body and comparing it with other women's. I see how free they are and how gracious they are and it's something I want for myself. When I see an attractive woman who really moves well and feels comfortable and uninhibited with her body, that's when I start to feel inferior.

In those cases I would like to be able to get out of comparing and say to myself, "I am different; I don't have a body like hers, but I have other qualities that are just mine and they are important. So just relax and be me." That's what I'd like to tell myself. When I feel pretty good

I am able to do that but when I'm feeling bad about myself, it's easy to start comparing and feeling inferior. It's not as easy as it sounds and it's not something I can talk myself out of all the time. That feeling good about yourself is intellectually simple to say, but it's not like a button you push and something happens.

That's when I really need people, when I get into those moods of feeling bad about myself. I know I really need the help of a good friend. And I go to them and we talk and we explore what I'm afraid of and feeling bad about. And sometimes my fears seem pretty unrealistic and I can see that; other times they are realistic, but I see that I can face them and survive. But I need someone else's help to see that.

JEALOUS

Jealousy feeds upon suspicion, and it turns into fury or it ends as soon as we pass from suspicion to certainty.

In jealousy there is more self-love than love.

François Duc de la Rochefoucauld

⌣⌣⌣

Ron Lunceford

I get jumpy inside when I get jealous; a little anxious, nervous and I find it hard to control that. It's a very visceral thing for me. At first I try to avoid it, try to pretend it's not there. Mostly that works for me; my jealous feelings are fleeting things anyway. They never last very long.

I know that jealousy is real and I don't want to deny it in me, but I don't like the physical feeling it gives me. I sometimes like the feelings behind the jealousy and being made to feel jealous. It says to me that I care enough, like someone enough to be moved in that way. It means that I am still in touch with someone in a relationship and that the relationship is important to me, whether it's a male friend or a woman.

When I am jealous it's as if someone was intruding on some private territory, some space that I have and I don't want anyone else there. But once I understand what's happening I can talk about it with the people involved and understand it's not threatening to my relationship, it seems okay. It seems like me giving permission to come into something that is personal and private. It can start out to be very private, but that can be negotiated.

I can feel that way about friends, Judy, the kids . . . it used to be that I would be jealous of the kids because they got more attention than I did, but I worked through that. I don't always say much about my jealousy, but it shows up on my face, my actions or my tone of voice . . . the hurt, anger, withdrawal, feeling sorry for myself.

Sometimes I wish I could talk about it more with the person that causes me to be jealous, but sometimes I don't think that's a way I should be and I don't talk about it. Somehow I get confused with an idea I have that "strong" people or "together" people, whoever they are, should handle jealousy better. On the other hand, jealousy is real and I don't want to hide it. Sometimes I don't want to talk about it because the person I'm dealing with is not important enough for me to spend the time and energy it would take to straighten things out. If it's someone I care about and am going to be spending more time with, I think I can and would talk about what's bothering me.

When I get down to it, I think my jealousy has to do with low self-esteem, low self-concept or feeling inadequate. I can begin to doubt myself and think people don't care about me the way I want them to or that they'll see something in me that will cause them not to like me. Mostly it's built around insecurity. But I don't know as I'll ever become that secure as to not experience some jealousy. I don't want anyone to be that meaningless to me. It seems kind of dangerous to me to be that sure.

I don't think I can say to someone I really care about: "Sure, do whatever you want and don't worry about me." I don't trust that in situations either. Some people think that is the ultimate in caring or trust and sometimes I think it's insanity. I doubt that people are really that way.

Part of the reason that I get jealous is that I have some things with Judy that are personal and private and I don't have them with anybody else. I can love other people and share things with them, but this relationship seems private and unique and I don't want to share that with anybody.

Kay Carlin

Jealousy immediately makes me think about times past when Larry would be working with a female client and spending a lot of time with her. I'd get to wondering how potent I was in our relationship. I'd begin this mind-fucking thing about how he'd rather be with her than me and start questioning my importance to him. I really feel beyond that now; I feel I understand that much more than I used to. But I used to feel that way even when Larry would spend a lot of time with a male friend of his; I was wishing he was with me.

It all boils down to wondering just how important our relationship is to him. I start to feel sorry for myself and start taking myself apart, bringing up all my bad points, saying "Well, no wonder he's not here." It's very painful. Then I start to overcompensatae instead of being myself with him. I try to be perfect, everything that he could possibly want . . . agreeable, nice, trying to psych out what he wants and giving it to him. I get to be other-directed and feel terrible about it.

But the more I tried to be that way, the more it had the opposite effect, the more it pushed Larry away. When I could be stronger and more myself, the closer we would be.

Another part of that . . . I would get into feeling like he was leaving me, that he's found somebody else—"He's found someone who means more to him than I do," I would say to myself. Then I'd start poor-mouthing myself and then I'd start on Larry—all talking to myself: "What's he done for me lately?" that kind of thing.

When I got that way, I cried a lot. I cried and cried and cried. It was a bad scene. And at those times it seemed like I had saved up a lot of bad things about our relationship that suddenly came to the surface. Thank heavens that hasn't happened in a long time.

I would hope that now I could start to share those feelings with him when they come up. If I began to feel jealous I want to let him know, right away, and to let him know some of the things behind it . . . that I feel left out and not wanted . . . those kinds of things.

Jealousy seems so tied up with my own feelings about myself. There is a threat to our relationship and I feel as if I'm competing with someone who might have more to offer Larry. It would be a scary thing to share that with him, but I wouldn't want to avoid it. Our relationship is so important to me that I would hope he could hear me in the way I wanted.

What I don't want to do is constantly worry about our relationship. That's the worst thing to do. It's a case of me moving away from complete dependence on him to an interdependence between the two of us. For that to happen, I have to become more my own person.

John Wood

Jealousy in me nearly always has to do with the love of a woman. I rarely find myself jealous or envious of possessions, money, or roles; I don't seem to want what others have. But when there is a threat to the attention and affection of a woman I care about, I can become threatened, jealous and possessive.

Extreme jealousy produces—or taps into—a deep fear of losing someone who loves me and whom I love. When I feel really threatened, it feels nearly like panic. The moment of jealousy—and it starts with a moment of fear—is a sudden rush, almost like the sudden rushing of wind out of myself. There seems to be a very quick hollowness inside and I am left with prickly, sensitive skin, surrounding . . . what? . . . emptiness?

I am suddenly emptied of something or someone. My first reaction to that, and a fairly quick one, is to rush into action. To bolt out and regain the woman who is leaving me. "To arms, to arms, your most valuable *possession*, your woman, is about to be taken from you. Fight! Defend! Hold on!" A voice inside me spurs me on. If I don't act, surely I will . . . lose . . .

I remember feeling that way recently about the woman I was involved with (can I say loved?). We were feeling somewhat distant from each other and things weren't going as well as we wanted them to go, when she became interested in someone else and acted on it. To arms! After the initial hurt and fear surged through me, I sprang into action to get her back Nothing else mattered, no promise seemed too great, no detail of my feelings too small. The important thing was to return her to the fold.

How absurd I am. How threatened and afraid I am. How human. Insecurity reigns!

At times like these I can rationalize until my head swells to twice its normal size with words and reasons, but it does no good whatsoever. I am ruled by my hurt, my rejection, and my fear, and I want to be loved.

It's funny; as much as I can get into this feeling, I don't consider myself a jealous, possessive person. I seem to myself to encourage my partner's freedom and relationships with others. Only when the threat is specific and concrete am I thrown into this state.

Two words keep coming back to me with regard to jealousy: insecurity and control. My insecurities about myself are easily tapped into when I feel threatened in this way. The more insecure I am with myself, the more I am susceptible to glomming onto things and people. If I am insecure and/or uncertain about my relationship with my partner, every potential threat to that relationship is magnified. To the degree that I feel uncertain about how I am with someone else, assuming I want something with them, I want to control them and what goes on with us.

Born out of my insecurity is fear and jealousy. It quickly turns into a need to control and manipulate my partner and the interactions between us.

When I think about growing away from jealousy, I think about gaining more security with myself. I think about letting go, of not having to control the situation, the relationship, the world around me. How arrogant a view that is, to think I can do that in the first place. How tiring it becomes. But it is not that simple. I think there is a balance in relationships that is found in clearly letting my partner know how much I care, what feels good and what hurts, but not allowing those messages to slip into control and manipulation.

It is so easy for "I love you" to ease over to "I love you so much; don't be this way if you love me."

In essence jealousy means to me taking what someone else has or holding onto what I think I have. In my better moments I realize that I can't *have* anyone and that it is a hollow hope to want to master anyone else but myself.

Gay Swenson

I feel very shaky when I get jealous; my stomach quivers and my voice shakes. My hands feel cold. I just get scared, I think, when jealousy becomes intense.

When I get into the kind of situation where I am being compared or competing with another woman, those feelings come to the surface.

Most of the time I back off, feeling like it is not going to be me that's preferred. Underneath that, I guess, is a basic inadequacy.

Just this morning a woman called that John has been friends with for some time. I've been jealous of her since John told me some things about her and that she was attracted to him. She called asking for him and it really brought out those jealous feelings. She has many of the things that typically make me feel that way . . . she's bright, young, pretty and a *certified* counselor.

When John told me that she had "worked through" being attracted to him, I could see that what she was doing was letting him know she was attracted to him in a safe way; if he didn't say "yes" to that, she could save face. My reaction right then was to be scared and feel vulnerable and angry.

When I learned that she was a certified, legitimate counselor that really got to me; it taps into things I want for myself, I guess. I'm sensitive around qualified, competent people who have done the work to get there and have the title, but sometimes I feel brighter and more competent than they do.

Just after he told me about his friend I started crying. I feel so loved by him and so loving and when all this came out I felt terribly vulnerable and powerless. There was nothing I could do if he were to respond to her or flow toward her and at that instant the love I had seemed so tenuous and vulnerable. I felt very sad.

Then I started saying sarcastic things, I questioned her motives and said how dumb he was not to see that. I got really shaky talking about it. Now we joke about it, we talk about her calls, and it seems better, but I know it's not completely okay. She wants the four of us to get together and whenever that comes up I am actively opposed to it. I just don't want to do it.

I have met her. The last time we went to the Center she was walking down the street toward us and when she saw John's face, her face just lit up. She came over to the car and we said hellos . . . she's lovely.

I feel particularly vulnerable now. My health is poor—this damn back of mine—and I'm not doing any kind of graduate work or making much personal movement. So it makes me feel less attractive and more vulnerable to those kinds of threats. When I do things that get me out of here and more in touch with some of the things I like about myself and am feeling more of a whole person, I feel much better and I feel better about John with other women.

I really want to internalize the belief that it doesn't make any difference how pretty or qualified this woman is in how John feels about me. I'd like to know that enough so that if John really wanted her to come over here, I could do that and do that with ease and not in a phony way. In a way, that would be confronting my own fear.

I just hate to get into that comparison thing. And I especially hate it when I'm feeling down on myself to begin with. I don't seem to mind when I'm feeling confident and doing something I really like, like teaching or leading encounter groups. I know that I'm going to come out okay and the comparisons don't seem harsh; it doesn't seem at my expense to say how great a teacher someone else is or at anyone else's expense to think I'm very good. When I'm not sure about that, I always end up short changing myself in the comparison.

But something that's very important . . . for the last year I've felt steadily, basically good about myself and partly it's because I haven't had somebody intimate continually implying that I'm *not* good. That went on for so long with me; my low image was encouraged and supported by my husband so that I bought it lock, stock and barrel. Now those moments of jealousy and doubt seem like momentary lapses instead of basic feelings.

JOYFUL

*This is the true joy in life, the being used for a purpose
recognized by yourself as a mighty one; the being
thoroughly worn out before you are thrown on the
scrap heap; the being a force of nature instead of a
feverish selfish little clod of ailments and grievances complaining that the world will not devote itself to making
you happy*

George Bernard Shaw

〜〜〜

Carol Ahearn

I think joy is something I'm just learning about. Lately my life seems to be a lot of not-joy and little bits here and there of almost-joy. But I like the direction it's changing in.

I can tell you about the last time I felt joyous. I went to the Chicago Symphony Monday night. Now, I don't know that much about music, but I knew just enough about the Mozart to appreciate it and follow along with it. That was a lovely thing for me because it's quite new. I got very engrossed in it and felt like I could hear all the different things that were going on in the orchestra, every instrument, and I got this shivery-tingly feeling all over my skin. My hair felt like it was standing out and this surge just kind of moved through my body. I knew that every ounce of my being was caught up in that experience. Every time I surrendered to all the things, all the music I heard, all the parts together—not separately —I got that feeling. It was truly a joy.

The idea of surrender that I mentioned is important. It's as if I let something penetrate me. I experience a lot of the opposite of that in my relationships with people—I don't let them penetrate me, but when I finally do that, I get a lot of excitement and it comes to a kind of climax, like getting shivers all over. To the degree that I let them in, is the degree to which I get filled up by them and I fully resonate when I'm filled up like that. I want more of that.

Sometimes joy is a very quiet thing. When I'm with someone I know very well and feel very close to, I can get a joy out of just sitting close to them and drinking them in. I get a great pleasure out of visual things and sometimes the form and substance of what a person is becomes so beautiful to me that I just want to absorb it. At those times I want to become softer and softer and softer to them so they can touch me more and more and more, just by being there. I want to let myself melt.

The less rigid I become, the more I can melt and the more receptive I can become.

Other times are not quiet times. When things excite me and I have space and it's appropriate to react in a physical way, I might jump up and down and clap my hands and laugh. Just by doing that movement I am letting myself into myself, into my body.

What I want to do more of is recognize the opportunity of those experiences more than I do. There are people that always give me that opportunity and I'm trying to take it as often as I can. But I want to learn to spot those opportunities in life by myself and not have to have them pointed out to me all the time. I seem to be waiting for someone or something to give me permission to enjoy. I want to take more opportunities for myself to be soft and receptive to people I'm with. I would like to be unafraid enough to be that way always, to not feel intimidated, but to let experiences in.

Sometimes what most people see as an unpleasant experience can be joyful. Recently I got really mad at someone I'd been wanting to get mad at for some time; I just let go of a lot of things I wanted to say and it was an exhilarating experience. That's joyful to me, not happy, but joyous. I experience joy when I know without a doubt I'm alive, I'm whole and not killing any part of me. When I'm happy I can be altogether happy, when I'm mad I can get jumping up and down mad. It's letting my own power go out, letting go and being fully me.

John K. Wood

There's one experience in particular that comes to mind when I think of joy. I was in Stern Grove in San Francisco; it's like a crevice or canyon in the earth right next to the sea and it forms a natural amphitheater. It's a deep canyon that has these giant eucalyptus trees all through it, like a forest, and in the center is a little meadow. It's just a lovely place. In the summer the San Francisco Symphony gives free concerts there.

I was there a couple years ago and I remember lying on the grass, my face to the sky, amidst thousands of people, listening to the orchestra play Tchaikovsky. I was looking up into this vivid blue sky framed by tall eucalyptus trees and this feeling came over me of just leaving my body. I was just lifted up and became the music, the place, the people. It was just like being taken out of my body and into everything else that was around me. It was fantastic.

That seems a different kind of joy than another kind I experience sometimes, of being ecstatic and happy and dancing around. It's more exuberant. But both kinds of feelings are certainly joyous.

Falling in love is full of joy. That's one time I'm sure I'm alive; I'm using all my faculties . . . I see everything, I feel things anew, I hear . . . everything is operating at full bore. I feel worth-while and valued and I'm able to give myself up to another person.

It's funny. Sometimes I have those same feelings falling out of love too, or when I'm losing someone I love. I feel like I'm using all of myself then too and while it's not the same thing as the kind of joy we're talking about so far, it's a very real, very deep feeling.

My joyful occasions seem to happen without much planning. In fact when I try and make them happen it fails. I say to some people, "Let's get together and have a really good time." That doesn't seem to make it. I think it's a matter of being open to experiences when they come up.

What seems to be a common denominator in the experiences I have that I'd call joyful is a feeling of power. I don't mean a power over someone or a physical power to lift a huge boulder, but a feeling of "super okay" about myself. It's not a power of offense but of defense, an indestructibility, anything that I do will be okay.

But further than that, as in the example I gave of the Stern Grove concert, there's a feeling of the self and power being irrelevant questions. Maybe where I went at that concert was *into* everything; I was the sun and the sky and the sea and the music and the crowd—everything all at once. That makes those ideas of power irrelevant.

One thing that helps me to be joyful is thinking about death, my own death. It brings me back to a center of myself where I take more notice of things and use all of myself in the present. What that seems to do is strip away all of the irrelevant busy-ness I seem to surround myself with and brings me back to a place of *essentials*. It's like wanting to say to you "I love you," wanting you to know that for sure, because I might die tomorrow and I'd want you to know that. I don't want to put those important things off. I have been wanting to say that for a long time, but I keep thinking the time hasn't been right. Thinking about my own death makes the time right for everything.

John Wood

I remember one of the first scenes in the movie "Dr. Strangelove" . . . Slim Pickens was in the bomb bay of a B-52 as it was over target, desperately trying to free a jammed atomic bomb so it could drop out. Suddenly the bomb released taking Slim with it, straddling it like a bronco. He ripped his hat off and waving it in the air over his head let go with a rip-roaring, bronco-busting yell. He was headed for glory. Thinking about joy brought that to mind.

Yesterday I was in the ocean, playing around with the clear, blue-green surf, riding some waves in, teasing some others. In one moment I turned around, away from the shore, and swelling up over me, about to break over my head, was one of the biggest waves of the day. I threw back my head and whooped an animal-like yell into the wave and the yell became part of the wave and so did I. I was overcome by the sight, the feeling of the wave around me and the raw power I was a part of. I was at the same time, powerless and in touch with so much power. It was joyous.

I think about other experiences of joy, in nature, with people I love, and it seems they all have one thing in common: surrendering.

I find joy in sex when I surrender myself to the natural power of my body and what I want to do and when that's matched in a partner. It's as if a third thing is created out of the union and it is somehow larger than both of us. Often I stand in awe of what the two of us have created.

I also find joy in dark green woods, at the tops of snow-covered mountains, in the cool blue liquid of the ocean and in the hot, baking heat of the summer sun. I am outside of myself and so very rich inside. I am emptied out, yelling out, rushing out, yet I am full, warm and glowing. What I do at those moments is unrestrained, unconfined and oblivious to the "whys" the "shoulds" and the consequences. The force of life is within me.

There seem to be two ways that I react, or behave, during those moments. One is to be quiet, awe-filled, reverent, and peaceful. The other is explosive; I whoop, smack my hands together, run, jump, hug somebody . . . anything that is a pouring out of energy. It feels like my energy bounces off whatever's around me—people, other animals, the walls, whatever.

I have other instances of joy that, on the surface, don't seem to fit these boundaries. There are moments of sadness or of anger when I am being totally myself, fully into the moment and lacking self-consciousness that, in retrospect, seem joyful. I am full of myself and have surrendered to the experience. The sad moments in particular feel as if they are carving out hollows or caves within me, opening space inside that can be filled up with warm, happy, more full feelings later. I know that I am alive.

I get real joy out of creating and that can be alone or with people. When a dream comes up in my head, rumbles around there for a while and then, through my hands, becomes a reality, I am joyous. When friends are together, building ideas or barns, giving and taking, feeding on each other and feeding each other, I am joyous.

There are so many opportunities—not plans or structures—but opportunities that present themselves, that I am seeing that I didn't use to. There are moments I can take to full-fill. myself. There are times with others I can choose to wade into. There is a world that awaits me and invites me to swim through it. My enemies are fear, control, and apathy.

My comrades are devotion and openness. My wish is that I will be fully me . . . and let go.

Doug Land

When I think of having joy, I think of experiences that represent for me a kind of total coming together of all parts of me. I think about hiking all day in the mountains, in the cold air, and finally arriving at a spot to make camp, totally tired. I make myself a small fire, sit down and look at where I am . . . I just feel like I'm going to burst. It's a total physical exhilaration.

That's one kind of joy for me; another has to do with something really different. I think about sitting with Jennifer in my lap and doing nothing, just enjoying it, just *enjoying* it. I suddenly know, I acknowledge to myself, that this is the greatest joy I could ever have. It's so peaceful and quiet and calm; it wouldn't matter to me if I died the next minute. That would be enough. That's the kind of joy I'd like to get back to.

The opposite of joy seems to me to be anxiety or fear, being afraid that I might die before I do something. That's just the opposite of feeling "This is it, this would justify my life, all that I have been and have had is enough for me." I've had that feeling, that completeness, and it's generally around my family. It's a feeling that I am complete. For instance, in a very good painting, at various stages it is complete in its own way . . . as a sketch, as a drawing, as an outline of the painting itself and filled in as a painting. Each of those is a complete thing yet it can go on. In those moments of joy for me, it is as if I have completed a cycle and I fully realize that completeness. When I go on I know it's going to be incomplete again, entering another cycle. I think I'd like to die in a moment of joy.

Another thing about joy is that I don't think we can tell others when or how to have it or that it can be programmed. I'd hate to live in a place where someone had planned out when I was supposed to celebrate, to be joyful, to appreciate certain planned things. I wouldn't want to be there. I really want to be surprised. I want my celebration to come out of my life. So joy for me has got to be like a gift, a surprise, that comes to me out of the blue.

I invented a great theological axiom for myself the other day; it has to do with the way we live our lives. The experience of grace, to me, is the experience of joy or celebration or fullness. I was thinking that the only efficient cause of grace is trust and if you can get people to trust their own process, they would have plenty of joyful experiences. They would be surprised by them. If we could learn to trust life, ourselves, it would cause us to experience joy. It really depresses me to hear people say, "I know what people want and I have been successful giving it to them. *This* or *that* is what people really need." We don't really trust each other to decide; it's stupid. If we could learn to trust ourselves and our own experience we could find more joy in so many experiences in our daily lives. We could be surprised to find out how much grace is in our lives if we just learned to let go.

LONELY

So lonely am I
My body is a floating weed
Severed at the roots
Were there water to entice me
I would follow it, I think.

Ono No Komachi

∽∽∽

Howard Saunders

Loneliness for me goes back a long time. I have been through several different stages of it and it is always different. And I see myself growing in the ways I approach it. I haven't been lonely a lot lately and sometimes I've wanted to be lonely, just to experience what it was I used to experience a whole lot.

The classic lonely situation for me was Friday night. There I was, watching a series of shows on television, resigned to being alone. "The Interns," "The Name of the Game," and some other hour-long show—I knew they were coming and I knew how predictable the plots were going to be, but there I was.

But before I had settled into watching them, sometime Friday late afternoon, I zapped around like crazy, trying to get something going for Friday night. But I would never start until Friday evening, until it was much too late. I became desperate. It was like I *had to* get somebody to be with and time after time it wouldn't work. I'd waited so long that I knew no one would be available; calling people and knowing they wouldn't be home and, if they were there, they would be busy. I would get myself really worked up. It was crazy. Then I'd just resign myself to watching the tube.

Sometimes, if I couldn't stand it any longer, I would go out and see if there were people out looking for rides. I'd find myself driving along routes where I might meet people. I might even pick someone up and not say anything to them. We'd ride for 10 or 15 blocks, I'd take them where they wanted to go and I'd go on. I wouldn't have said anything, but I'd say to myself, "Well, I met somebody else tonight. There was another body in the car with me."

But Friday somehow, was the worst time to be alone. I just felt dead. It was very painful.

I can remember being frantic at times. I would walk around the house screaming—"What am I doing to myself? Why me?" All those times, I wasn't down on myself; it was a very "up" period for me. I liked myself. I didn't have the excuse that I was an asshole. I knew if people were around, if there would just be somebody, that they'd like me a lot. That was the most frustrating part of it. It makes me very sad to feel again that part . . . that I was worthwhile and didn't have anybody to share it with.

Now, I think I could go for a long period of being alone without experiencing loneliness in a destructive way. In a way, being as lonely as I have been in the past was good for me; I became compulsive about seeking out people. That's the best thing that happened to me about being lonely—getting aggressive about seeking out people and demanding time. Even though I'm not lonely now, I'm still doing that—not out of loneliness, but just letting people know that I want to be something to them and want them to be something to me. That seems like something very productive I learned out of my loneliness and not being lonely now doesn't keep me from doing that.

When I am lonely I am hopelessly unable to do anything else but express it in some way; I am almost incapable of keeping it in. That's just the way I am.

Bill Stillwell

I usually know when I'm lonely when I find myself doing a lot of things to take up time, scheduling myself very tightly, filling up time with more than one thing. Like I'm washing dishes, listening to the record player and watching TV. Sometimes I'm lonely with people, but most of the time I'm lonely when I'm alone. Lots of times I choose to be alone and then I find I can't handle it; then I start filling up my time.

Lately I have become more willing to admit my loneliness. And I can remember going out to people, trying to start or further relationships, writing letters to people I care about but haven't seen for a while. That seems to help. I go into a lot of fantasies too, about being close to people, being loved.

I can remember being lonely when Ann has been away, but I get help with that by knowing that we will be back together. Recently she was gone for two and a half weeks and during the last week I had a lot of trouble staying with, in an emotional sense, the people I was working with. I was so much wanting to be with her and wanting us to be close, that I had to say to them that it was nice being there and they were enjoyable, but I was really having trouble devoting myself to the situation. Saying that, getting past it in a way, helped me get through that last week. It was like a big part of me wanting to be with Ann and a smaller part of me wanting to be there with them. Somehow the big need for Ann covered up my other part that could be there working with them; it was blocking those other people out. But sharing my feelings with them, helped them and helped me be more in that situation.

Lonely is something I don't like to be and I can avoid it, but generally I don't like it until I can be in it, *until* I let myself be lonely. Then I can appreciate that. I seem to be getting better at allowing these negative things in myself. When I can say "I am lonely" and fully accept it then I can go about finding out what some of my lonely needs are and try and take care of those.

Betty Meador

My loneliness has to do with not so much how many people are around me but where I am in my own development. When I remember the really lonely times in my life it was because I was not doing what I really wanted to be doing, not being able to do those things (I thought) and not even being aware that that was so.

In those times, I didn't have any good, strong sense of myself and I was really frightened and insecure. If I had somehow the sense of what I really wanted to do, or someone to help me find that out, and had the courage to go after that, it would have been a big step away from my loneliness. I think I realized that I was lonely, but I didn't have any notion that I could have taken care of it; that I could have changed my life in such a way that I wouldn't have been so lonely.

When I think back I was just extremely depressed. I felt purposeless, full of despair, frustration. I can remember wishing so much that I had a friend who would read books with me and talk about them and be interested in the same kinds of things I was interested in. Now, it seems I was just hungry for somebody who, in a way, represented a step in my growth, who would help me go the way I wanted to go. It turns out I did find a friend like that, it was uncanny; we met each other at the library. We're good friends still.

Thinking about that, it seems that my loneliness had a lot to do with not being who I was. My background, surroundings, circumstances had put me in a place where I was being a person I didn't really want to be.

Sometimes still I long to be with people who are more where I am and, while that's a kind of loneliness, it doesn't carry nearly the weight and rest of the emotional package that I felt years ago. When I get into that, I fantasize a lot; I think about what it would be like to be with those people, to have what I want. And I vow to do something about my fantasies, to go find people, to call people. That's one of my resolutions, is to do something to make those kinds of fantasies come true.

The whole thing seems like reaching to be more of myself. My drive to be with others like me, the places I want to be are in a way beyond where I am, the next step in my development. When I get that—when I am with those people—it feels like a growing, expanding thing.   ↰

Steve Doyne

It's very hard for me to say that I'm lonely. I tend to let it out in other ways; I tend to get angry, say hurtful things. It seems like the world is against me or there's something wrong with the people around me. My first reaction seems to be to get mad.

I'm not sure what makes me lonely. I can be lonely with a lot of people around. If I begin to sense that the person I'm with is not really caring about me, giving me recognition or acknowledging my feelings, then I can begin to feel very lonely. Sometimes I can make myself lonely by cutting off those very things I want, by withholding, withdrawing.

When I do that—isolate myself—I start to get more negative, more irritable. I really can get snotty. And it's not an easy thing for me to get out of, because it's so subtle; I seem to be so good at hiding my loneliness. It's easier for me to see things I don't like in others than to deal with myself and the reasons I seem alienated. It makes me very uncomfortable when I'm lonely. I think no one cares about me, and, in a way, I start to do things to them because they don't.

When I'm lonely for a long period of time, I really start to wonder about myself. Who am I? Do I like myself as a person? Do I want to accept that there are parts of me that others don't like?

Often I do just need to spend time by myself to sort out some of those questions and answers. Sometimes I just need a good cry and I allow myself that. Sometimes it's important to share my loneliness with someone and just the sharing makes me feel better—if I have some understanding, some togetherness about what it is. Just saying "I'm lonely" doesn't do it.

In any case it's better for me to look at myself and what I'm doing than it is to start to set up things to "cure" my loneliness. 'Cause it will just come back when those things are gone.

One thing I know . . . it is very important for me to be involved with people, to care about them and have them care about me. That's a very strong need for me; I don't know if I could do without that.   ↰

John Wood

Sometimes it seems as if I don't really let myself experience my loneliness; or I don't express it as loneliness; I say it's something else. Or I have so many people around me, what do I know about loneliness? It seems as if I never need to say, "Hey, I need some people around me, some bodies." But I do get lonely; I really get lonely.

When I'm lonely, I can almost see myself standing out in a crowd. There are people all around me, but they don't see me. I'm kind of crouched alone in the middle. I see myself and I know I'm there among them, but they don't. They're all tending to something else. I'm there but no one cares about me.

I can begin to resent people for not meeting my needs and that alienates me from them and I resent them even more and I can get into a vicious cycle that perpetuates my loneliness.

When I am the loneliest is when I don't want to be with me. Then I'm saying, to myself, "You're really a shitty person. What you did or what you are is not something that I like." Then how can I expect anybody else to be with me? When I get like that it really pushes me way out. At those times, there is a deep sadness and sometimes tears and those tears are saying, "No one understands me. No one knows me. I don't even understand myself."

Sometimes I think about the irony of my loneliness and how I deal with it. I say I'm lonely and I withdraw and isolate myself. It seems like what I should be saying is "Hey, I'm lonely. I want to be with people." At least that's the way most people think of loneliness. But it seems different for me; that my loneliness is not so much a separation from other people as it is an alienation from myself.

When I take the time to get back in touch with myself and what I need—I still might be lonely—but I feel better about my alone-ness.

Then going out to get what I really need seems to be getting myself in a way. It seems like a realization of myself that is away from loneliness, an expansion of myself. Loneliness, then, seems a narrowing, a cutting off of myself or a part of myself that needs to be satisfied.

Maybe loneliness simply means not having my needs met; my needs to be known, understood, loved, growing. Loneliness is like having all my needs inside, stirring around, and not have the contacts, the relationships to take care of them.

Sometimes it's scary how much I need other people and how reluctant I am to admit that.

LOVING

↩↩↩

Ron Lunceford

I get confused about loving sometimes. I feel all kinds of different love for people . . . for individuals . . . for people as a group . . . and I feel like I love a lot of people. I don't feel like I'm actively in love with them, but that I love them.

I would find it very difficult to be promiscuous though; I'm lazy and that would mean I would have to give a lot of energy to romantic, loving relationships with more than one person. I reserve that kind of loving and energy for my wife and for my kids. So while I think I'm capable of loving more than one person, it seems too difficult to carry on lots of satisfying love relationships.

Loving for me is a very mellow feeling . . . lots of warmth, contentment, excitement too. It's good to love somebody and feel that way and to have it returned is even better.

Sometimes I feel in love with my students, as I watch them move in different directions, when I see them fully experiencing things and see their real struggle with something. I get a real warm, caring feeling for them. I can even enjoy the pain they go through and love them for being real.

Some of the things I love in people are simplicity, honesty, a "realness," being able to express their feelings, being able to show love. I love people who are able to reach out to others too. With Judy, I love her encouragement, support, understanding, all of her talents and skills, her unselfishness . . . all of these wrapped up together in one package.

I wish I could express that more. I say to students sometimes how much I care about them. People need to hear that more, but sometimes I get lazy about not wanting to go any further into it. Often I think it's that I just like the feeling I have and I don't want to talk about it. The more I talk about it, the more it becomes just words. I can express it in other ways. Sometimes I just sit and enjoy the good feeling.

I used to think that there ought to be an equality in loving relationships, that one partner should love the other one just as much as he or she was loved. But that seems like an ideal to me and I think some people's capacity for love or ability to love are just different from others and that can be worked out. That makes me think about the degrees of love. Some people say that the epitome of love is giving up the one you love and still love them. If, for instance, it came to a situation where Judy found someone that she fell in love with and that meant more to her than I did and I was a hindrance to that, it would seem a loving thing for me to do to let her go. It would be painful, no doubt about it, but I think I could deal with it.

The one thing I think I wish for myself is that I could express my love more. I can express my love, but sometimes I have the fear of talking about it too much. I like being loved and I like giving love and sometimes talking about it changes that feeling for me. Sometimes too it is sad for me to talk about love and loving feelings to people who don't have someone to love or anyone to love them; that's sad.

I want to say sometimes to people, "Hey, you can love me and we don't have to make promises to each other." Some people can handle that and some can't. Some just need permission to express love and be open to it; sometimes it helps to begin to take that risk.

But for me, I want to say, "I love you" more. I don't want anyone I love to go without knowing that.

Larry and Kay Carlin

LARRY: When I feel loving it seems like I can't keep what's inside inside; I have to reach out, touch, embrace, hold, kiss. That's my first response when that warm feeling starts to come out of my tummy. It seems to be centered there and it comes out as kind of a slow explosion, reaching out and widening. It feels as though I can't contain it; I have to express it in some fashion and the easiest way for me to do that is in a physical way. I can talk about it, but it's much more important for me to reach out physically.

KAY: When I'm feeling that way around you and the kids, I have a similar kind of feeling; it's like overflowing. I want to hug, touch, squeeze. There's a warm feeling deep inside and it seems like brimming over of many emotions. Sometimes when happy tears come to my eyes it seems like a physical overflowing that's like my loving feeling. Things seem very close to the surface in me.

LARRY: It's also a feeling of one-ness. At that moment when that loving, caring feeling comes up, I have a one-ness or unifying feeling that manifests itself in my grabbing and holding the person I'm loving. It kind of makes us one. It seems like it's limitless, like there are no boundaries on the feeling. I have this little saying with the kids—"I love you more than the universe"—which is my way of saying to them my feeling for them is infinite, boundless, totally encompassing and beyond imagination. At those moments, I would do anything for them.

It's hard for me to think about loving when it's not in relationship to someone specific. And I'm thinking about people who say they're "in love with life" and that sort of thing. I experience that but I experience that in a relationship. I can feel that way, but it seems to be when I'm with Kay and the kids. It has something to do with sharing it. Sometimes I just reflect and feel good about how great things are going for me, but I can't divorce that from the people in my life. It's hard for me to think about it without Kay and the girls. It's like that explosion, but there's no one there to grasp it, to share . . . or to say it back to you.

KAY: Another feeling that comes up in me, secondarily, is that I'm very lucky to be able to feel this way. Like looking at the kids when we're all together doing something . . . camping in Mexico, watching the sunset, looking in tidepools, in the tent at night reading together . . . I just feel so lucky to be who I am at those moments.

I also think that when I don't feel good about myself, I have a hard time feeling loving. I can care for someone or do things for them, but I don't think of that as loving necessarily.

LARRY: I like what Kay said about loving and how she felt about her. It's hard for me to be caring, accepting and open without feeling good about myself. When I feel bad about myself, I find myself blocked from other people. I am absorbed into feelings about me and cut off from Kay and the kids. I am much less tolerant and accepting and more critical and short-tempered.

KAY: When you're that way you don't even love yourself. And in that stage, I can't be loving to you. I can care about you and be concerned. But I have to let you be where you are. I can't say to you: "Don't feel that way." I want to give you as much room as you need and trust that you'll find your way out of that.

LARRY: That suggests a critical thing to me . . . it's a bond and in those tough moments of a relationship, because that bond is there, it allows Kay to accept me in my terrible mood or vice versa. If the bond wasn't there and I act the way I do in those crappy moods, there would be nothing there to keep us together. Love, in that way, acts as a glue or a cement in the relationship.

When I'm in love with someone, besides being physical with them and telling them how I feel about them, I take a great deal of pleasure in doing things for them—giving gifts, literally giving gifts I have bought or made, or a gift of doing something for them . . . making them breakfast, helping with chores.

KAY: That makes me think of the time I got sick and it really scared me not to do much of anything, not to be much of anything. But I was involved in a lot of things at the time and I told Larry "I just feel sick and weak and swamped with things to do." And he said "What can I do for you?" And we got in there and did things together . . . that was such a gift to me.

LARRY: I like that when it happens to me too. It's a doing for someone else that doesn't include the expectation of something in return, without any sort of reciprocity. It seems like love is unconditional; it's not a tit for tat kind of thing. The love is within me and it's mine and I give it without expecting a response.

KAY: I think all I expect is that my love be honored, at least recognized. And if you love me don't expect me to love you in any way except in the way that I want to love you. When you start putting conditions on it, it messes it all up. I used to do this to Larry all the time. I wanted him to be with me all the time and when he wasn't I thought it was because he just didn't want to be with me or he didn't love me on that day . . . it was terrible. Now I know what that's about and realize how much freedom has to go along with my love.

LARRY: That suggests words like faith and trust to me. And what Kay was saying earlier, about feeling better about herself, seems to be a critical element in that. I can't love someone else unless I have love for myself. I think that's absolutely essential. It has to start there.

I think of love as dynamic. It can't be static; it's either growing or diminishing. I don't think of it as ever standing still. Therefore, it seems we have to "work" at keeping that loving relationship growing. The first and most important thing we had to do along that line was to begin to really communicate with each other including expressing anger to each other. In any kind of relationship there's going to be negative feelings, abrasiveness. I've had difficulty in expressing those and the extent to which I hold those back, the more they fester inside. I think that's toxic; it kills the relationship and diminishes the love. So I really needed to be able to get angry. And I needed to own up to those times when I don't feel loving and not feel guilty about it, just to accept that as part of any normal relationship. I don't have too much difficulty expressing loving feelings, but I do with angry feelings.

Another big thing for us was to consciously find out and do some things that we had in common, to share more with each other. Those things for us include a lot of physical things . . . swimming, backpacking, camping. Most recently we've discovered classical music together. So it means sharing things that we have together and, on the other hand, having things that are mine and Kay having things that are just hers and respecting those areas of privacy. That means some time alone.

I think I need to grow even more in the area of expressing myself to Kay, about my negative feelings and things about my hopes and aspirations, my own feelings of inadequacy . . . not keeping all those to myself so much but bringing Kay in on them. I have all kinds of people I could share those with, but the point is I want to choose to share more of them with Kay.

KAY: I think I need to start trusting that it's okay for me to be a little more selfish. Like I come home and I really want to work on my weaving and I want to be more able to say "To hell with the clothes that are waiting to be folded." That's very hard for me; I'm not used to it. I feel guilty when I'm home and everything house-wise and kid-wise is not being taken care of; those are my roles. And to work on my communicating to Larry. My part of that is learning not so much to communicate my negative feelings like anger, but to learn to receive them.

LARRY: I remember how it was when Kay and I first met. It was like there was a seed there between us. There was some good fertile soil for it, some nice things between us—we had common interests, we worked near one another, we enjoyed each other's company. But it was not a Hollywood, romantic, flash-bang-boom kind of beginning; it just wasn't. It was a steadily growing thing. And it still is. I love Kay more today, 12 years later, than I did when we were married. It's just been growing—it's been rocky—but growing."

KAY: I'm thinking of what a good portion of the "glue" we talked about was for me during some of the bad times; it was a good ol' compatible sex relationship.

LARRY: I think for us that's absolutely true.

KAY: That took us over some of the rough spots.

LARRY: For us, there were times in our relationship where that was the one thing that kept us together.

KAY: It seemed to be the one pleasant experience we had.

LARRY: Had that not been there, with all the other things that were going on, we might not be together today.

KAY: At different times during our relationship, different things were important to us . . . common interests, our sexual relationship, the children . . . and at this time in our relationship we seem closer than ever to lots of those things coming together and being important at the same time.

LARRY: It's like a maturing process. The seed grew. But not without some effort and commitment.

John Wood

Loving is tender. It is moist, multi-colored—but mostly orange—wet eyes and an expansive feeling in my chest. It's a radiance, as if I have a sun inside of me and it is shining out and basking the one I love in warmth, support, encouragement, and food for growth.

The idea of nourishment is very important to me. I often think of love as manure and my role in loving is to spread this supportive, encouraging manure at the feet of the growing things in the person I love. I think this is the most important thing I can do for another person; it is what I want the most from a partner. It is difficult though. Sometimes I get into a bind about whether or not it's my partner wanting to grow or just me wanting that for them. Also I may want them to grow in certain areas they're not ready to step into. In these cases it's easy for my encouragement and good intentions to cross over into pressure on another to change to meet my needs. It is also difficult to encourage a person to grow in ways that take them away from one or create even a temporary distance. Though an occasion or an activity may be the best thing for my loved one to do on her own, my own self-interest may not help her to that decision. All in all, that is a critical part of loving for me, to help the ones I love go where they want to go.

Loving means, obviously, that I *care* about that person and have an investment of sorts in what happens to him or her. It is like they have claimed parts of me and I of them. When they hurt, I hurt. When I rejoice, they have a part in that rejoicing. It is an active process instead of passive, exciting instead of boring, present or *with* someone instead of distracted and preoccupied.

Loving energizes me. It's like that sun inside; I have a power and a radiance that does not exist at other times. Perhaps it is not so much another person giving me energy as helping me tap into my own, serving as a catalyst for my potency and a reflector of my energy.

I think they also need a sun inside them to be that way. To be loving helps me to be creative—open, sharing, giving of what's inside me, looking at the world with new eyes, putting myself into things. So often I flip-flop between two basic ways of looking at the world. In one of my moods, I view people and their actions with contempt and disrespect and don't trust anyone's motives. On more "loving" days, I watch people carefully, with a wonder and interest that brings a smile to my face. I'm not at all sure what makes the difference, but I know it is in my eyes (or heart) looking out—that the reality outside me is the same as the day before.

One important way I show my love to someone is to share myself. That sounds so simple, but it has many aspects. I share my past, my hopes, my disappointments, my excitement, my anger, my sadness, my tenderness, my body, my time, my secrets, my skills, my energy, my reactions to the world . . . it is an opening process that gradually gives another person the gifts I have to give. To the extent that I give less of those things and withdraw into myself is the measure of being out of love, with any one person or in my other relationships.

I worry about not loving someone, about becoming heart-weary and retreating from the vulnerability of love into the safety and sufficiency of my own private self. I see myself doing that temporarily—I think most people do—and when I feel that happening, I worry about the possibility of that becoming a way of life. I remember that Simon and Garfunkel song that almost got to be my theme song when I was younger:

> I am a rock.
> I am an island.
> And a rock feels no pain.
> And an island never cries.*

Luckily, those retreats are temporary so far. I see how tight and dark and lonely it is in there by myself and I come back outside, to the light and the nourishment of others. To go backwards seems too much like dying.

I think I have learned some things about my loving. They are bandied about a lot, but they ring true for me. I need to love myself—that includes acceptance of myself, responsibility for myself, nourishment and self-support and the realization of my ultimate alone-ness and the strength of that. Until I take care of myself I don't feel as if I can take care of another.

Another important growing process for me is a devotion to the present. It is so easy for me to get wrapped up in anticipation and expectations or to be burned by my past hurts and disappointments. I think it's impossible for me to escape my past or not have hopes for my future, but I don't want them to govern me. Attention to the realities of the person I'm with and the gifts they bring to me helps me to be much more loving and hence feel better than if I'm expecting, pressuring, dreaming of what we *might* have.

As simply as I can put it, loving means being the sun, soil and rain for someone's sunflower. I think I'm in love with the feeling of being in love.

Bill and Audrey McGaw

BILL: Love has gone through a real change in me. In my youth, a very important thing for me was wanting to be a better person than I really

---

* © 1965 by Paul Simon. Used by permission of the publisher.

was for the one I was in love with. I don't feel that need anymore; I'm not conscious of trying to be good, to present only the good, attractive side of myself. It used to be hard work to do that. I think it's a big change from the heroic, deep, tragic, always serious feeling to what I feel now. It seems much more mature, satisfying, comfortable, more secure; I need and feel needed, I feel tolerated and understood. I share more of all parts of myself, including the stinky, weak feelings I have about myself. I used to be much more private about those kinds of things.

AUDREY: I like the kind of love we have. I think about how it's changed too. Especially in the last three or four years we've done some big changing. Once upon a time Bill was king in the house. It wasn't so much that he wanted to be king, but we all made him king. Then about three or four years ago I began to feel myself more strongly and I didn't want to live with the king anymore. That was a tough time for us, to get Bill down off the throne, a throne he didn't even realize he was on, but enjoyed all the benefits of. We all did sort of special things for Bill, the king. That change was traumatic for us because I think it said to you that I didn't care about you anymore.

BILL: Yes, it did.

AUDREY: But the truth of it is that I was caring about you more than ever, as a more whole person. I wanted to meet you on the same level instead of looking up to you and treating you like something special.

BILL: It was traumatic. I didn't want to abdicate the throne, although we hadn't conceptualized it in king and throne terms then. I thought it was a whole bunch of awful stuff she was going through and I didn't quite understand what I had done.

AUDREY: All that change wouldn't have happened and couldn't have happened the way it did if there hadn't been a lot of love between us. I began to feel really loved by Bill and the more loved I felt, the stronger I became. It took me a long time to believe that I was loved, but Bill is such a loving person that it finally sunk in, to the point that it "healed" me in a way. I started to become more whole and stronger. What we had up to that point was good, but it wasn't as real as it could be. It was really scary to rip out what we had at the roots, to try for something better. I had grown into a different person and we had the same old relationship, as if I were the same person, who was a lot weaker. Then we had to meet each other as the people we are. It was very, very hard and it took a lot of love. That was hard to get across to Bill at first. What was I doing to him? What was I trying to accomplish? The message he kept getting was that I didn't like him anymore. I kept trying to say, in as many languages as possible, that it was because of his love and the strength I had gotten from it, that I was doing this.

BILL: An important part of that is the more the roles we play go out the window, the more reality sets in and the deeper, more satisfying the relationship becomes. My role as king of the house was very much in the way of us getting together as real people.

AUDREY: It seems like a real liberation to me, more a people's lib than a woman's lib. There have been changes in the way we relate to the kids as well as the way we relate to each other. There's more freedom for everybody in the house.

BILL: As I escaped my role it freed me more too. Here I was stuck in the role of king and while that might be an enviable role for many, it put me above and away from my family. But it was tough to realize that and come down off the throne. When I am without a role of any kind, and just my self, I think I have much more ability to give and receive and it's just one less filter between me and somebody else. Not being jammed into a role frees me from expectations, my own and others, and lets me be more parts of myself, more whole.

AUDREY: Living with a king is exciting and fun, but along with that goes a lot of resentment. As long as I could see myself as subject, I could be comfortable in that role. But the more I began to see myself as a whole person, I'll be damned if I wanted to be a subject and take orders anymore. For a long time, I didn't understand the resentment and it was easy to put all the blame on Bill for being authoritarian and handing out all these kingly orders. The big change was when I began to realize that we were this way because I had put you up there. I needed that from you then. Gradually I began to take responsibility for myself and stopped blaming you or anyone else for it. I had to face the fact that I had the power to put you up there, a strong, whole man, and it was scary to face it that I could influence you so. It was in this time that I formulated one of my simple rules for myself; it's "What do I want and what can I do to get it?" I wanted to live with a human being not a king, and I could change that. I looked into myself to find my own answers. At that point it was a tremendous risk, a risk of tearing the marriage apart, taking the roles away and asking "Where can we go from here?" Where we went from there is just great.

BILL: I think that's so important, getting rid of roles, and my definition of a deep, swinging love relationship is where the parties are free of roles and there is freedom to be just self.

AUDREY: When I'm in that kind of relationship and really feel loving, I feel physically healthier as well as emotionally healthier. I feel a lot of energy. I want to touch and play and cook and have sex. I want to do things for and with the people I love. I feel courageous; I can reach out to people. My skin feels younger and smoother and I breathe more deeply. When I'm not feeling loving, I feel more like a raisin, sort of closed in on myself and I don't want anybody to do anything for me and I don't want to go out to anybody. I feel old and sullen and I want to close the door and be alone.

BILL: That pretty well matches for me. When I don't feel loving or loved I'm very much oriented towards taking and demanding. I'm a much more giving person when I'm feeling loved and loving. I do feel younger, more energetic too. Being out of love is an empty, depressing feeling as opposed to a full, sweet, rich one.

AUDREY: This is different from you, Bill; I don't want evidence that I'm loved when I'm not feeling loved. I want to push it away and isolate myself. I tend not to believe it. Even when the kids, who are marvelous, sensitive people, reach out to me at those times, I don't want it; I reject it. That's terrible.

Another thing I do when I feel loving is look forward and not backward, as I tend to do when I'm not loving. I look back to my past and dig up all the unhappiness there, wrap it around me and wallow in it. The future doesn't seem interesting or appealing in any way. I don't like evidence that anyone else feels good.

That feeling, of being loving, is so important to me that when it's not there, it's like the world has ended. I think I'm just learning to love, to *really*, love. I think a lot of people might say, or have said about me, that I am a loving person, but the change I feel has opened up a whole new area of loving in me. I think I've been good at giving, but that's different from loving. I spent a lot of time giving, like a lot of women and mothers do, but there's an idea of giving and giving and giving and expecting something back. Or giving to fix something, to repair things. I don't have any need to do that kind of giving-intruding anymore.

My son pointed out to me that he didn't see how it was possible to be loving without patience; that has become very important to me too. It's learning to keep my big mouth shut sometimes and let things alone. I don't have to fix things so that everybody loves everybody else. I used to kind of step in and be responsible for other people. Bill had a way of saying "The helping hand strikes again." I think that's marvelous; it sure was me.

Now the loving that goes on around here is straight loving. It's healthy and robust.

BILL: I think one of the most important things we have going for us is a process of deep, on-going, communication. There's trust, openness, honesty and that seems like a big part of a loving relationship to me. I feel understood. That's so important to me and it's come out of the way we communicate with each other.

AUDREY: I don't think there's any part of me that I hide from you, that you don't know about. At one time or another, every part of me has come out. The result, for me, is not so much loving as feeling loved and accepted. You know exactly who I am and you love me; that's exciting. Along with that goes no guarantee that we'll continue this way though. I used to need a guarantee, I think because there were parts of me that were unknown, not out yet, and I lived with the possibility of losing Bill when and if those parts of me surfaced. I don't have that need for a guarantee that we're going to live together for the rest of our lives anymore. I take just what we have now and don't have to stick anything from the future on it. That gives me the freedom to be myself and do whatever I want. That's exciting.

It used to be that I depended on Bill for the things that were my life blood . . . my love, my security, my joy, my excitement. I used to say I would die if he ever left me. And I think I might have. But there isn't that feeling in me anymore and that's got to be an enormous pressure off of you.

BILL: Yes, that really is.

AUDREY: Each day we're together we choose to be together. My accepting the fact that we might not be together has made it easier for us to be together. That doesn't mean I don't need you. I need our relationship, right now, to bring me the joy that it does. It's very important to me.

The really nice thing about loving is that it's such fun; it's really such fun.

REJECTED

There is not a woman in the world the possession of whom is as precious as that of the truths which she reveals to us by causing us to suffer.

Proust

~~~

Betty Meador

One of the first things I do when I'm feeling rejected is ask "why?" I start searching around for reasons, things I've said, impressions I've given.

I quickly become frantic, panicky about it when I fully realize what's happened. I feel like I'm going to cry. And I have to do something about it. It's as if I start mobilizing protective, defensive measures. They're defensive yet they're active. It's a feeling of "Boy, I'm going to do something about this." Most often, and this is not typical of me, I just get in a fighting mood when I'm feeling rejected. I'm just ready to come out swinging.

There's something strong in this whole thing about not being noticed. It's as if the world is going to go on and I won't be noticed. It's a feeling of being left alone and the other people involved are going on living life happily and not noticing me. My panic is needing to be paid attention to. I don't know if the fighting changes anything, but it makes me feel better. "By God, I've told you how I feel about this and you're not going to get away without knowing how bad it is."

It seems different when I'm feeling rejected by a man than it does a group of people rejecting me or being turned down for a job by someone. In a romantic relationship I don't fight. I'm much more passive and accepting of what's happening. I do look for the reasons and when I find them I tend to say "yeh, he's right." When I think about the situations that don't involve men, it seems as if I've been rejected for reasons that weren't valid. They were wrong in their rejection and I fight back to tell them that. The man was justified in his. That's so funny.

When I have felt rejection from a man it's almost always a case of him choosing someone else over me and I tend to accept that, to think I can't change it. It seems like, typically, he is choosing someone who is more whole, more mature, more of a person than I am, someone who is more equal to him than I am. Maybe I sense that from the beginning; maybe I set that up.

I wish I could begin to feel more equal. In relationships with men I care a lot about, I tend to put them way above me. I wish I didn't do that.

In other kinds of rejection, I think I like the way I react. I like the fact that I fight, that I can get angry and say clearly what I feel. I really feel done in and wronged in those times. It seems unfair and I like it that I can fight back.

I can't seem to get past the unfairness of it. What rejection so often seems is the unfair choosing of someone else over me. I have a hard time fully realizing that the choosing of the other person might be realistic. I tend to think it's unfair because I haven't been known fully. Maybe that's just a case of defending myself and not wanting to admit that the other person really is a better choice.

When rejection comes I really need to talk it out with the people involved. I need to find out the reasons. And when I think it's unfair I have a strong need to say that and have it heard, to fight for myself. It seems like I have to talk that out or go crazy. When that happens in a romantic situation though I say to myself the rejection came because I wasn't a full enough person and I start working on ways to make myself fuller. I do a lot of self-improvement kinds of things. That comes after a period of deep hurt though; I experience a lot of pain at times like this.

John Wood

Rejected. Flat. Denied. Offered in the store window—looked over, handled, appraised—and left there alone. Not good enough. Not pretty enough. Not together enough. Not secure enough. Just not enough.

Rejection cuts me to the quick. It slices right down inside and says: "I've seen who you are, sonny boy, and I don't want any more." Right away I'm afraid. "What are you doing to me? Why are you doing it? Where are you going? How can that be better than what we have?" The questions spring out, launched from my fear of being alone and testing for the last time the reality of losing a woman I care for. Yes, a woman; what else matters as much as rejection from the woman you love?

There is a quick emptiness inside. The fear. And nothing fills it. I am empty. Part of me is leaving and there is no replacement. Nothing fills the void. Am I in there? Yes, but tiny and afraid, not enough to fill out my own self. I can almost feel the wind whistle around in the emptiness.

But soon come the defenses. The reasons, the rationalizations, the denials of importance—all rush in to fill the void. I am okay. It wasn't good for either of us anyway. It was just a matter of one or the other of us having the courage to end it. I seem to be piling up sand-bags to halt the flood of fear and sadness that would wash over me if I let go.

I think about two kinds of rejection—rather two ways I am in a relationship that affect how I react to rejection. One way is to reveal or act out some parts of myself and not others; the reason is not always clear. I am giving part of my time and energy or being only part of who I am with the other person. If rejection comes I can say to myself: "Well, that's to be expected; they only know part of me." To the other person I can say: "Wait, you don't know this about me. I am more." This doesn't seem to make much difference in the long run. The seeds of the separation have been sown long ago in the partiality and fragmentation of my giving *and* the reasons for it.

Another way is to be as fully into the relationship as I can be, to know another and be known and, when you are known, to be unwanted. This is the big bomb when it hits, saying: "Yeh, I know you and you're too ——— to be with. I just don't want you anymore." Boy, that hurts. All that I am is not enough.

One tragedy is of not being known and things left unsaid. The other tragedy is of being known and not being wanted. Both cut to very tender parts of me.

Is rejection always a tragedy? In my saner moments I think not. Sometimes "rejection" seems just a matter of timing, of one person realizing a growing apart before another. Keeping silent about that (a choice one might make to avoid "rejecting" the other) can only increase the emotional distance between partners.

Rejection has often been a healthy thing for me. There seem to be blessings, though sometimes well disguised, in every rejection I have experienced. A person's obvious refusal to live with a certain part of me can be important enough to consider changing that behavior. Perhaps not; perhaps I want to stay the same and take the consequences, good and bad, of being the way I am. Either way, it is a learning experience for me IF I can get past the defending and the anger and *listen* to what someone else is saying about me. Again, it's my choice to accept that or not. I need the realization here too that only a part of me is being rejected, not my whole person.

Another thing I'm learning—and this seems most important—has to do with choosing, commitment and risk. "I want to do what I want to do" is one way of saying it. I want to make choices, in situations and relationships, that I feel good about and can commit myself to. Anything less, for me, sets up the failure/rejection in being half-assed about something or someone. I also want to risk more—to be full, to be direct about what I want and risk not only the rejection, but the acceptance I'm looking for.

The lack of joy in my life is not so much rejection from others as it is my own fear of giving myself fully to anyone or anything.   ↰

Muriel Keyes

Rejection makes me fold up. I kind of cave in my stomach and feel things going on in there. My voice cracks, I cower and move away a little. It's a hunching, protective kind of maneuver.

Often when I feel rejected I use that information to put myself down; I reject myself. I'm so able to do that without someone else helping me that when someone else rejects me, I can get to a really bad place. I think I get through that part of it quicker than I used to and sort out what part of the rejection is mine and what part is simply what the other person needs.

Generally, rejection says to me "I'm not good enough." Typically, that hurts me very much. In those cases I don't think I bounce back very readily; I don't come back to that person and say anything about how I'm hurt. I just tend to be wounded and stay with that until it's over.

I see an end to my hurting more quickly than I used to. When I was in junior high school and dancing was a big part of my life, I applied to the high school of performing arts and "tried out" to attend. Well, they mailed me a letter turning me down. I was hurt by that for years. I was constantly knocking myself over the head thinking how lousy a dancer I was. In fact, I stopped dancing for a long time.

Now, if that situation came up, I think I would be able to say to myself: "Yeh, by their standards, I'm not a very good dancer, but I don't want to be the dancer they're looking for . . . narrow, stiff, disciplined." I don't think I was really willing to commit myself to the discipline and training it took to become a professional dancer, but I wanted to be accepted and then be able to say that. It seems I have more of a sense of who I am and when I feel rejected now for being something that I'm not, I don't have to take it. It's living up to someone else's standards.

When I think about that coming up now in a relationship, I think I'd first have to decide how important that relationship was to me. If it were important enough, I'd want to go to the person and let them know that I felt rejected and hurt and try to clear up where that came from and what I was being rejected for, if that was indeed true. I'd like to sort that out together, whether or not, in the end, it meant a rejection in fact or not. That wouldn't be as important as my learning from it. Sometimes it's sorting out how much of it is theirs and how much is mine. If they rejected me for being a certain way that I felt I wasn't, I'd want to straighten that out. From my point of view, sometimes I can reject people or write them off by thinking they're more a certain way than they really are. It's a neat discovery to sit down and talk and find out that those terrible things aren't true and find out what we have in common.

What I often find myself doing lately is clearing up for myself who I am. I kind of review my strengths and weaknesses, my various parts and how they come off to other people. "Is this something I want to change? Do I like it in myself?" I start to ask those kinds of questions. That helps me sort out my own rejections and acceptances of myself.

David Mearns

Rejection for me almost always has to do with a woman. It's the lowest of the low; the ultimate in low feelings. There's nothing to compare to it. It feels like the total spirit has been sucked out of me.

It's something I can get into easily; it seems like it's happened to me a lot, in varying degrees. Many times I could see it coming and I am so scared of ending up in that state of rejection, that I do things to make it not so bad. I start getting defensive or denying the other person and what they mean to me or saying that what we have isn't that important anyway. Other times I just wade in with both feet and face it squarely, remaining as open as I can and saying what I want and how I feel.

Actually I like myself better when I don't hedge the bet, when I just go right in there with all I've got. The rejection is total and miserable, but I like that I was able to be myself in the situation.

When the ax falls, when I know I've been rejected, I have a real ambivalence. I'm totally torn between saying something like: "Okay, fair enough" and act like it's not important and, the opposite, to bare my soul and say what I'm feeling and how I'm hurt. That's what's going on in my head. In my gut, everything sinks down; my heart drops, my intestines sink down. I get smaller and get into a crouch inside myself. I get very heavy. Yet, when I've been myself and not pretended, I feel relaxed about it—sad, heavy, but relaxed. I can do no more than be myself. In those times when I'm trying to be something else, defensive and pretending, then I'm more tense, tight and nervous.

Those feelings of rejection, fully experienced, are really intense for me, really heavy. I used to get worried about myself; I would have suicidal thoughts. That was the most extreme I ever became.

There's a bit of the feeling of I'm not good and not wanted in all of this, but a stronger feeling for me is realizing that I won't have this utopian happiness that I thought I might have with this person. That's the most important thing it says to me. I won't have this happiness I've been dreaming about and thought was so close at hand. There's no way to avoid that feeling, for me, when I face the rejection and fully realize the end of a relationship.

Of those two ways of being—walking into the rejection head on or being defensive about it—I'm really not sure which way I'd like to be if it happens to me again. Thinking about it almost unemotionally now, I can say that I'd probably like to get on with it, go into it. I'm not at all sure though. It's very heavy, very heavy. I don't think I would decide until the moment before it would happen. It's like going down the road and all of a sudden you're face to face with the rejection and it's like a Y in the road and you make a split-second decision. One of the ways, being pretentious and defensive, might take a week, and the other, walking right into it, might take just ten minutes, but it's one hell of a trip.

The more I live, the more I'm able to just let it be, even though it hurts. I look back on the times when I've done that and I feel good about them, I remember them with a strange kind of fondness. The other times I don't have many feelings about them. It just is getting more important to me to be what I am.

REPULSED

I'm repulsed by the things I'm afraid I will be.
John Wood

ᔑᔑᔑ

David Meador

One response I usually have to feeling repulsed is to turn away, to remove whatever it is that's repulsing me from my awareness. I might cringe and kind of draw into myself. My adrenalin starts to flow. My hunch is there's a lot of fear tied up in my repulsion.

I think of coming upon a bad automobile accident, with people laying all over the road bleeding and maimed. I can imagine that and imagine feeling repulsed, afraid and helpless all at once. The fear, I think, is a kind of empathetic fear—I am somehow identifying with those people, imagining myself in the situation.

That same kind of thing holds true, in a way, when I feel turned off by people or qualities in people. A guy I spent some time with recently seemed so weak and so unable to respond and take care of his own needs that I didn't want to be with him. I wanted to leave as soon as I could. I felt like I was carrying all the responsibility. What made me want to move away from him was his reminding me of those parts of myself. There are parts of me that want to acquiesce and hand over responsibility to others. I don't like that in myself. I'm sometimes repulsed by parts of me that I see in others.

Whenever I feel a negative response about someone, I do a little checkout thing on myself to see what part of me they're touching. I guess I go through life with the assumption that when someone does repulse me they're tapping into a part of me that I don't like. I try and take responsibility for that instead of accusing them or dumping it on them.

I see repulsion as turning away from something, avoiding it and leading nowhere. That doesn't seem good to me. Anger I see as leading somewhere, it's directed at someone. Maybe that would be a healthy way for me to deal with my repulsion, to get angry, to direct my strong feelings of discomfort at the person. It seems to get me beyond the repulsion.

It's hard for me to do that though; it's difficult for me to talk about things that repulse me. I think it's scary for me because I sense, or assume, that the other person is very sensitive about the thing I'm repulsed by. If I mention that "ugliness" I assume it'll scare them away because they don't want to deal with it anymore than I want to deal with the ugliness in me. But I don't know that.

I wish I could just state my dilemma to them. Saying, for instance, "Hey, I'm having a problem and I need your help. I'm afraid to talk to you about 'ugliness' or how you're relating to me or how you deal with your husband, or whatever. I'd like to relax with you, but this is getting between us and I'm not sure how to talk about it."

One thing I've learned is that people aren't as fragile as I usually assume. I often respond to people as though they were weaker than they really are. I could stand to be more open and honest, more direct than I usually am, instead of trying to take care of or watch out for others all the time.

I have this ideal that being powerful, responsible, strong, and grounded has to do with my ability to respond to what's going on inside me. If what's going on is my repulsion, I want to respond to that in some way and not filter that response with what I project to be the needs of the other person. At the same time, it seems to serve me to sometimes delay or modify a response based on what I see in others. But I'm not sure if that's a cop-out or not.

It's a pretty heavy message to say to someone: "You repulse me." In essence that sounds like I'm telling them I can't love them, that they're not loveable because of this thing standing between us. As I accept more and more parts of myself, that I might have been repulsed by, I get more loveable and am able to be more loveable to others. When I'm on shaky ground with myself, I don't have much of a base to reach out from and much of my energy is going into maintaining the little self-respect I have. Then the risk of encounters and being open seems greater. I seem less secure.

Some days I am more easily repulsed than on other days. When I'm feeling good about myself, stronger, more secure, then I'm able to take in and accept more and different kinds of people and situations.

John Wood

I think about being attracted to someone or something as being drawn to them as if we were magnets, so it's natural to think of repulsion as the opposite end of the pole. Someone else and I are meeting "negative to negative" and there are things between us that keep me away from them, repel me.

There are a couple of ways I might react when I am repulsed. One is to draw back, physically and emotionally, and remove myself from the person or situation that's repelling me. This takes the object of my repulsion away, but, in a personal sense, it isolates me. Another way I have reacted is to become angry. This sometimes comes out in an accusing way and makes the other person defensive. Though this may be hard to work through, it is at least a start in communicating and seems better than isolating myself.

There are things that repulse me in people that I don't know too much about. I call those prejudices, biases or "sets" that I have that I seem ignorant about. New Jersey accents are in that area for me. There seems to be no reason in the world to be repulsed by a New Jersey accent, but they really make it hard for me to be with a person who has one. It's like a dripping water faucet in a way, an annoyance, a block to my attention.

There are other things, qualities, that turn me away from people that I know a little bit about. I am repulsed by people who are arrogant, cool, act superior and judgmental. I know that I am very capable of being those things myself and I am afraid of being them. I am repulsed by my own arrogance, just as I am repulsed by arrogance in others. I am afraid to be arrogant; it is a terrible way to be with people, but there are times when I slip into it. I'm repulsed by the things I'm afraid I will be.

That is not 100 percent true. There are things that turn me off in people that I have never been and don't see myself becoming . . . boring someone by talking too much, being deliberately cruel, physically punishing another person or an animal . . . but those things seem so removed from me that they are not areas of growth for me. While it's possible, I suppose, to be one of those things, it is too remote to deal with. I can only be turned away or angered when I see it in someone else.

But the other qualities are closer to me and crop up in day-to-day relationships with people I can learn from. In those areas, my repulsion tells me I am turning off and refusing to admit to a part of me. With the things I mentioned—arrogance, coolness, superiority and judgment—I want to face those things in myself. This is where I need a gift. I want help from my friends in confronting my own arrogance. I would like to let it go, to be arrogant and have someone call me on it. I hope I'll be open to how it is affecting them and ready to change as I understand it more. As long as I bury it, I can't change it.

I suppose that if that's true for me, some others will feel the same way. That gives me a clue to how to act when I'm repulsed. If I can be aware of my own repulsion and share that in a personal, first-person statement from me—not an accusing, angry, or sarcastic way—then there is an opportunity for me and the other person to learn from it. In this way it could be a gift to share my fear, my repulsion with the one who's turning me away.

Bob Lee

Repulsion has a sticky, slimy, gooey, quality about it for me; I don't want to put my hands in it; I don't want to get involved. There's fear and anxiety in it too. I draw my hands back from whatever it is and they start perspiring.

Sometimes with public or political figures I get repulsed, like with a John Birch Society type doing his number, and I realize that it's a part of me I don't accept. I know that's in me, that you are me and I am you, but it's a part of me I'm not in touch with. I don't accept it.

Intellectually, I know I can be an Adolf Hitler, in terms of his personality; I can be as paranoid as he was, as self-centered, as prone to temper tantrums as he was. It's "Do it my way, god-dammit; I'm not going to take anything else." I have that in me . . . fears, selfishness, craziness. Those things are parts of me that I'm not in touch with most of the time and choose not to act on in other instances. I am repulsed by those things and I won't accept them, but I know they're a part of me.

In the past a typical reaction to something that repulsed me might have been to walk away from it or to contain it inside myself and control my reactions somehow. But the energy would come out in other, cutting ways later, I'd be judgmental, critical, but through the newspaper, in indirect ways. Now I like to think I am more up front with it. I can tell others how they affect me, how I see them. It turns out to be a powerful learning experience for both of us.

I like it when I can do that. I tend to sort of search myself and to find out what my reaction is all about. When I discover it, I report it.

What I've seen myself doing with things that repulse me is going to them, confronting them. It's like being afraid of the dark and just going out and being in it until I can be comfortable there. I don't want to be repelled by life, by people, and I don't want to repel them from me. When I find myself in situations like that I tend to put myself further into them, to explore and find out what it is I'm afraid of or repulsed by.

Sometimes I see this like lighting bulbs. We are all electricity and covered by hundreds of light bulbs. The thing that repulses me lights one or more of those bulbs; it's turning a part of me on that I don't turn on, that I don't like. I know I'm more alive when that happens though, because I'm more fully lighted. All these experiences light up areas in me that have been dark. They're there for me to learn from.   ⤺

Carol Ahearn

Sometimes I have the feeling of being repulsed, panicked almost, by the demons that are around me. I was going through my journal recently and found an entry in 1971 in handwriting I didn't recognize at first. It was mine. I had written about a real panic I was in. I was looking out the window at this tree and I couldn't really focus on the tree and they looked like tunnels and caverns with sharp edges. They were scary. The whole tree was scary. I had the distinct feeling I would like to throw that up, get it out of myself, purge myself.

That feeling of throwing up has a lot to do with repulsion for me. It's like I'm in a situation where I can't accept something—it's just too awful—and I want to throw it up.

I can feel that way about men sometimes. I remember having an affair with a guy, a brief one, and running into him in an entirely different context later. I was afraid of being repulsed by him because the affair had ended up kind of nowhere and had been mostly a physical thing. But the point is, I was afraid of getting physically close to him and being repulsed; it was one of my demons coming out at me. In this case, the "demon" probably was my shame and my bestial desires and he was reminding me of those.

In a lot of cases, I see that my repulsion is a matter of something in me that I want to send away, to purge myself of. Sometimes it's almost a panic. And most of the time, I run, in one way or another.

Last night, at the dinner table, I said something to one of the people I live with and I immediately regretted it; it was a stupid remark. Well, she got really self-righteous with me and instead of being able to say I was sorry and didn't really want to say that, I got really choked up and kind of nauseous. I got this horrible feeling and couldn't say anything. What I had said really turned me off and the way she reacted turned me off . . . the whole thing . . . and I just started to gag. I wasn't able to handle it—something about it repulsed me.

There's something changing in me lately that I have to deal with. There are lots of things that need resolving. A lot of new things are happening to me; I'm having to take in a lot and sometimes I find myself gagging on it. There are things I can't readily accept. Often I don't know whether I'm keeping something down or keeping something from going down, but I know that feeling of being gagged and choking is centered right here in my throat. There's a lot of pressure there.

When something repulses me and I feel strong, I can confront it. When I don't feel strong, I try very hard to control my reactions and my emotions in the situation. I tell myself: "Keep cool, keep calm. Don't fly off the handle." That seems to cut me off from whoever I'm with. They're so different from me that if I let them into me, in a sense, there'll be chaos in me.

Saying to someone "you repulse me" is like saying "I have limitations where you are concerned." I usually won't do that; I'll attack them in some way instead of admitting my own limitations. Something about the person that repulses me is too much for me. I can't take it, and to admit that openly somehow makes me less accepting, less perfect . . . that's when I have that idealistic picture of myself.

On the other side of that when someone says to me that some part of me turns them off, I want to be able to hear that more. It could be valuable to me to hear that. I wish I didn't have to defend myself or use up energy separating myself. If someone is repulsed by some part of me, my reaction is to defend. If I am repulsed by something or someone, it seems like a separation. Repulsion is separating myself from something in me, from something in my environment, from something in someone else . . . and it could become a part of me if I would let it.

In the best of worlds, I would like not to be afraid. To defend, to resist doesn't help me. It is like choking myself—keeping something out, or keeping a reaction of mine down. Using that kind of energy to keep things and people out, by saying they repulse me, is a terrible, tiring way to live.

RESPECT

Respect is love in plain clothes.
Edward Dean

ᴗᴗᴗ

Gaye Williams

Respect is something that I *have* for myself or I *have* for other people; it's almost like a condition instead of an active feeling for me. Sometimes respect seems like a hard word to me . . . concrete almost. It seems more like a man-made word than other feelings do.

When I think about people I respect I immediately think of Betty. I respect her professionalism, especially because she does it quietly and with a poise that I like. In that, she maintains her woman-ness. I really respect that because that's something that's been very difficult for me.

I also respect someone who takes responsibility for himself. That makes me think of the man I'm with right now. I respect him for that and I respect him a whole lot for his ability to care; he really loves to love. I don't see that in a lot of people and I really respect it. He says, by the way, that respect is love in plain clothes.

Sometimes I think of respect as a verb. It is an active way of responding to someone that says you respect them. When I'm with someone I respect, I listen to them very hard. I let them know how important they are to me too; I want them to know that. I share more of myself with them, because I think they care about me. Respect gives me a certain commitment to the relationship too. If I don't respect someone I'm not committed enough to take time to work things out between us if we get in a difficult place.

I respect people who are doing things that don't come easy to them. And I wonder about that. I wonder why I can't just unconditionally respect people.

I think about self-respect in kind of fragmented ways; that is, there are qualities that I respect in myself and some that I don't and that holds true for others too. I don't respect it when I'm very ambivalent. I don't respect myself at all when I'm a bitch, when I'm feeling bad about myself and it comes out at other people. I don't respect my not listening to people.

I respect myself when I have courage; that's important to me. Or when I can be centered when there's a lot of chaos around me. I respect myself when I work through confusion. I respect my wish to be fair to people and for trying to see a situation clearly.

The movement I'd like to make with regard to respect has to do with accepting a larger number of people and becoming accepting and respecting of more of the less obvious things in people. It seems like the things I respect are so "large" and obvious sometimes. I'd like to appreciate some of the plain clothes instead of just the fancy, frilly ones. That holds true for my self-respect too. Instead of having to go through a big struggle to prove myself, I'd like to respect myself as I am.

John Wood

I don't think of myself as growing up with a great deal of respect for the kinds of things we traditionally respect. I haven't spent any time following father figures. Institutions like churches and schools have drawn what I consider a healthy dis-respect from me and I've never had a professional mentor or guru I have modeled myself after. I have never placed anyone or anything in that exalted position of awe and reverence that respect, in capital letters, carries with it for some people. I think that has to do with respecting images, not people, with setting people on pedestals who will eventually fall from grace.

What I really want to say is that I think that's an "old" way or, for me at least, a useless way to think of respect. I seem to have a very long yardstick for people to measure up to before they meet that "old" definition of respect.

I can't talk about respect without talking about self-respect. As I see myself, I see others, and I can't respect others unless I accept and respect my own human-ness. It's as if there is another me outside myself that will respect who I am.

I think about having respect, in general terms, like having respect for the human race, for other animal life and for our life system on earth in general. I think I have that, or a better way to say it might be, I operate out of that framework of respect. I try to do things that honor those things instead of violate them.

That is different than an intense respect that is focused on someone. Those come for me in moments of interaction. It is tough for me to worship from afar. My most intense respect for individuals has come out of our lives rubbing up against each other in a way that something of value has been revealed about them. It is in those moments that I am awed, that I set them in a special place in my attention and that they have all of me focused on them. I am in attendance.

Those moments pass. They change. I change. But they have carved out a niche of respect in me, as well as other niches I guess. We have a bond.

I respect openness, confronting, struggling, tenderness, honesty and a person who respects him/herself. I realize that I respect someone who has met or is meeting challenge. For instance, I have an instant respect for people I see that are physically handicapped and doing something like swimming or playing touch football. My heart just leaps out to those people. I think it's because my physical-ness means so much to me and I don't know that I could do what they're doing. I get tear-eyed just talking about it. Just knowing the road they must have traveled, the battles they must have gone through inside and the odds they must have overcome gives me that respect without knowing more about them.

I have a notion that if I find something difficult, I respect someone who does that with ease. If I have trouble with self-discipline, for instance, as I do, and I see somebody who is good at that, I respect them for it. I admire them because it's a struggle for me and they seem to have made the same struggle and conquered it. What I don't always know is whether or not that quality has been a struggle for them or if it just comes naturally and they take it for granted.

I don't seem to have any respect—or it isn't even an issue—for people who are not struggling with issues like I am, struggling with their life and facing challenges. They seem to be apathetic, to have it too pat, too settled. Perhaps that is just a case of wanting company and being envious of someone who has it all together. (Is there anyone like that?)

So much of respect for me seems to be wrapped up in yardsticks, judgments and expectations. I expect myself and others to really measure up before I'll hand out my respect. I'd like to throw a lot of those out and just respect the individual in front of me for who he or she is. That doesn't necessarily mean loving them or treasuring all that they are, but taking them for what they are at that time in that place.

Applying that to myself, I want to respect my totality. I want to honor all of myself and know that I am made up of many parts—many self-contradictory. Then I can allow those parts—the loving and the indifferent, the angry and the tender, the arrogant and the humble—and know that any one of those parts is not all of me. Respecting my whole person, and yours, I don't want to take away any of our parts. (Perhaps they will grow away, but I don't want to squelch them.)

Norm Chambers

Respect for me starts with self-respect. It's respecting and celebrating me as I discover myself through frameworks and structures that are truly mine. That's the essence of my "self-system." My range of emotionality, for instance, is unlike anyone else's . . . I can be aloof, quiet, indifferent in one moment and be involved and angry in the next . . . that range is within me to experience and act on. It's only mine. If I respect me, I don't judge that or penalize it, I just accept it as me.

I think I spent a number of years seeking respect from a variety of people and kinds of populations, starting with my family and moving out to various kinds of social systems. That certainly included black folk for me because we're sometimes caught up in a "blacker than thou" kind of thing and I had to demonstrate a particular posture if I wanted the respect of the black community. That got to be too tiring for me; I got weary of fitting into different slots for different people. So my focus has become to take a good look at me and respect myself.

That includes self-acceptance, a celebration of my own system, stroking myself, and spending time on myself—not necessarily at the expense of others. I don't think I can "move" with other people without this kind of attitude. It's a really healthy thing for me in my relationship with others, this moving to my own self-acceptance at a deeper level. This is not black-white stuff necessarily, this is about Norm, his limitations, his questions about his essence, his intellectual ability, his drive . . . all those things.

When that moves out to others, I have an understanding and a deep respect for them and where they are. I find myself not punitive at all when I'm in that posture of respect because I understand where people are in their stages of development. Sometimes I don't like it, but I respect it deeply. I feel myself moving toward an unconditional acceptance of others, but that includes maintaining my own integrity.

I respect risk-taking people, I really do, both verbal kinds of risk and behavioral risks. Recently I was doing a black-white training group and we were into a very intensive part of it; the blacks were in one room, really getting their stuff together, feeling very close to one another, and the whites were in another room presumably doing the same kind of thing. One white guy had a need to walk in on us, which was very, very risky. He took a tremendous amount of verbal abuse and there was some talk of physical stuff too. I really respected his balls for walking in at that point, out of his own need.

I respect people who are honest . . . honesty with judgment about where the other person is. I respect honesty with self too, when I don't put my stuff on anyone else and own the fact that I'm frustrated or don't like what's going on, sometimes taking an unpopular position and saying "this is not where I am." I also respect intellectual folks, not the traditional kind of intellectual, but a person who is bent on searching for the truth, who is curious and exploring.

When I'm with people I respect I tend to be quiet and unassertive outside and on the inside, I'm collecting data like a sponge, trying to understand all the dynamics of what's going on. It's much easier for me to be myself with people I respect too, and we don't have to have a long history together. That can happen pretty quickly.

I think I need to spend even more energy on my self-respect, because I see the residuals from that pile up in respect for others. I believe that if I'm less punitive on me, I'll be less punitive on other folks. I can't accept the notion that I can respect the world and not respect myself. As I become more known to myself and accept, honor, celebrate myself, that goes out to others.

My growth in this area of respect has a lot to do with the whole area of expectations. I guess I put fewer expectations on myself and others now than I used to and it helps me not to get into conflict. If I respect where you are now I am free of expecting you to be a certain way. My own expectations of myself are not as heavy on me. I respect myself and respect other folks enough not to expect them to be super human.

Tony Rose

I start to know I respect a person when I find myself looking toward, listening toward him or her consistently. That doesn't mean moving toward them though; there's something about distance in respect for me. It's a kind of a distant admiration, an appreciation, a looking up-to that makes me say to myself: "Watch, listen, respond, but from afar." I seem to sense the person needs space, or at least I give it to him, and I want to see them in a larger perspective.

I had a great deal of respect for my doctoral committee chairman, John Seward. Of all the professors at UCLA he was the one I had the most respect for as an undergraduate. He had incredible integrity in my eyes. Everything he did seemed to fit together. He seemed to be a man who didn't know he was enlightened, which made him even more enlightened to me. He was a complete experimental psychologist, completely involved with every experiment, rat, and monkey he handled. He did everything with the animals he worked with, raising them, feeding them, cleaning the shit out of their cages, operating on them, and ultimately destroying them when that time came. He felt the whole life and death of each animal he worked with. He was also totally involved and nurturing with his students.

There was a distinct-ness about him, an aura around him that said "I'm just as human as everyone else, yet I'm unique. I need, but I'm the one, ultimately, who must meet my needs." Those things about him made me watch every move he made, listen to everything he said when I was with him, but I kept a distance. I absorbed him. Then I began to model him and behave as he behaved; that's a sure sign I respect someone.

Generally with people I respect, I come in with a humility, a modestness and willingness to listen and learn. I'm also willing to be known, to say what I think and feel and what I believe in. At the same time, I know the person I respect will respect me and be gentle with me. I seem really open to suggestions and alternatives from them. That person has power and influence on me; I am really susceptible to impact from them.

When someone says to me "You should respect your elders. Respect your superiors," that's dangerous. To me, respect means they can influence or change me, so I want to be careful and decide for myself the people I want to honor. That seems critical to me.

Being with someone I respect is a comforting feeling. There is a base on which to stand, there's a model to follow or reflect off of. There is someone with his feet on the ground and I feel solid with them. I get a sense of earth and continuity out of connecting with them. There's also some heaven, some creating going on that inspires me.

Sometimes when I look for people to respect or get close to someone I respect, I discover the idol has feet of clay. I feel that way about me and Carl. Some of the times now when I get angry at him, it's realizing he has feet of clay, that he's not all I set him up to be. I feel a little bit let down in those cases, but in a real sense, let down onto my own ground. I come to respect myself more when I discover the other person isn't as integrated as I thought. Instead of standing on them, I'm standing on the ground; they break out from under me and I'm left on my own ground.

In a sense I'm transferring my respect from them to me. The situation seems more parallel; I am standing on my own and they are on their own. We are more equal. That's an important transition, from respect for others to self-respect. As I gain more self-respect, my respect for others is going to grow and the way I express it will change. I'm standing on my own earth and creating my own heaven and I can look, in very different ways, with respect at others.

SAD

[Our sadnesses] are the moments when something new has entered into us, something unknown; our feelings grow mute in shy perplexity, everything in us withdraws, a stillness comes, and the new, which no one knows, stands in the midst of it and is silent.

Ranier Maria Rilke

〜〜〜

John Wood

Today I feel a large reservoir of sadness sloshing around with me. It feels as if it's been there a while, but today the movement of the water seems greater, the tide is stronger. I think I am afraid to go to it. It is dark, deep. I could drown in it. At the same time it entices me, calls me, pulls me.

It rises in my body and laps at my throat and my eyes and they become moist. My skin is cold and tingly and very sensitive to my touch. I am deep and full. I am aware of myself as a single entity. I am alone.

My sadness today (I feel tender talking about it) is about leaving and failure . . . the passing of a relationship . . . slow, hard good-byes . . . a part of me going away. It is about being tired of fighting . . . fighting to stay with someone I love. It is about confusion; I am trying to flee the confusion of indecision I feel, the pain of fragmentation. I want badly to be whole and peaceful again. It feels as if the relationship is dying a slow, painful death and would like a gun put to its head.

I am sad for myself, that I will not let myself need or love. Giving myself seems so hard sometimes. I don't trust that whoever I give myself to will handle me with love. I am becoming more alone by my own choices. The hesitation is my own; the holding back only mine. I see the loneliness in front of me all too clearly and it makes me deeply sad.

I am sad when I isolate myself from others, especially those who love me and want my love. And I am equally sad when someone I care for pulls away from me, into their own sad and lonely place, and will not come out to meet me. I am sad that we make ourselves so lonely.

Most of the time I will go to my sadness; a better way of saying it might be I let myself go with my sadness, wherever it will take me. And it will go to the source, if it is specific and if I let myself go. I know that when I am "good and sad" it is a deep, meaningful experience for me; it is plumbing me to my depths, gouging out spaces within me, and I have no doubt that I am alive and caring. That seems to be a good part of sadness for me, to find out how alive and intense I am feeling about someone.

Sometimes I seem to encourage my own sadness. I seem to have a talent for melancholy. I think if I had been a singer, I would have been a blues singer . . . there is often a noble, honored, romantic, tragic aura to my sadness that is legitimate and beautiful as long as I don't wallow in it. I do find myself rolling around in it sometimes. That seems okay (I do the same thing with my joy) as long as it's not artificially prolonged and I don't become a martyr about it.

I love Rilke's quote about sadness and I think about things leaving me and things entering me. I think what I want for myself is to let things leave that are ready to leave and fully experience their leaving. Only in that way can I make ready and be open for the new part of life that is blossoming in me or about to come into me.

I also want to share my sadness. This seems hard for most of us to do. But I know from experience how isolating it is to pull away from everyone when I'm sad (or to have someone pull away from me) and how painful and fruitless it is to try to avoid or stifle sad feelings. Sharing such a deep, meaningful feeling has never failed to bring me much closer to the one I care about enough to share it with.

Jack Bowen

I'd like to distinguish between being depressed and being sad. Sadness has a melancholy, wistful air about it, whereas depression has an element of guilt in it for me. I experience sadness when someone very dear to me goes away . . . when a very good friend goes away or if Maria and I would ever part, I would be very, very sad. It has something to do with people and relationships. Depression has more to do with screwing things up or feeling bad about just myself. Sadness is more clean, clear, uncomplicated; it's something I feel free to experience, but depression is something I feel entirely too much of and I don't like it.

Sadness is also something I experience when I get along with my son, Andy, badly. Like yesterday I just got furious at him; I yelled at him and hit him, really got out of control. I really felt sad about that. I don't want to hurt him; I don't want him to be afraid, I don't want to alienate him . . . that makes me sad.

I think about sadness too with my friend, Paul. He's going away and I'm going to be sad about that, but not depressed. It's exactly what he needs to do and wants to do and I don't have any sense of dependence or possessiveness about him. The ending of this part of our relationship makes me sad; it's a joy to have him around and I'll miss the joy.

I usually want to experience my sadness, not avoid it. I'll cry easily, which is something I don't usually do when I'm depressed. It's like I'm mourning when I'm sad. I feel it intensely, I don't block it out. Sometimes in a way it's welcome because it points out how important people are to me. Sometimes it seems sadness is something I experience for people like love.

I remember getting sad and lonely when I took LSD. I spent the day with Paul and in the afternoon I spent two or three hours with him holding me and I was realizing that that was how I would like to spend the rest of my life, with someone who cared for me holding me, when I realized that couldn't happen, that was sad; it was an emptiness I encountered in myself. I fully realized that I couldn't have that, or it was leaving . . . that things I love and want have to all pass and it makes me mourn. At that time I remember wanting to experience my loneliness, my emptiness. It was as if I wanted to start over from that basic nothingness.

In that way, my feeling sad is a new awareness, encountering an awareness that I am empty, bottomless, not able to be filled up permanently. Sometimes deep sadness comes after a long period of trying to hold on to something I know must pass. Finally I see that it must go out of me and I mourn for its leaving.

I don't want to deny my sadness. I'd like to really let go and experience it. There's another part of it too . . . I would like to know that the one I'm feeling sad for is feeling sad for me. I would like to know that it makes a difference, that I'll be remembered and missed. My sadness seems mostly connected with people leaving me, going out of me in a sense, and it soothes me to know the feeling is reciprocal.

Bruce Meador

I think of several ways I am sad. One I like, in a way; I'm even a little proud of it. It's a capacity that I wish everybody had. It has to do with empathizing with characters in books, movies, plays and songs. I can really get sad with those people. My whole body can cry with them; tears just roll down my cheeks. I remember seeing "Camelot" in Washington, D.C., and I had this fantasy that John Kennedy had seen it at the same theater. After the movie was over I was walking out while the audience drifted out and I was feeling very sad and crying. In a way I didn't want anyone to see the tears coming down my cheeks, but somehow I was proud of it. Somehow it was good or noble or something like that. I felt like it made me strong; it was inspiring.

Another kind of sadness is a down kind of sadness, when I think life is not all it's cracked up to be. It might be over something I've done or haven't done or some relationship not working out. I don't feel good or strong about this kind of sadness. I feel inoperative. It feels more akin to depression, a kind of down-in-the-dumps sadness. I don't like it very much when I get this way and I think I'm really indulging myself to stay in it very long. I guess I think if I stay in this depressing kind of sadness, it's negating the basic ideas I have about life being good and beautiful.

I used to think about my children dying and being sad. I can remember driving down the road, thinking about that and crying while I was driving. But that's not a bad sadness for me. It is not without hope somehow. This kind of sad has something beautiful and expansive about it; it's getting in touch with something. I'm not dead. I'm alive and I'm open to what's around me. It's an opening instead of a shriveling up, which is the way I see the down-in-the-dumps sadness. I like to let this kind of sadness run its course until it goes out of me. I often want to write down or capture somehow the beauty that is in this kind of sadness for me.

When I get into the depressed state, I try and do something different to get out of it. I might go out and buy something I've been thinking about getting. I might seek out a new person or try to change my outlook or thinking about something. I used to play the piano a lot when I got in this state; it was cathartic, self-expressive, creative—it was great. It was getting rid of something and getting something positive in its place.

I think I'm better than some people at not, if you'll pardon this expression, wallowing in it. Either some people like being depressed or they're unwilling to change or jump into another milieu. I seem more than willing to do that; in fact, I get impatient with myself when I don't. It doesn't do anything for me to stay there.

I really have learned that I don't like this kind of general depression enough to do almost anything to get out of it. My tolerance seems much lower than that of most people. It's almost not legitimate for me to be there, and I seem to be willing to make some big changes to get out of it if I need to.

Bill Coulson

Recently my sadness has been an awareness of the inevitability of the thing that's making me unhappy; there's a sense of resignation, even justice, about it. It seems very appropriate to be sad at that moment. Nothing else would do except to feel bad.

The things in my life that make me sad are kind of given; that inevitable quality is there. Like I can get very sad about the bombing of Cambodia, but I'm cynical about it too and have no hope that they will stop bombing Cambodia. I also know that, after a while, I'll stop being sad about it. Something new will come up, in our society or in my personal life, to make me sad—that's what I mean about being resigned to sadness as a part of my life.

If I'm misunderstood, I get sad. I no longer think that it shouldn't be that way or if I were better at communicating it wouldn't be that way. I just think that every now and then I'm going to be misunderstood and sometimes it's going to feel real bad. I hope that at the same time I'm feeling sad, I'm hopeful that it will pass. There's an awareness in me of the comings and goings of the major feelings. Just as sadness will pass, so will the happiness that I feel.

It seems like I now know enough to realize that things won't always be well. I used to hope that, as long as I did things right, everything would go well. I don't feel that way any more. Now, when the sadness comes, my body almost goes into a state of readiness for it and it becomes a matter of waiting out the sadness.

At those times I slow down, I want to be alone, I sometimes want to pray or meditate. I also might sit down at the typewriter and work it out in words; try to understand the elements of my sadness. Lately, when I can locate those elements and the "whys" of my sadness, it just seems right that I should feel that way.

So I know that it's right to feel that way and know that it will pass. But the working on it, in the sense that I try to understand it, is a way of being active, of trying to understand myself and that helps the whole situation. It's not talking myself out of it, on the contrary, it might be a permission to go ahead and feel that way. Sometimes, in this way, my sadness will mobilize my curiosity or my cleverness.

What I want to be able to do when I'm sad is to recognize it and to get everything out of it that I can. There's often a delicious feeling about sadness. I sigh deeply, maybe I cry, maybe I get out my trombone and play something sad. At those moments I feel quite alive. It certainly isn't an everyday experience and I don't want to court the feeling, but it does add something to my life.

I know that sadness isolates me. One thing I am not likely to do is go tell somebody that I'm sad, thinking that they should be involved in fixing it or that somehow sharing it is the ultimate thing. I might as well go ahead and feel it and be big about it.

In the future, I might pay more attention to myself when I'm sad. I might ask myself some of the things we've talked about today and explore my sadness a little more. I can't think that will be a very bad experience, though I'm not going to go away from here wishing to be sad again quickly so I can check that out.

My sadness then, can be a positive experience, particularly compared to depression. Depression for me is awful, suppressive of myself and almost anti-human. My sadness sometimes confirms my sense of aloneness and therefore my own potency. Depression takes away my potency, leads to thoughts of self-destruction and awful things like that. Depression seems continuous, hopeless, on-going. In my sadness, I can feel it, let it go and know that it's going to pass.

SATISFIED

What do you suppose will satisfy the soul, except to walk free and know no superior.

Walt Whitman

ꜱꜱꜱ

John Wood

There is a deep long breath and a sigh when I feel satisfied . . . I have finished . . . I have done enough. I feel "used" in a good way. My mind and/or my body have been chugging along at full capacity. They've been stretched, challenged, exerted, and have lived up to it. It is a curious feeling sometimes of being empty yet full.

Sometimes I think I will never be fully satisfied. I bore easily; I have a restless, wandering nature. I want to explore, sample, experiment. Things seem enough for a while, then I am driven onward. That is on a rather general level though, like that "big satisfaction in the sky." On other levels I have learned some things about satisfying myself.

The beginning of satisfaction is realizing that I am responsible for satisfying myself. A wife, a friend, a parent cannot ultimately be responsible for my satisfaction or disappointment; that is up to me. The more I put my hopes for being satisfied on someone else, the easier it is for me to be disappointed, start blaming, and become bitter.

Sometimes it seems I have to keep a running inventory (or at least periodic) of what I want and need to make me happy. I ask myself: "What do I want from this occasion? What do I really need now to satisfy myself?" Then I map out ways of getting it. Others may be involved in that and, as hard as it sometimes is, I want to be able to ask them clearly for what I need from them. At other times my need may be to be with myself.

Sometimes the difference in being satisfied in a relationship or an occasion is the difference between needs and expectations. If I go into a situation with high hopes I am more likely to push hard, be tense and pressure others to meet my expectations. When I can go in fairly free of expectations and go about getting what I need once I'm into it, I will more likely end up satisfied.

Commitment has a lot to do with satisfaction too. I have trouble with that. I can find myself expecting to be satisfied by someone or some occasion when I am not giving myself enough to the relationship to make it happen. How can I hope to be satisfied when I don't choose to commit myself to what I'm doing? If I'm half-assed about it, I will be half satisfied (half satisfied seems like a contradictory term).

It follows for me that I must then choose people, tasks, living situations that I can to commit myself to. I want to seek out situations in which I can be full. That can be something that lasts 10 seconds or a lifetime. I am much more likely to satisfy myself (not *be* satisfied by someone else) when I can give myself to it fully.

Sex has taught me some lessons about satisfaction. Being in sexual union with a woman that I can be *total* with leads to much more gratification than when I am occupied with distractions, fears, expectations or bent on proving something or manipulating someone. The giving of all my energy and the focus on what is in front of me at that moment is the difference between good and fantastic. I am fully there, I am doing what I need to do, I am surrendering to that moment, I am not afraid.

That says so much to me about satisfaction . . . and about life.

Bob Lee

Being satisfied is being nourished. I have a lot of connections with being at my mother's breast, being warm and comfortable and sucking that warm, nourishing milk. I still get that feeling around women I'm attracted to sometimes. When I'm satisfied, I'm vibrating, I'm alive, I'm feeling this warmth flowing through me . . . it's like a humming inside.

It's like I'm being totally taken care of . . . that's the feeling. But I can't expect, as an adult, for that being taken care of to come from other people. I have to be receptive and I have to do some taking care of myself. A lot of that has to do with being aware of my own feelings, my own urges, and being open to following those. I need to switch from that external being taken care of, like a child, to turning inward and doing something about meeting my own needs.

I am more "inner-oriented" than I used to be and more present-oriented than ever. Becoming satisfied doesn't have much to do with my environment or with the future or the past in me.

I experience a lot of people wandering around searching for the key to their satisfaction outside themselves—in cars, food, money, entertainment—that's not where it's at. I had to realize and trust that all the truth I need to know is inside me, not out there. It's a matter of letting go of my own feelings and being fully open to people around me, of letting them come into me.

I used to have this thing about candy; I'd go out and buy three candy bars at a time and wolf them down. I had this craving and needed to satisfy it, but I really wasn't *satisfied*. I'd want more. It's a very temporary kind of thing. Well, I'm not doing that nearly as much any more and I know it's because I'm more satisfied with the day-to-day way I'm living my life and my ability to get my attention in the moment. That's really different than saying "I can't wait until I get that candy bar" or "I can't wait until that party tomorrow because it's going to turn me on so." For me, it's been candy bars, for others it might be ice cream or booze or dope—just taking something from outside and thinking it's going to satisfy them. It doesn't, not in the long run.

Sometimes I think about people as candy bars. It's like satisfying myself by eating someone else and that's a false satisfaction. What I want to do is consume myself; I want to eat me—validate me, listen to me, take in all of me—that's when I'm satisfied. I feel much more alive when I can do that.

I think the biggest thing I've learned along this line is to listen to myself, to really pay attention to what's going on in me. When I get caught in other people's things, that's when I lose me. I can easily slip into that, but it's a trap, meeting other's needs or expectations. Where the risk comes in is to be what I hear when I really listen to myself. That's very difficult, very difficult for me.

Carol Ahearn

Being satisfied is having me totally at my command. I am not using myself in any way that I don't want to. I am aware of everything around me and I don't have to defend myself from any of it; I can *include* everything.

When I can be with another person without feeling that I'm putting anything between us, I'm satisfied. There are no barriers and no need for us to fight. Then there is opportunity for anything to happen. It means not frustrating myself . . . letting myself be satisfied is satisfying.

Things that appeal to my senses, that really fill my senses, satisfy me . . . a meal that is so delicate and so beautifully orchestrated that I reach some sort of height of enjoyment using as many senses as possible. Music satisfies me. A person can fill me up in that way, sensually. It seems to be a case of using all my receptors and having them wide open and good things come in. It takes some concentration and focus to get there.

Often being satisfied is a pacifying, calming kind of feeling; it tells me I am not at war with my environment and what's going on around me. When I'm satisfied I'm not still striving or reaching for something, I'm just *in* it.

Satisfaction has a connection in me with being loved. It's difficult for me to allow myself to feel really loved and I am especially aware when I'm not satisfied in a love relationship. For instance, I know when I'm inventing barriers in a relationship. Getting satisfied is a result of not inventing barriers or removing old ones. It's a matter of very slow learning for me that the barriers are mine. I don't see them that way at the time—I see them as outside me—but to keep learning, little by little, that they're mine helps me to lift them away. That happens as I feel safer.

Satisfaction also is tied in with keeping my own power or giving it away to others. It has been hard for me to hold on to my own power in a relationship sometimes, particularly when another person says "I love you." I start to give them a lot of power, because *I have* their love and I want to keep it, to hold on to it. They can become very powerful and manipulative, even monstrous, when I let them. It's a tyranny I set up for myself. Until recently, the man in my life has been willing to accept that power and manipulate me.

That is not true now. The man I'm involved with doesn't want that power over me; he won't take it. So I have to realize and live the fact that it's all mine. It's my power that I'm giving away. I know that until I feel sovereign in myself, I won't be satisfied in that relationship. I won't be able to feel vulnerable to him or be able to surrender what we have together. This is something I want very much and I'll probably learn it.

I cannot give myself up to a monster. But if I feel sovereign, there is no monster because I haven't invented him.

My goal is to *allow* myself to be satisfied in that relationship and I know what I have to do. I have to allow him to be with me and to be able to accept his statement "I love you" without the demands, promises, expectations and threats of manipulation it has meant to me in the past.

That's when I'll be satisfied, when I can stop working to maintain that separation. I don't know that this will work out perfectly or will be forever, but I'll never know that unless I let go and try it.

It's funny, sometimes I think I fight the hardest to keep someone out who is what I want the most. When I really fight to keep that thing or person or experience out, it's a clue to me that it's something big enough to fill me up. It could be big enough to overpower me if I'm weak or to fill me up if I'm strong. What I want, of course, is to be strong and filled up.

Jack Bowen

Being satisfied is feeling no push, no needs, no hurts, no ambition . . . I'm just very comfortably sitting on the beach, in a clean white spot, with no place to go and no deadlines to meet. I associate satisfaction with my body feeling warm, held and cared for and it doesn't hurt or feel tense anywhere.

One time when I feel satisfied is very early in the morning, when Maria and Andy are still asleep and I get up and fix myself a cup of coffee. I go sit and look outside my big window, watching the trees swaying and the birds fluttering about. It's quiet . . . no noise to impinge on me, no demands to be met. I seem to keep going back to the idea of demands;

it's hard for me to feel satisfied or rested when there are demands to be met. That could be anything that intrudes, annoys or ticks away at me.

Running on the beach, walking, working at something I want to do, like to do, usually satisfies me. There's something about really throwing myself into something and getting consumed for a while that's very good. I don't feel split and I don't have to look back at what I did with any regret or look forward to doing something I *should* do. There's something about demands again.

I like to use my time well, to do what I want to do, and also to accomplish things. I felt quite satisfied yesterday after we had finished laying that concrete. I felt tired, hungry, pleased with the work we'd done and happy we had accomplished something I had wanted to do for some time. I made gin and tonics for everybody—we were all ready for a drink —and I could throw myself into that gin and tonic and my dinner just like I'd thrown myself into the work I'd done. It was a good feeling; I was satisfied.

I think of some things that keep me from being satisfied; procrastination, taking on responsibilities that I don't really want to, spending time with people I don't like, putting off things I want to do, fear that keeps me out of growing experience. I get dissatisfied easily when I have more obligations than I have time for; I don't know what to do in those cases. It's something about obligations haunting me, hanging around inside. I don't do anything about them nor can I forget them.

I realize that I'm much more satisfied since I have started working for myself instead of working for someone else. I've learned something too about going ahead with the things I really want to do, instead of putting them off because I'm afraid they'll fail or whatever. I also let myself have fun, give myself more permission lately. I play more than I used to. I am much more apt to follow my own nose instead of doing what others want.

I am more likely to be satisfied if I am moving, doing, changing. The more I let myself do the things I want to do, the things I feel excited about, the more open I am to my own energy. That makes me happy.

SHY

❧❧❧

John Wood

I don't live my life in fear, but there are things I am afraid of; so it is with shyness.

I am shy about things I'm not sure of. I am shy about tender parts of me and/or things that express my tenderness. I am shy about my "accomplishments" sometimes and would rather people discover them than having to bring them out to show.

I think about my poetry. I'm shy about that and particularly reluctant to show it to a man unless I'm very, very close to him. I'm not at all sure it's good and it expresses some soft, tender, "feminine" parts of me. I think sometimes men would find it cornier than women do. I seem more willing to share it with a woman that I may be getting close to because she, I assume, will be much more open and positive about the tenderness expressed (exposed?) in my poetry.

Dancing comes to mind as well. I am not sure that I dance very well, that my rhythm and the steps I know will fit in with what others are doing or will be seen as good. I am afraid, in my dancing, of trying and coming out looking like a fool. So sometimes I don't dance, even when I want to and I feel the music within me.

That is a clue to shyness. That I am afraid I will try something and end up looking foolish, exposing my absurdity; my weakness and my soft spots will be naked to the cruel world. My shyness, expressed in this light, seems like a shield or a way of closing down so as not to expose something I think will be misunderstood, laughed at or treated cruelly.

When I am shy I mostly just clam up; I don't see myself becoming bashful or embarrassed the way some people do. I just quiet down, fold up and wait for the situation to change or the person to go away. My behavior reminds me of a turtle pulling in when you threaten him. All efforts to pull me out of it only drive me further in.

I don't seem to be shy about other people approaching me and asking me questions about myself. In fact, I rather like that. There are no subjects that I won't discuss. But I am reluctant sometimes to offer myself freely, to jump into situations with all I have to offer and be myself without coaxing. Parts of me will go undiscovered by my acquaintances for a long time unless they show interest and ask me. Then I'm often accused of being secretive or closed.

A conclusion I've come to about my shyness and my way of relating to people is that I lead with my strengths. I meet people initially, when I'm unsure of the situation, with the part or parts of me that I feel best about, most comfortable with. Typically the picture I would present would be one of a strong, quiet, subdued, intense, and attentive male. Generally I will be more sexual and more direct with a woman. I will tend to hide feelings of being playful, silly, tender, sad, confused, or fragmented. I believe this is true of first meetings mostly and it seems to be an effort to present a typically dominant male picture to new people.

Most of the way I've talked about shyness so far seems to be negative. I also realize what might be shy behavior can be a genuine humility or a centered peacefulness; only then I probably wouldn't call it shyness. Mostly, my shyness is a shield, a reluctance. There are times when I want to honor that reluctance and try and find out the reason for my hesitancy, but generally I want to step out from behind the shield and make myself known to those I care about.

I am missing something in my shyness. It somehow robs me of spontaneity, of dance, of explosions, of passion, ultimately, of some real opportunities for joy. I am missing parts of myself by trying to hide them from others. I wish I could risk looking foolish.

Tony Rose

Shyness is a blush, a sensual feeling, a hiding, a good kind of embarrassment when I meet a person who strikes some surprising chord in me. I discover, to my embarrassment, that I may love that person, in a moment, that I have sexual feelings for them or sensual feelings. It's a blush of blood rushing through me. I avert my eyes, pull back and savor where I am. I'm not at all sure what I'm feeling is appropriate or that I want to allow that person into my world.

I consider myself a shy person in some ways. I surprise myself at the openings in me and how often I let newcomers into those openings. Occasionally I feel I have to withdraw and close those openings. Also I seem to have developed some strong ways to overcome that shyness. I can close off the openings, in a sense, and kind of barrel through in an assertive, masculine way that doesn't as much take in who they are and what we are together as it asserts who I am. It's a way of overpowering or even bluffing through my shyness.

There are times when I stand back and don't offer my hand to people; I'm waiting for them. That comes off as aloof I know, but what it really is is my shyness. I'm afraid of the impact they will have on me;

I'm too vulnerable and open. In those times I can't reach out to someone very well, but I may be very receptive to someone reaching out to me.

Meeting new people sometimes makes me feel that way. It's hard for me to meet three or four people in a row, for instance. Shaking hands, for me, can be as deep an experience as I let it and I never know how deep he or she that I'm meeting may want to go or how I'll react to some intimacy. I can tell when that hand-shaking ritual, which is down pat for so many of us, doesn't mean anything. For a typical salesman, for instance, it seems to be a way of asserting himself and not knowing the person he's meeting.

When I meet people I try to look them in the eye, I may get embarrassed, I may giggle, I laugh, I get scared. I feel their hand; sometimes they hold tight, sometimes not, sometimes I don't want to let go. It's different every time. All kinds of messages come through in those first looks and handshakes that can become incredible intimacies if I'm open to it. It's like I have to break the ritual first and breaking the ritual opens me to that person, shows my embarrassment or whatever instead of barging through.

Lately I've discovered how good it can feel to let myself be shy. I've realized how many qualities of it can be a treat. I think that started with the sensual and sexual qualities of it, being shy with women, blushing and hiding from a kind of turned on feeling. I started to accept that and let myself be shy more often.

I want to be able to make a choice . . . to let that shyness go and be shy with people or to withdraw, pull back and cover when I think I need to. I think there are situations in which I just don't want to be open and I want to be able to keep a particularly vulnerable part of me protected. I want to be careful about what I show some people. There's a tendency for me to show people what I think they will like about me first, at that first meeting.

One of the reasons I think my relationship with Sandy is still so exciting is that we're shy with each other. There's still a mystery about us, a wondering, and that's attractive. I'm not sure what's going to happen between us. There's something in shyness that is a slow beginning. If I get to know everything about a person in a week, we may be done. But if we spread things out, we keep growing. Sandy is growing faster than I can get to know her and the same is true of me; I think that maintains a mystery that is good.

Norm Chambers

It's kind of difficult for me to identify my shyness unless I think of it in specific categories or examples. I guess I don't think of myself generally as a shy person. I have noticed that I've been reticent, hesitant, withholding lately about confronting people; that's been an area where I've been a little withdrawn, especially with some black people I've been with.

At times during the past year, I've been sort of artificial with these people I'm thinking about and I really don't like me when I'm that way. Part of this came about because, after a real confrontation with some of them, I was "penalized" in a sense for confronting them. Some good friends and people who were important to me said it wasn't fair and other things that kind of put me down for doing it. Ever since then, I've been reluctant to open myself to them. It seems to be the best policy to keep my damn mouth shut. But I haven't liked myself for it.

I've found my self blasting out at others, displacing a lot of anger and things I should have been saying to the people involved. When that reluctance to talk and be myself gets a hold of me I find myself smoking more, being more nervous. For some reason I write more; I guess it's instead of talking. I find myself removing myself from the people I am involved with on a social basis, not dealing with superficial stuff with them. I find it very, very draining.

I guess if I had a pure definition of shyness it would be a reluctance to reveal Norm. One of the things that strikes me as a reason for that is I have a tremendous need to be heard, to be really listened to, and I guess I choose carefully when to let go. It's like I want to be sure I'm going to be fully listened to. It's not that the material I have is devastating but that, at this stage of my development, I'd like for others to hear me.

Another part of my shyness is something like having the burden of insight. I think I understand people really well and it gets in my way. I understand, sometimes more than they're saying, and I don't want to explain. My openness and freedom comes around people I don't have to explain to. Sometimes other people and situations seem to be tied up in knots for me. I find, too, that often I get wrapped up in that counselor-therapist role and that comes off as shyness, but I'm really just sitting back and trying to sense the people I'm with.

I've gradually lost the kind of shyness I had as a child, when it seems I had a purpose in no one seeing me. For instance, I would do well on an examination or something and hope that the teacher wouldn't point it out. That had something to do with not wanting to be attended to publicly; I didn't want anyone to call attention to Norm. That was kind of a push-pull thing for me. The things I said suggested that I didn't want any attention, but everything I did and ways I behaved said that I did want it. I did things that I would be good at and that would get attention.

Now I openly like to be attended to, when it's authentic. I think I'm the kind of person that can't get enough. I've never been ignored because I always knew things to do to get people to pay attention to me. I could still do that, but it wouldn't be as authentic because I designed it. Today it feels much better; I see people working to get closer to me and I like it. I find it means much more when it moves beyond traditional, structured ways of getting attention or praise. Sometimes I am ways that are perceived as aloof, but it's really a posture that's sitting back and saying I'm not going to settle for half a loaf. I want all of your attention or none of it, in a way. The alternative is to withdraw, to back off.

I guess when I feel those feelings of shyness and withdrawal coming up, I'd like to say so, to own it, and instead of running away from it, take some step out of my hiding place.

Gaye Williams

I think of myself as quiet, but not necessarily shy. I think my shyness comes out in certain situations or with certain people. I've been told that I look very snobbish with groups of new people, but what's going on inside is I'm feeling shy about revealing myself.

A friend said to me recently that shyness was the manifestation of a wish to divulge something to someone coupled with the fear that they wouldn't understand. I really like that; it fits for me. I think I am afraid that most people won't understand what I want to say when I'm really being myself.

I've come to some conclusions about my own shyness. I don't like it as a posture for myself; neither do I like the position it puts others in around me. It's putting me down, somehow saying I'm not okay enough to divulge myself. It's also putting others down to make the assumption that they wouldn't understand me. Sometimes, however, shyness has a good feeling about it, a feminine, soft kind of feeling that I like.

I feel shy in groups of people where the others in the group seem to be connecting with each other and I don't feel a part of that. I don't like the work I would have to do to become a part of that. I am shy around people who I think are important or who are important to me by reputation. When I first meet someone that I think will be important to me and I want them to be, I have a hard time talking. I want to do the "right" thing.

I know my shyness really inhibits me. If I don't do anything, I won't do anything wrong seems to be the rule in those cases.

In some cases, my shyness may get me some attention. I might be noticed if I'm shy and retiring and not just talking like everyone else. That does leave the other person in the position of having to reach out to me and in a way it's not being straight; I don't like that part of it. I also might get ignored, especially if I'm with people that take care of themselves and think everyone else will. If someone is being straight about themselves and onto the game of people being shy to attract attention, the straight thing would be to ignore them until they came out themselves, instead of playing into their bid for attention.

What I'm learning to do is recognize my shyness and what's behind it and *do* what I'm not wanting to do. It becomes a case of making myself say what I have to say instead of waiting until someone else asks me. I really have to make a conscious effort to do that. I can remember that happening to me often and I could really feel it in my body; I'd get all nervous and my heart would start to beat harder and faster. I'd have to speak very precisely or my voice would quiver. I'd have to rehearse what I was going to say. That is different for me now, mostly, but I'm still initially afraid in some groups and in some intimate situations.

I'm shy about other people's expectations of me too. For instance, when you asked me to talk to you about shyness, my initial reaction was "Sure, that'll be fun," but as the time got closer, I got shy and reluctant. Typically, I think that I don't really want to do it and began thinking up reasons not to. I think that comes from my not being sure I have anything to say that you would want to hear. What I try and do with that is go with the initial feelings of liking it and wanting to do it.

It's a matter of pushing through my own fears. I can be afraid and still do what I need to do. I don't want my shyness, my fear to be a handle that keeps me from doing things I want to.

SUPERIOR

How nice it is to be superior!
Because really, it's no use pretending,
one is superior, isn't one?
I mean people like you and me.—

Quite! I quite agree.
The trouble is, everybody thinks they're just
as superior as we are; just as superior.—

That's what's so boring! People are so boring.
But they really can't think it, do you think?
At the bottom, they must know we are really superior
don't you think?
don't you think, really, they know we're their superiors?—

I couldn't say.
I've never got to the bottom of superiority.
*I should like to.**

D. H. Lawrence

ᔕᔕᔕ

David Mearns

I think about being superior, much of the time, when I'm not feeling superior at all. The intriguing thing is how I can put on feelings of superiority, in a very convincing way, to others and myself. It frightens me to think I can do that so convincingly.

I relate a lot of this to years ago when I was tremendously inferior; I not only felt inferior, I *was* really inferior. It was in high school. I got through high school somehow, though I really was a puke, as far as most people, and myself, were concerned. After my first year of college I decided I would change my personality—I just decided I would. I wrote down things I would like to be and decided to become those. It is terrifying, thinking back on it; I should have become totally deranged. I found myself forcing myself into things . . . approaching girls, taking dancing lessons . . . just pushing myself into awkward kinds of things for me. Part of what was operating in me was I was saying to myself: "I'm inferior. I come across to others as inferior. I don't like it, so I'm going to be superior and act superior."

Somehow those feelings enabled me to do things I wouldn't have

* "To Be Superior," in *The Complete Poems of D. H. Lawrence,* ed. by Vivian de Sola Pinto and F. Warren Roberts. © 1964, 1971 by Angelo Ravagli and C. M. Weekly, Executors of the Estate of Frieda Lawrence Ravagli. All rights reserved. Reprinted by permission of The Viking Press, Inc., and Laurence Pollinger Ltd.

ordinarily done. I could do things with this attitude and my feelings about myself were raised in some areas. Also, at the same time, I got these fantasies of superiority; I still do. I would have these wishes to be great at something and my mind would float off into how *great* I could be. It would be in sports or academics, even being a great criminal; I would have these dreams of greatness.

The greatness fantasies are always tied in to how I am in relation to other people. It has little to do with what I've done before or the content of the work; it just means I am greater than others.

When I get those superior feelings I tend to act slower and much more coordinated than usual. My movements are smoother and much more together; not my usual jerky self. I stand taller than the person I'm with, even if they're taller than I am. I speak slowly and deliberately with well-pronounced words. I even hold my head differently, sloping down in a way. All in all, I am very composed. That's a way of setting up a dominant-submissive type of relationship.

I don't like it. I get some enjoyment out of it at the moment, but I think about it later on and I really don't like it. It's a terrible game, an act, and I don't like it in myself or in others. It produces barriers between me and others and somehow I can only know that person in that context of superiority or inferiority. I really like it when that turns around and in situations afterward I can by my playful, normal self with that same person. It's all a fantasy; I set that up because I define myself as superior and it doesn't have to have much basis in reality.

Often I see it as a way of getting through a situation that's uncomfortable. If I can muster up feelings of superiority and bluff it through, I'll come out of it okay. In those situations I'm totally oblivious to the feelings and needs of the other person. It's just as though they're a tool to be manipulated or an object to be overcome.

I'm trying to gradually eliminate those occasions in my life. I don't want to play that game, with myself or with others; I don't like it. I really need to talk to myself because it's a strong urge in me. I need to keep saying that the feelings are based in fantasy or assumptions at best and that if there are ways I'm superior, they're only a part of my existence and the other person's existence and they're not generalized. I want to be able to stop and listen to the other person, because in that dominant position I don't really listen to what the other person is saying, I just take it and fit it into a "submissive"-"inferior" box.

Betty Meador

There's a real difference for me in feeling good about myself and in feeling superior. I think feeling superior is defensive. It has more to do with feeling inferior and compensating for it by inflating yourself. Feeling good, for me, is feeling real and with people and has nothing to do with how I'm looking to other people. When I feel superior there's a self consciousness about how I'm looking to others.

It's so rare for me to feel really good and with people and not feel superior or inferior or shy and any of that crap. Somehow it's useful for me, in a way, to feel superior; I can feel better about myself and get more work done.

Most often it happens in comparison with someone else though and I don't like that. I think I start to feel that way in situations where I have some doubts about myself; somewhere in me there's a question. There is a potential threat from another person to my position or self-concept so I puff up and get superior. There are times when I can feel *beyond* another person or feel like I know more about myself than they do, but that's not feeling superior. I don't feel a comparison, a threat.

That's not true with Gaye, for instance. She was the student and I was the teacher, but now she's more a colleague; she's a woman and she's very pretty and very capable . . . so she's a threat to me sometimes and I have to march out those superior parts of me to face that challenge. I feel lots of good things about her too, but it's when the threat comes that I get defensive and pull what rank I have. I realize that there are seeds for both things in the situation—to feel superior to her or inferior and I go back and forth.

When those feelings of superiority come up I feel like I look haughty, snotty, stuck up; I feel condescending and solemn. Inside I'm tight and narrow. The ways I can react are limited; I'm constrained. I don't feel at all open and giving. I'm limited, it seems, to just maintaining the act of being superior and it's hard to stop. I just hate it. It's so false and I say such shitty, put-down things to people.

For instance in our women's group the other night, this woman was saying that it wasn't the kind of group she wanted and that it wasn't good enough. I got real uppity and told her she was misinformed about what the group was and we weren't going to do what she wanted. Then someone else pointed out that the group could probably do whatever it wanted. I realized that, but I was so busy being better than they were that I said: "Sure, you can do what you want, but if you get into discussing issues and ideas, I'm leaving. That's just a head trip and I used to do those, but I know better now." Or something similar. It really is not true that I won't discuss ideas; I love to, but I was so intent on cutting her down to size that I stayed in that superior, leadership role. It really seemed like I was trying to win and in those times I choose to say things that will keep me one up, not the things that are true for me and really mean something to me.

Immediately after I said that the other night, I felt bad about it, like a real creep, like I'd "won" but she'd been hurt by it. I thought to myself how shitty I'd been. I fought with myself about forgiving myself for being that way. Finally I forgave myself—all this is going on inside—and admitted that I am a creep that plays that game sometimes. I was tempted to apologize but I don't trust her and I don't want to put myself in a vulnerable position with her. In a way, being superior is a way of keeping distance between us, of maintaining some kind of control. I don't trust her and the situation if I let go of that superiority.

What I'd really like to do is tell her about that whole dialogue that I had with myself about her—that there's a part of me that plays superior being, that I feel bad about it sometimes and that I don't trust her—all of that.

It seems clear to me now that I feel superior, or need to feel that way, in a situation where I'm threatened, where I feel competitive. It's like a defense I throw up. Almost always when I feel superior, I say something that hurts someone and I feel sorry and guilty afterwards. I feel terrible when it's over and it's hard to apologize to someone who threatens me. I see another way to deal with it and that is to tell them the whole story of what's happening with me, not just the superior messages and the apologies, but the threats and the conflicts inside me too.

John Wood

Aloof. Higher than. My head is up, I am higher, looking down at someone. I am in control, sure of myself and what's going to happen, more sure than the others involved. I have height and distance from others. I am somehow on top.

I think that I am seen by others as aloof a lot of the time, but I am certainly not feeling superior a lot. My aloofness comes from being into my own thoughts and fantasies, but it is still a way of keeping others away, a protection.

When I get to feeling superior, it is easy for me to get sarcastic. It's still part of a way of saying "I know something that you don't so I can kid you about it and tease you." I do things and say things that keep me one up and keep the other person wondering or confused about what's really going on. It's manipulative. The things I do seem to be designed to keep a person in their place, and me in mine.

There are times when I recognize myself behaving that way and it disgusts me and I want to change it. Mostly then I just shut up and stop the verbal games I'm playing. Other times I don't know I've acted that way until after it's over.

I think about doing that with Joann. One of the ways I feel superior to her is verbally, saying more of what I mean and saying it in a "better" way. When I start to feel that way it's easy to just overcome her with a barrage of words. I mean what I'm saying and I want to say something important, but I get into a comparison thing when she's not able to articulate her own feelings in the same way. So I say "You're really shitty at that. I'm better than you." That's just an immediate distancing thing, in me and in her. I realize the distance then and I really don't want it, but I get confused about how to get out of it.

There's a bind here though. It has to do with being cautious. If I feel better than someone, like with Joann and words, for instance, I tend to be careful about that part of me so we don't get into the better-worse thing a lot and hassle about it. But that makes me feel like I can't fully be myself at times because it'll end up making me feel superior and her inferior. So I avoid that kind of interchange with her, or at least I have that tendency, and it is a part of me I really want for myself and miss when I'm not acting on it.

I don't want to give away things I feel strong about, to subvert my own strengths in order to bring myself to someone else's level. I don't want to give up a part of me I value. It makes me want to seek out relationships in which I feel more equal, and not inferior or superior . . . in fact, not comparing at all. It seems hard to find people in whom those parts meet at the same level. But it's what I want.

I don't want to feel superior to people in general; I don't want to feel that way around the people closest to me most of all. It's a distance that I don't want. I can't be together with a person when I'm feeling either of those things; I'm either above or below them. What I want to do is find the ground where we're together and travel that and not get hung up in the comparison game. The comparisons are always about only one aspect of me and one aspect of the other person.

Neither do I want to continually be with people who constantly give me the permission to be superior by their own feelings of inferiority. It means that I need help . . . I want to get out of that. It seems to me that two people are in that together; I can't feel superior by myself. I just am. It's when I compare and compete that those feelings come up.

Competition, hence comparison, is part of the American way of life though. It is ingrained, to one extent or the other, in all of us. I am learning that personal competition produces bad feelings in me and that "better" or "worse" are places I don't want to be in relation to the other people on this earth. I see that, in some ways, I set this up myself. If I act superior, no matter how much of a bluff it is, it drives off others or sets up inferior feelings in them. They are not inferior, just inferior as I see them. Sometimes I sense superiority as having more gifts to give someone than they have to give me. I know that this can come from not being ready to receive the gifts they have to give or not looking hard enough for them. My awareness may be so centered on what I want that I don't see who they are. Finally, I see that it profits me to come down off my pedestal of superiority by admitting and acting out my human-ness, sharing my weaknesses, my confusion, my vulnerability.

Above someone is not nearly as warm as beside them.

Bruce Meador

I grew up believing that it was really not a good thing to feel superior to someone else, that it was good to be "a good ol' boy." That was a common expression in Texas in my day and that included being modest, *not* being superior. That was very important in the circles I traveled in. For instance, I remember in high school it was okay to make all A's, though that might have been suspect, but you certainly didn't tell anyone that you did.

It was the acceptable thing to do, to be an "aw shucks" kind of guy and you were that way so that your peers accepted you. I see that in the Navajos too. You don't try to do better or seem better than your peers. You became an alien or even a traitor.

The democratic ideal, that all people are created equal, has a lot of personal meaning for me. I happen to believe that. Most people I ask say, "Of course, that's not true." I don't mean that everyone can run the 100-yard dash in the same speed—that's not it at all—I mean that there is a sense in which nobody is superior to anyone else. You show me two people, I don't care who they are, and I'll show you two people that in a real sense, are equal.

Given that basic belief, it's difficult for me to get into the set of feeling superior to many people. I don't believe it or avoid it or something. Like it's a problem for me when another person communicates to me, in one way or another, that he feels inferior. I don't know how to handle that; it makes me feel uncomfortable. It makes me think the person has a broken or disabled arm and how do you shake hands with somebody that has a broken arm? It's like I become aware of a handicap, in a way, a person is putting on himself, but being aware of it I don't know how to react to it.

That makes me think about a guy who used to come into WBSI to kind of hang around and find out about what we were doing. He acted inferior, like he wasn't as good as the rest of us. I didn't like him. I felt imposed upon and didn't want to be with him at all, though I didn't say that. But I don't know which came first, not liking him or feeling superior to him. Somehow it seems if I like the person and feel superior, it's much more okay; in fact I kind of like that. It seems like I have a broader world view or see more than someone else does and I meet them, teach them perhaps, something about that.

But it is true, that in my life, it has been easier for me to feel subordinate or inferior than to feel superior. That's been the arena I've had to wrestle in rather than feeling better than people. And I've made so much progress in the past few years, you wouldn't believe it.

There are times, when I'm in a leadership position, say the leader of an encounter group for instance, that I can sense people looking up to me. It's very tempting to do things to preserve that station, to perpetuate that above-ness. Sometimes I ask myself about things I do or say to test whether or not I'm just doing it to maintain that leadership position.

In those instances, I think of people looking up to me like I used to look up to teachers that I have had and respected and liked. I like that feeling, but I don't like it when I do things that perpetuate that just for the sake of perpetuating it. It keeps others from getting to know me.

If I withhold things that would make me more equal or do things that perpetuate the superiority, I wouldn't feel like I was being true to myself.

It seems like either way you go, it ends up as a comparison. I don't want to spend too much time worrying about being superior or inferior, but devote time to other ways of relating to people.

It's a separation, no matter how you look at it, and separation from people is not what I want. I would like to be respected and thought well of, but to think I am superior is for someone else to short-change themselves and short-change me because we didn't get close to each other.

A friend of mine used to complain that people always thought he was so smart and it kind of set him apart from people. I told him to say something stupid once in a while. It's a matter of being honest. I think if I'm really honest with somebody, I don't come out as being superior. I think if we knew the true feelings of the people we stand in awe of, we wouldn't stand in awe of them for long.

SUSPICIOUS

Suspicion is the companion of mean souls, and the bane of all good society.

Thomas Paine

~~~

Doug Land

It seems to me suspicion is a little like guilt . . . there are two kinds, one is paranoid and one is real. I think that I'm pretty good at being suspicious about someone that no one else is suspicious of; I mean it turns out that I am most of the time right about my suspicions. In a way I trust my mis-trust of people. That seems to compound the problem for me when I'm suspicious illegitimately because I can rationalize it so well, find the evidence and justify my paranoia to prove that I'm right.

It boils down to those bad feelings coming when I don't feel good about myself. When I feel inadequate or not being what I want to be—effective, productive, strong—that's when I'm likely to be suspicious of people around me. I attribute my own currently known faults to them and will not trust positive things about them.

For instance, when I start getting in a suspicious posture toward the world, the first thing I start suspecting is that my family doesn't love me, that they don't *really* love me. Then I can find evidence to support that, little things that happen confirm my suspicions . . . the table is set and everyone has a knife but me and I can say "there it is; there's the evidence." That's a terrible way to feel and, as I said, the fact that I can rationalize and verbalize it when they're legitimate somehow makes it harder for me to get out of when it's illegitimate.

Being suspicious is like having a screen or a filter in front of me that picks off certain things as they come in. I think that I can get to a place pretty quickly where the filter is open wide, where I'm letting everything in, when I'm letting people have access to me. What I think I'm good at is not opening that filter naively. I think I am careful about who gets close to me, but I don't think I'm hard to get close to. I am in control of how close I get to people. Some people seem always open and you're always able to get close to them and they don't seem to get hurt by that. Perhaps because I have been hurt I don't maintain that kind of open-ness. I believe in it, but I don't do it naively. So I analyze people's motives and psych out what's going on in them.

There are times when I purposely avoid doing that. I say to myself "I'm going to trust this guy. I like him on the surface and I'm going to trust him." I can be wrong at that. If I decide that I'm going to trust in spite of my doubts, I can make a mistake, but I'm not sorry. I can always say it was my decision and it's no one's fault. I also say the other thing; if I'm careful and pick my way carefully, I can say that this is where I want to be and I'm in control of myself. I don't think trust is lack of control; I don't think trusting someone means giving up your control.

The thing about motives gets confusing sometimes. On a crass level, I think I care about motives. If a guy comes into my house selling encyclopedias and he says "I really like your house and I really like you" I'm going to doubt him because of his motives. But beyond that crass level I don't want to doubt people's motives because I believe the closer you get to people, the more mixed your motives are. The more honest we are with each other, the more we find how confusing our motives are. I want people to feel their motives are okay whatever they happen to be. I *do* care about their goodwill; not so much the why of what they're doing, but the spirit in which they're doing it.

I think that I am a contradictory person, a paradoxical person. I have a characteristic of being both very insulated, protected, distant, and at times very close, intimate, open, and sharing. I rationalize by saying that I choose the way I'm going to be, but that's not always true; there are certain things that trigger responses in me. I think about being hurt when I was young and the simple explanation is that makes me careful about getting close quickly. Yet there's something here I want to work out. I don't commit myself very wholeheartedly to people or situations and being suspicious is a tool I use. Perhaps it keeps me from being hurt, though I feel I can absorb and deal with that pretty well. What I can't do is get myself to go over the brink; to say "I will commit myself to this person or situation." By being careful at getting close and picking my way, I make sure that it's not going to require more of me than I want to give. That care and suspicion has to do with not committing myself. It's hard for me to say that I'm going to suspend my suspicions and stick with it. Then, at the end, after I've done the thing wholeheartedly, I'll decide whether it was worthwhile or not. I don't do that; I always imagine ahead of time what it's going to be like.

It's like I'm suspicious of myself. I don't trust myself to be all I think I'm going to be. I don't think I'm afraid of failing. Maybe it's the success I'm afraid of. Or maybe it's the committment itself I'm afraid of, the total giving of yourself to one thing or one person. Because if I give all of myself to one thing I can't give it anywhere else.

In my life, that's what I want more than anything else, to settle down and invest myself in something, in one thing and do it really well. I wonder what I'll choose.

John Wood

My eyes narrow. I get quiet and still and begin to observe another person carefully. It's as if I am trying to see through another, to capture the essence of what's going on because what is apparent is not "real." That's the picture that comes to my mind when I think of being suspicious.

Suspicion in me includes lack of trust, a loss of innocence, a cynical outlook, questioning motives, assumptions, and facades. I guess if I trusted everyone all the time and believed that all I saw was real on the face of it and that's all there was, that I would never be suspicious. As I grow older I find myself less and less suspicious. I think that's tied in with accepting things more as they are and people as they are, but more with seeing the actions of people as rooted in their own selves and not directed at me. That's an important distinction. When I see other people's behavior directed at me, it gives me much more cause to be defensive, regard them from a distance and suspect their motives. The more I grow toward knowing that words and behaviors are rooted in their own fears, hopes and prejudices, the more I can regard our interactions as events or happenings and not attacks aimed at me.

Cynicism makes me suspicious of the good in the world. My cynical self suspects that everyone is out for their own good and has selfish reasons for everything. Sometimes that's a way of denying that they could feel good about me, that they could find me attractive for who I am.

Constantly questioning others' motives, another way of saying lack of trust I suppose, is a suspicious posture too. This can really wear me out if I let it. For much of my life the question "why" was very important to me. It was a way of getting to the meaning of life and I seemed compelled to get to the reasons behind actions. "Why" has become very diminished in importance to me; I am much more interested in "how." "How" doesn't seem as tiring. I can see the hows of people's actions and they have a communication and meaning all their own. For me, it's been a slow, hard process to believe and live the axiom that actions speak louder than words. Learning that, I can see that I don't need to know motives all the time.

Assumptions are wrapped up in both sides of being suspicious. I can assume good things about another person and our relationship . . . good intentions, good feelings . . . or I can assume something worse . . . that someone is out to get me, that I'm not thought well of, and so on. It is when these perceptions begin to change that I need to check out my assumptions and clearly state how I see what is going on.

Facades have to do with the idea of looking hard at someone to see through them. When I have a feeling I am getting a facade presented to me that is covering up something much more real, more important, I become suspicious. I want to know what's going on behind the facade and I become quite guarded until I find that out.

People who are vague, closed, and not in touch with themselves make me suspicious. It is as if they are avoiding me, avoiding some truth in themselves. It is until that truth about them or between us is revealed that I think I have to be guarded. I know that I am often vague and closed and not sure of what's going on in me; what I want in those times is for someone to be patient with me, to listen well and trust that behind my suspicious behavior is a good person. Likewise, when someone is doing something that hurts me or that I question I want to "suspect" that there is a good person behind that and their intentions are good. I wish I could do more of that; perhaps we'd get together sooner.

Carol Ahearn

I had a dream last night that kind of deals with suspicion and some of the movement I've been making in my life lately. I was in a theater, in a performance of some kind. I was in the audience and one of the performers came and sat by me. I gradually became aware that his arm was behind me supporting me and the question came up in my head "If I allow this is it an invitation to intimacy?" As the dream went on somehow this person seemed to touch more of me in a quiet kind of way so that by the time the phone rang and woke me out of the dream, I was sitting in his arms, cradled by him. The thing I noticed was I made more or less conscious decisions all along during the dream that I would relax with this and that I wouldn't be suspicious of him wanting to use me in some way. I suspended suspicion, in a way, and allowed myself that whole experience.

Most often I get suspicious when I think someone is going to take advantage of me and I quickly put a lot of distance between them and me. Somehow I am experimenting now with not doing that so much. Typically someone would approach me, physically or verbally, and I would begin to question their motives and immediately guess that they have the least desirable motives. That keeps me safe.

I really see the dream as significant. It's reflective of what's going on with me in my "waking" life. Somehow, lately it is not so frightening to me that somebody might get control over me. That seems to be a key thing in my suspicion, whether or not someone might get control over me, that I might be subject to their power.

When I feel that coming on I get very calculating; it's the beginning of a strategy, the beginning of all kinds of defensive maneuvers. The first thing is to not let the other person know what I'm thinking. I seem to be in a situation where somebody is trying to gain an advantage over me so I try and gain an advantage over them. It becomes a question of who will go away less "taken."

I become very observant when I become suspicious. I seek out mannerisms and things you might not be aware of, because I'm not believing what you say. I'll believe the other messages you send me. I think I try and look as trusting as I can, so as not to hurt your feelings, so as not to make an enemy, but I will be really frightened at the same time. I'll be very much on my guard.

It seems like the suspicions I have are ridiculously exaggerated; I feel like I have exaggerated fears. They don't seem rational at all but seem on a different level, where I put myself in relation to others. I make myself little and powerless, like a little child, and you are big and powerful and you can do with me whatever you want. A lot of that has to do with sex . . . that a man is going to try and be intimate with me without really being intimate, just using me. Someone is going to want to touch me and not recognize me and my needs. Or I have something someone needs and they're going to manipulate me until they get it. I am suspicious of people who hire me, people who are my bosses, and I'm very careful that they don't take advantage of me. Again, people with power over me make me very shaky.

What I don't like about that is the mapping out of strategies I get into, that I can't look someone in the eye and deal directly with them. I lose part of myself, my authenticity, when that happens. But when I feel so threatened it's hard for me to be myself. Ideally, I wish I could be brave and just report out what was going on in me. It seems like they have an advantage though and they wouldn't need to respond on my level and respect my feelings. If someone is trying to get me into bed, I can deal with that directly, but if it's a matter of someone giving me a job, a matter of food and shelter, it gets trickier. But I may be missing the fact that I can be myself on a job and that would be okay.

When I am suspicious it means that I have compromised, that I am not living up to my values. I don't have to feel that weak and try and manipulate someone, even if I suspect they're trying to manipulate me. It seems immoral in a way to buy into that game.

I realize that I can be hurt by giving my trust to someone and having it betrayed. It seems like a trade off. I can be trusting and vulnerable or suspicious and safe, defended. And when I'm suspicious I'm also cut off and isolated and I know that doesn't work for me. The whole point of my life now is not to be isolated. It's been a trial and error method of finding out that I can't be isolated. For most of my life I have thought it was possible to be that way and I have experienced that to an extreme that I don't want to experience it again. It is an inefficient way for me to live; it wastes a part of me.

John K. Wood

I think I get suspicious most often when a person's words don't match up with the other messages they're sending. People will say one thing with their words and be saying something entirely different with their posture, or eyes or movements. That makes me suspicious right away.

Sometimes suspicion just gets down to a different way of looking at things. I can look at a situation or a relationship in one way and it seems fine and then something in me will cause suspicion to rear its head and I will begin to see it differently, to entertain other notions of what that event was. Maybe suspicion is involved in that process of looking at things in different ways. That can be a creative thing by that definition, as when an artist or a scientist discovers something by looking at it in a new way, but it seems to be a bad thing when it makes one defensive and puts distance between him and the rest of the world.

When I get suspicious I might start puffing on my pipe a little harder, wrinkle my forehead, narrow my eyes and look a lot more carefully at the object of my suspicion. I'd slow down and get generally more attentive. I want to examine more closely and determine if I'm seeing what I think I am.

When that happens with a friend, I bring it up. For instance, with Charlie, he has this way of asking for favors without being direct about it. Sometimes it's a cunning—but charming—way of manipulating me. I often don't know about it until later and when I find out I tell him that I have "discovered" him and he blushes and admits what he was doing. But the next time I'd look at him out of the corner of my eye and wonder what he was really after. It seems to get back to reasons and if the reasons behind what you're doing affect me, I want to know about it.

I wonder what makes me question it. Most times I don't question what people say to me and I wonder what makes the difference. A guess is that when I'm defensive and not feeling good about myself, I question others more. I don't know if that's true or not. I do know it's connected with my own defensiveness; when there is some kind of effect on me, it does something inside me to make me question and possibly defend. It's like I have an investment in what's going on and I want to protect that investment.

I have thought of it in terms of loss and gain. Up to a certain point there is a gain in being suspicious, beyond that there seems to be a loss. I see that range of suspicion in others. There is the very naive person who never questions anyone and takes everything at face value. A vacuum cleaner salesman comes to the door and says he wants to see the whole world clean and this woman believes it and buys a vacuum cleaner. She's not suspicious at all, but I think she's missing something; a greater awareness would enrich her life. She could be a fuller person.

At the other end of the scale is the person who is suspicious of everything, who just tortures himself questioning the intent and motives of everyone around him. I think he's missing out on life too because he can't trust or believe. It's one thing not to believe the Jehovah's Witnesses' view of the world, but another to be so cynical, narrow and untrusting that you cut yourself off from people. You limit your whole existence.

TRUSTING

As soon as you trust yourself, you will know how to live.

Goethe

ᴗᴗᴗ

John Wood

Trust is a verb. While I was thinking about this section, I came across Buckminster Fuller's quote, "truth is a verb" and it struck me that the same emphasis could be given to trust. For while trust can be thought of as a general condition, I find it most often is an active give and take, an interaction, an alive thing that has to be nourished or it will die. I often think about it in terms of secrets—the more real secrets about myself I share with you, the more you will trust me and vice versa. If I am keeping secrets to myself—particularly about me in relationship to you—the less you will trust me.

Sometimes it seems like a test, though I don't think of it in that way at the time, when I say something that I think is silly, tender or I'm ashamed of. If the other person receives that in an accepting way, that really helps me trust them. If they also think it's silly, I may feel just neutral about them. But that's the only way I know how to go about it, is to go into it slowly, to offer something and see how it's received.

I think I'm spoiled. I really trust—very much—several people in my life; I think of it as a lot of people. It is a very nice feeling to think about you, David, Joann, Howard and some others—somebody I can say anything to, do anything around them and it will be okay. It makes me feel good just thinking about it. But then I think of all the people who say "I just don't trust people" and how bad that must feel.

I find myself getting angry with people who say to me "I can't trust you" when what they mean (I think) is "I can't predict your behavior." I think they are asking for guarantees—assurances that I won't do something that will hurt them. When I experience someone's distrust of me, I start to feel hurt, guilty and defensive. I begin to question my own motives. The defensiveness sets up barriers between us. I am wary. So are you. In this way, "I can't trust you (because I can't predict your behavior)" becomes a prophecy that fulfills itself. Trust breeds trust. Mistrust breeds mistrust.

When I experience myself not trusting someone, an accurate way for me to say that might be: "I don't trust this situation enough to be myself in it," or "I don't trust myself with you, to say and do what I'm really feeling." That way of thinking about it puts the emphasis on me—the only one I can realistically do anything about in the situation.

From now on when I hear myself say, "I don't trust you" I hope I will remind myself that I'm feeling my own fear and that admitting that out loud, in a distinct way, might be the start of that "secret sharing" leading us to that verb, trust.   ↰

Maria Bowen

When I trust someone, it means I believe they care enough for me to spend the time and energy it takes to deal with whatever comes up between us. I think that is the essence of trust for me.

Trust is a funny word. When I was growing up, someone would say "I really trust you to do what you want to," but when a decision of mine ran counter to what they wanted, there were feelings of betrayal and guilt. Trust apparently meant that they could predict my behavior.

Sometimes I don't see trust related to actions at all. It has more to do with attitudes. For instance, I have a great deal of trust for Jack. That doesn't mean that I know what he is going to do, far from it, but I know that he will spend the time and energy to stay with me and deal with my reactions to what he does. Trust is so related to caring.

I think about different levels of trust, of trusting most people in general, of trusting others to a somewhat deeper level, but that one deep level of complete trust is hard to get to and I believe it takes a lot of time and work to get to.

When I am with people I trust, I really feel free. I am not concerned with being stupid, infantile, ugly, or crazy . . . it's a very nice feeling. Trusting someone doesn't mean they have to like everything I say or do though; they may not like something I say, but they will say so openly and directly and, again, take the time to work it out with me. What usually happens is people don't say anything, but inside they are making judgments, rejecting me and removing themselves from me without making me a part of that decision. When I have that kind of feeling about people, I hide myself very well because I don't know what the person is going to do with the information. I sense that I won't have any influence on what he or she does. In a way, it's like having a piece of the action—I want some of the action that's going on between us. It's a matter of mutual exploration, mutual involvement, instead of a secretive, one-way kind of thing.

I appreciate feedback. I think I am a person who is open to feedback, but I need two conditions surrounding that. One is that the person giving me the feedback really cares about me and what he is saying. The other is that he'll stay around and work through it with me. I don't like this practice of dropping "honest" remarks and running. A lot of people go to encounter groups and learn to be honest and they go around being "instantly honest" without dealing with the consequences of their remarks. I wonder whose needs they're meeting. I don't want to be used in that way. I want to be cared about enough so that my needs are taken into consideration as well as the other person's. If I believe that, I will trust someone.

One thing I've learned about this whole area is learning to trust myself and trust others to take care of themselves. In my counselling, I have a basic sense of trust in the other person's competence; I like that. I used to have to save people but discovered that I don't have that power. It has a lot to do with learning to trust myself. If I'm not willing to deal with something with other people, then I figure no one is going to do that with me.

Trusting has a lot to do with liking yourself too. If I don't like myself, it's hard to believe others like me. If I don't trust myself, I don't see others as trusting me. I had to learn to like myself first.

Bob Kavanaugh

When I trust someone I immediately notice a decline in my apprehension. My anxious need to please or to test or to conquer is gone, or almost gone. My tongue moves as if liquor-loosed; I am anxious to tell foibles, secrets and goofs.

For years I had instant trust for those with the proper authority labels—cops, nuns, priests, doctors. My trust was role-tied. Now I still feel trust for labels though I hate myself sometimes for so doing. I find I fear blacks and all "other-looking" people at pre-cognitive contact. Only when I correct my original feelings do I give them a chance to be trusted.

Now I am almost able to feel trusting toward everyone, but it is because few can hurt me any longer. I trust easily when no risk is involved and with most I meet there are decreasing risks.

I feel trust as a general over-all relaxant in the presence of those who give me permission to be human. It feels like a good sauna or jacuzzi, like nakedness after wearing tight clothes. I do not find it running around in any particular location, but rather all over me, inviting all parts of me—little boy, bastard, lecher, saint—to come out for play.

It is so hard to discern trust or mistrust as feelings. They are always linked to certain reactive feelings that accompany them. When I trust joy, ebulience and relief are there too and I cannot identify the specificity of trust. And so with mistrust; anger, suspicion or similar feelings block or cloud my ability to describe mistrust.

Steve Doyne

I know I'm trusting when I'm so relaxed with myself that I'm content to just be myself with the persons I trust. When I don't hesitate to talk or act. When I don't have second thoughts about saying or doing something. When the voices in my head which sometimes keep me from being free become inaudible. When I can cry if I need to.

I'm never sure how to obtain trust. Caring is somehow important in my trusting another person and, I think, vice-versa. Having the ability to really share with others is important, too.

When I find a situation or people I can trust, I really rejoice in that; I bathe in it, immerse my being. It feels so good to drop my roles, my "shoulds" and just be me.

Joann Justyn

I trust you; do you trust me? Do I trust you? Can I tell you all the things that even I can't tell myself? Can I accept your judgment of me if I tell you these things? Do I not worry about my esteem, my value, in your eyes? Am I more honest with you than myself? If I am then I know I trust you.

Trust is so like love, perhaps less exhilarating, slower, more gradual, more long term. Sometimes I think that people who have been together for years and years—have more a trust relationship than a love relationship. It's trust that keeps them together. Trust that your partner won't hurt you, forsake you, tell your secrets. It is having this total trust that is so hard to live without when a relationship ends.

I think I've never been hurt more as when my trust has been betrayed. It's so much easier to have someone fall out of love with you. But trust is built, painfully, carefully. It's much more rare than people are aware of, more rare than I am aware of.

When I trust someone, I am totally at ease, comfortable, safe with them. I am myself. What a neat feeling now that I think of it! Trusting myself is scary, satisfying, hard to do. When I trust myself I flow along rather than move abruptly. I feel strong and confident in who I am and where I am, and the decisions I am making.

I have just thought that trusting is like having an extra best friend when you're very young, your companion in everything. You do insane, wonderful, daring things with them that would be hard to do by yourself.

Some of my best times are with people I trust. I wish I could trust myself and others more. I don't really consciously distrust—but I am pretty reserved and conservative about what I disclose to myself and others.

How do I become more trusting? Perhaps by writing this. By doing things I don't ordinarily trust myself to do—taking risks.

The People
Who Are This Book

These are the people who have shared themselves with me so this book might be published. I apologize for the descriptions. In many cases they seem so terse, sterile and not at all a description of the people I know, but at least this is one way for you to know a little more about the people you're reading about. These people are, perhaps more than most, multi-dimensional and this is but one facet of them. ⤸

Carol Ahearn is a Goddard College graduate student attached to CSP.

Andre Auw is a marriage and family counselor, organizational development consultant, writer and a member of CSP.

Mary Bardone is a yoga instructor.

Jack Bowen is a psychologist and a member of CSP.

Maria Bowen is a counselor at University of California, San Diego, psychologist in private practice and a member of CSP.

Earl Burrows is a group leader, consultant in organizational development and a member of CSP.

Kay Carlin is a San Diego school teacher.

Larry Carlin is a consultant to governmental and educational institutions on human relations and a member of CSP.

Norm Chambers is head of black and urban studies at San Diego State University, a consultant and a member of CSP.

Janet Colby is a free-lance graphic designer.

Steve Doyne is a psychologist, educational consultant and a member of CSP.

Paula Ann Engelsman is a San Diego school teacher.

Marcia Jaffe works in urban redevelopment in Boston and was a participant in the 1972 La Jolla Program, a part of CSP.

Bob Johnson is a counselor and instructor at Washington State University and was a 1971 visiting fellow at CSP.

Joann Justyn is the CSP coordinator.

Bob Kavanaugh is an author, counselor at University of California, San Diego, and lecturer.

Muriel Keyes is an instructor in structural patterning.

Ralph Keyes is a free-lance writer, author and member of CSP.

Doug Land is an educational consultant, group leader and the 1974 director of CSP.

Elsie Land is a creative family organizer.

Roger Ledbetter is a consultant, group leader and member of CSP.

Bob Lee is a counselor, consultant on race relations and a member of CSP.

Chuck Lee was a participant in the 1972 La Jolla Program, a part of CSP.

Ron Lunceford is a counselor on race relations, marriage and the family, a member of the counseling staff at University of California, Irvine, and a member of CSP.

Charlene Mackowiak was a participant in the 1972 La Jolla Program, a part of CSP.

Audrey McGaw is a group leader, with Bill.

Bill McGaw is a consultant in communications and human relations, a film producer and director and a member of CSP.

Betty Meador is a leadership and human behavior consultant, a member and the 1972 director of CSP.

Bruce Meador is an educational consultant, group leader and a member at CSP.

David Meador is a group leader, consultant, and was the 1973 director of CSP.

David Mearns a Glasgow graduate student in psychology, was a 1972–73 visiting fellow at CSP.

Pat Rice is a counselor and consultant to religious groups and a member of CSP.

Paula Ripple was a participant in the 1972 La Jolla Program, a part of CSP.

Tony Rose is an author, film maker, organizational development consultant and a member of CSP.

Chris Ross is director of a family services agency in Calgary and was a participant in the 1972 La Jolla Program, a part of CSP.

Howard Saunders is a free lance graphic artist.

Anne Stillwell is an anthropologist.

Bill Stillwell is an anthropologist, counselor and member of CSP.

Gay Swenson is free of role definitions at this writing.

Cheryl Thurman is staff assistant to the Human Dimensions in Medical Education program, a part of CSP.

Terry Van Orshoven is an organizational development consultant and a member of CSP.

Gaye Williams was a Union Graduate School student attached to CSP and is a new member.

John K. Wood is a group leader, counselor at California State University, San Diego, and a member of CSP.

This Is an Invitation

I hope this book raises some feelings in you; that's what it's all about. If there are things you'd like to write to me about, I'd like to hear from you.

I fully realize, now, that this book is finished. I am a lot happy, a little sad and wondering what I am going to do next.

Keep in touch.

John T. Wood
Center for Studies of the Person
1125 Torrey Pines Road
La Jolla, California 92037